POLANSKI

POLANSKI

John Parker

VICTOR GOLLANCZ

LONDON

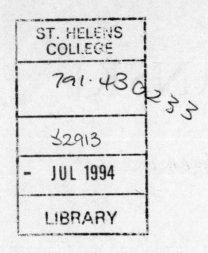
First published in Great Britain 1993
by Victor Gollancz
A Cassell imprint
Villiers House, 41/47 Strand, London WC2N 5JE

© John Parker 1993

A catalogue record for this book is
available from the British Library

ISBN 0 575 05615 0

Photoset in Great Britain by
Rowland Phototypesetting Ltd, Bury St Edmunds, Suffolk
and printed in Great Britain by
Mackays of Chatham plc, Chatham, Kent

Acknowledgements

Much of the information, detail and colourful reminiscences collected for this book is derived from rare and lengthy interviews with former friends, lovers and colleagues of Roman Polanski in Poland, the country where he lived for twenty-four years, from the age of three, after his parents moved to Krakow from Paris, the city of his birth. The author wishes to acknowledge the invaluable assistance of Polish journalist and author Marek Garztecki with the numerous interviews conducted in Poland which entailed many hours of listening, transcribing and translating taped conversations. Thanks are also due to many others, in Britain, France and the United States, for the time given to the author for personal interviews, telephone conversations, correspondence or the supply of relevant documentation from official sources, all of which provided considerable additional insight into the life of Roman Polanski. Finally, my thanks to Ivor Game for his help with picture research.

Chapter One

*E*very now and again, students at Poland's National Film School at Lodz gather to discuss the life and work of their most famous old boy, Roman Polanski. For more than fifteen years after he left the country at the dawn of the sixties, he never once went back. This was, in part, because his work was shunned by the Polish Ministry of Culture after the nation's hard-line leader Wladislaw Gomulka banged his fist on the lectern at the Thirteenth Plenary Session of the Communist Party of Poland and declared that Polanski's film *Knife in the Water* was neither typical of nor relevant to Polish society as a whole and as such had no place in its cinema.

Times changed. Polanski returned to Poland during the thaw of Communist oppression and at Lodz met students and tutors past and present who greeted him with a kind of schizophrenic reaction, on the one hand a welcoming warmth to the prodigal hero and on the other, hostility to the artist, a son of Poland, who had tainted his work with Western influences and scandal.

'Schizophrenic' is an especially relevant word when dealing with Polanski's life. Even when attempting an objective assessment, the writer is drawn one way and then another, experiencing at once admiration and disgust.

In the early days, when Polanski's work was less overshadowed by the troubles in his life, debates about him at Lodz would be spirited and forceful. The intricacies and nuances of scenes from his films, the subterranean movements of his plots, would be analysed and pontificated upon. Why had he done this? What were his inspirations for that? How did he achieve such stark, macabre portraits of human behaviour? Where did he learn those camera techniques?

The answer is easy. He learned them at Lodz, and peppered his plots with real people and real events drawn from his own incident-filled life, or dreamed up in his own hyper-imagination at times of despair or, occasionally, while under the influence of mind-expanding drugs. His screen images of women, often portrayed in scenes of brutal and deviant madness, were also a regular talking-point – and that trait also began at Lodz. 'You can blame me,' said his first wife, the Polish actress Basia Kwiatkowska, whom Polanski rechristened Barbara Lass when she gained her first of many starring roles in Continental films. She seldom speaks of her time with Polanski, but in a long, taped conversation at her home in Munich where she toils making life-sized dolls, she reflected, 'I think that it was his revenge on me, because it started when I left him. Afterwards, his women are only used, crushed.'

As an artist in film, Polanski is a respected figure in Lodz, but nowadays more for his curiosity value than as a leader and innovator. Several of his former contemporaries, now tutors and professors, frequently use the word 'genius' when referring to his talent. The younger generation, however, no longer regard him as anything more than an interesting figure of study in the history of Polish cinema since the Second World War.

One of his old friends, Henryk Kluba, a former actor and now a respected administrator, summarized Polanski in the nineties, as seen by Lodz: 'I personally have great respect for what he has achieved, and no one among Polish directors has achieved so much . . . even Andrzej Wadja, one of our greatest directors, is known mostly in Poland. But there is also controversy surrounding him. I have known him a long time, and have respect for Polanski's originality as an artist. It is only natural that the younger generation do not kneel before him. They see him as an artist corrupted by the big producers, for a mass downmarket audience.'

In fact, it would be more accurate to say that the corruptions were of Polanski's own making, when the lure of bright lights, movie stars, fast cars and high living became an overwhelming temptation to the young man who was the product both of Poland's austere post-war Communist regime and of Lodz, that unique training ground for a career in film.

There are many in Poland today who remember Polanski in the early days and several of them have contributed their reminiscences to give a rare portrait of Polanski for this biography. Lodz was also the source of a number of Polanski's most successful collaborators who from time to time were invited to work on his movies and found success in the West. One of these was cameraman Witold Sobocinski, who filmed two of Polanski's most recent pictures, *Frantic* and *Pirates*. Sobocinski says that within his professional circle, Polanski was always regarded as the only Pole who really made it big abroad. 'In a way it is sad that his career has been reported from the scandalous and not the artistic angle, but the scandals which followed him were the result of his own character . . . he likes it when the world revolves around him.'

Some who followed Polanski out met with tragic consequences. Krzystof Komeda, one of Poland's greatest jazz composers, died after an incident while working for him in Los Angeles. Komeda's widow, Zofia, sitting in her tiny house in a village in the Carpathian Mountains, bought with her late husband's royalties, reflected on a bitter-sweet relationship with their friend Polanski: 'I loved Romek . . . but at times he was an animal.'

Death seemed an all too frequent visitor to Polanski's circle of Poles who went west. Wojtek Frykowski, for instance, one of his best friends at Lodz, whose father financed a short film that helped his career, was one of the victims of the Charles Manson murders in which Polanski's second wife, Sharon Tate, also died. And never far from Polanski's sphere was Jerzy Kosinski, the novelist, born in Lodz, to whom Polanski introduced Peter Sellers for his best screen role in *Being There*, which Kosinski wrote.

Kosinski, who committed suicide by putting a plastic bag over his head in 1990, was a distinguished academic whose own childhood was even more tortured than Polanski's. Curiously enough, it was Kosinski's first novel, *The Painted Bird*, a classic in Holocaust literature, that helped draw media attention to Polanski's early life. Though semi-autobiographical, it was an account that reflected the experiences of many young people in Eastern Europe including Polanski himself.

Polanski's story begins in 1933. The year itself was historically significant for everyone in Europe, and then the world, and most especially the Jews, of whom Polanski is one, although he has never practised the faith. It was the turning point in the history of the twentieth century. Adolf Hitler's Nazis were put above the law by the German parliament on 25 March and Hitler became dictator overnight. Within a week he began his vendetta of violence and repression against Jews. Within a month they were being hounded out of office in Germany and their businesses blacklisted and burned; within three months they were being herded into concentration camps.

That year, too, a young mother who would eventually be gassed in

9

one of the most infamous of the camps, Auschwitz, gave birth to a son far away in the quiet back-streets of Paris, on a hot summer's day, 18 August. The awesome terrors which would eventually overtake this tiny, jug-eared infant were typical of those faced by many hundreds of thousands in the European turmoil ahead; his case was only made outstanding by the way he developed, by what he became famous for as an artist, and infamous for as a man.

His father Ryszard, a Polish Jew with artistic ambitions, had left his home in Krakow in the late twenties for the romantic, Bohemian delights of Paris, and became one of many in that international melting-pot of dreamers and escapees from the mundane. After divorcing his first wife, he set out to make a life of his artistic dreams but, like many a struggling artist, discovered that his paintings, while competent, were not good enough for the sophisticates of the Paris art world. In his search for work, he was drawn to the émigré populations of Paris and a community of White Russian exiles, where he met and fell in love with Bula Katz, a young beauty of dark features, half-Jewish. She was also married, and had a child, Annette.

Their romance antagonized both Polish and Russian friends and they were themselves exiled from the exiled, both in the community itself and in religious terms. Bula obtained a divorce from her husband and she and Ryszard married in a civil ceremony. They moved into rooms three flights up in a shabby apartment house at 5 rue Saint-Hubert where they remained for almost three years, both taking jobs to make ends meet.

Their son was born less than a year later. They registered his name as Raymond, which they had mistakenly believed was the French equivalent of Romek, the Polish diminutive of Roman. Later, in Poland, Raymond became Romek, and later still, in the West, the young Polanski chose to be known as Roman.

He was three years old when his parents decided they would move back to Ryszard's homeland, a decision motivated by shortage of money and the menacing political situation that was emerging. Anti-semitic demonstrations which had swept through Germany since 1933 had spread, on a lesser scale, to other parts of Europe, not least Paris, or London, for that matter. Jews were being cast out by many factory owners and businessmen, and Ryszard became an early victim when he was fired from his fairly menial job in a record factory and could not get other employment. He was not the easiest of people to get along with at the best of times. He always believed he had the intellect and

10

talent for something far better than factory work, and gradually that feeling turned to frustration.

Life in his homeland looked less threatened; he was not to know that he would be returning to what would become the first target in Adolf Hitler's expansionist plans. Back in Poland the Polanskis would be among many of their own kind. There were 70,000 Jews in Krakow itself and some 3.5 million in the country as a whole before the beginning of the Second World War. What could happen to such a large ethnic population? It is easy to imagine the reasoning.

Krakow Jews were dispersed in a fairly integrated population, although there was a Jewish quarter whose presence dated back to the eleventh century and which was now known as Kazimierz, after King Kazimierz the Great who granted the Jewish people full citizenship three centuries later when he declared that they had contributed much to the business and community life of Krakow and later to its development into Poland's finest cultural centre.

Krakow was one of the gems of Europe. Originating as a river town, located around the Vistula, it had retained the elegant flavour of the Austro-Hungarian Empire of which it was part in the nineteenth century. High on a limestone rock, known as Wawel Hill, stood Wawel Castle and the cathedral which had been the home and burial ground of Polish kings since the end of the sixteenth century. Sprawling beneath the castle, the city was famous for its civilized café society, centring on the magnificent Renaissance Market Square. It was the home of the celebrated Jagiellonian University where, Communist rulers would later point out, Lenin himself came to read in 1912. A flourishing cultural life supported nine full-time professional theatres as well as cabaret halls and art centres. Steeped in history, Krakow had survived two centuries of troubles with warring neighbours and seemed unassailable.

Ryszard, Bula and Romek departed Paris, leaving Bula's daughter Annette behind with her father for the time being, although she would join them later. They were looking forward to a more settled life and the new experience for Romek of having a grandmother, aunts and uncles and cousins to hand.

Ryszard found them an airy, freshly decorated third-floor apartment in a middle-class area of Krakow, at 9 Komorowski Street opposite a market from which the morning smell of fresh farm produce and newly baked bread wafted appetizingly on the breeze. Nearby was Planty Park, once the site of the ancient city walls, a haven for young children.

Life was certainly better. Work opportunities were only marginally

11

greater than in Paris, but they brought a higher standard of living, and the young Roman began to experience the normality of what would become an all-too-brief childhood.

Ryszard's dreams were still unfulfilled, but early in 1938 he joined one of his brothers in a merchandizing company, selling plastic trinkets to shopkeepers. Within the year, however, the business had become no longer viable as Poland prepared itself for war.

On 15 March 1939 the German army invaded Czechoslovakia, and Hitler drove triumphantly into Prague and raised his standard on Hradzin Castle, the ancient palace of the Bohemian kings. Krakow, located close to the border with Czechoslovakia, was the first major Polish city to see the effects of war. Down in Planty Park trenches were being dug, and all around houses were being boarded and windows taped up.

The Jews, fearing a Nazi invasion, began to close ranks, many of them moving into the Jewish quarter to share the houses of friends and relatives. Ryszard gave up the apartment in Komorowski Street and moved his family into his mother Maria's home in Kazimierz, an old, dark apartment building where Ryszard's family slept in one room. Outside, the sirens wailed in practice and, as the threat of conflict moved close, Ryszard Polanski devised a plan.

He decided to move his family to Warsaw, away from what he considered the danger zone, while he stayed on in Krakow. It was a serious misjudgement. Bula and the children had barely settled into their new home in an unfinished building in Warsaw when Germany invaded. The Wehrmacht force of 1.25 million men swept into Poland in the wake of sustained Luftwaffe bombardment.

It was soon clear that Warsaw itself was the focus of German attack when war was declared on 3 September. Within a week, German forces, striking south from East Prussia and east from Germany itself, arrived at the city gates, and for the next two weeks, the German air force completed the rout with sustained, devastating bombing raids. In the following week, Russia invaded Poland from the east, and Stalin came to terms with Hitler on the partition of the country, the Soviets getting 76,000 square miles of the eastern part of the country and its population of 12.8 million, while Germany got the rest, including Warsaw. Agents of the Gestapo and the NKVD (later the KGB) met at their newly drawn frontiers to do their deal: German Communists who had earlier fled to the Soviet Union were handed back to the Germans to face certain death, while the Gestapo exchanged Stalin's Polish enemies arrested by the Germans.

They would be sent north to labour camps in the frozen wastes of Russia, and in the early stages of the Second World War, Stalin murdered more Poles than Hitler: 1.5 million soldiers and civilians were deported to Siberia, shipped in cattle trucks to the Arctic regions. Up to 750,000 died of starvation and disease, among them 100,000 Polish Jews who died in a Soviet holocaust even before the Germans began their own, and 15,000 Polish army officers who were slaughtered by Soviet secret police and buried in a mass grave in the Katyn Forest.

It is worth remembering these statistics when considering the accounts of Polanski's 'traumatic childhood' for which he later drew much sympathy and publicity in the West, when he became famous. He was a tiny speck of dust on a vast desert of human devastation, and he survived.

In September 1939, the Germans were at the gates of Warsaw. Bula Polanski and her two children joined the rest of the city in the terror of the air raids and spent their nights, and many days, in dank cellars. Towards the end of the year, Roman's father managed to reach his family whom he had inadvertently positioned at the very heart of the conflict, whereas Krakow was so far relatively untouched. He bribed his way out of the city and began the trek back to Krakow.

By then, the Germans had started to organize regional controls, especially over the larger towns and cities, and for the first time Polish Jews began to fear for their very lives. For Roman Polanski's family, the situation was ironic. Ryszard and Bula had never followed the religious beliefs they had inherited, and had never enrolled their two children into the religious instruction necessary for the faith.

Even so, the Germans did not appear to be enforcing a regime of brutal autocracy in Krakow – yet. Life seemed calm and almost normal. Food rationing was beginning, and the Polanskis, along with everyone they knew, were sent to one of the new Jewish settlement areas – the ghettos – where they were given a ground-floor apartment on Podgorze Square, which they had to share with other families. For the time being, Jews could continue to move about the city with relative freedom; Romek even started school again. Soon after Christmas 1939, however, the next phase of the ghetto establishment was brought in.

One morning, Romek looked out of the window of the family apartment and saw workmen building a wall across the middle of the road. Soon every street and every door leading into the ghetto were bricked up and topped with barbed wire. Within a mere couple of weeks, Krakow's entire Jewish population had been interned in guarded compounds which they were unable to leave without permits.

13

The city still relied upon Jewish workers for many tasks, such as labouring jobs and menial work, and the Germans themselves hired Bula Polanski for cleaning duties at Wawel Castle, which had been turned into the command centre for the area's German administrators. She was one of the few in the neighbourhood with a cherished pass allowing her to come and go through the compound checkpoints virtually at will. But slowly the screw was turned, imprisonment looked to become final, and people were disappearing from the streets, never to be seen or heard of again. There was much talk about new concentration camps being built specifically to take Polish Jews, and by mid-1940, when this was confirmed, the ghetto-dwellers were struck with panic and terror, dreading the days when the Germans came through the checkpoints and began their house-to-house searches.

Ryszard Polanski had considered what he might do to save his wife and family from the troubles that lay ahead. He knew of cases where some of the more wealthy in the ghettos had attempted to bribe their way to freedom but ended up losing everything. In any event, he only had enough money to save one of them – the smallest, Romek – and, with objective pragmatism, came to an arrangement with a Catholic family named Wilk whom he had met some months earlier. They lived well away from the ghetto and were prepared to look after the boy as best they could for the duration in exchange for money and other valuables.

One afternoon, Bula used her worker's pass to leave the ghetto and take the boy to the Wilks' house so that he would know where to go when the need arose. By then, Romek was coming up to his eighth birthday. He was a small, shy child, never far from the protective arm of his mother. His slight build and thin face gave greater prominence to his long nose and prominent ears; his eyes were sad, his mouth was thin and unsmiling, and he looked barely capable of withstanding the troubles that lay ahead. The timidity would soon be forced out of him, however.

By the end of 1940, the Krakow ghettos were under the brutal control of sadistic guards. Stories of families and friends giving each other moral support, sharing food and necessities, were matched by other tales of treachery and back-stabbing. The ghetto was geared towards explosiveness, a total breakdown of moral and social values, which was all part of the Nazi psychological tactic of grinding the Jews into the floor. Public beatings and instant executions of offenders became regular occurrences. By the middle of 1941, when the first concentration camps which were to be mostly filled by Poland's 3 million Jews were ready, the raids on the ghettos became more frequent, until the first wholesale deportations began, with columns of men, women and children being marched away towards the city railway sidings.

Romek was a witness to many of the raids, and his own escape route was ready. He was so small he could slip unnoticed through a gap in one of the barricades and head off towards the Wilks' house when his mother or father gave the order. As the weeks wore on, he began making sorties into the other side, slipping through his escape route and darting in and out of alleys and cellars like a little fox; he would search bins and city tips for anything that might be of use, from bits of stale bread to discarded clothing. When word of his successes got around, boys from other families began to join him. Romek had discovered ways to get past the ghetto guards and through the barricades. He found sewer tunnels that took them deep into the centre of Krakow, where they could ferret around the trading areas and restaurants, the bars and the markets.

By the end of 1941, the Nazis were coming back day after day, systematically emptying the ghetto. The Polanskis were moved to another flat, in the block where Roman's grandmother Maria lived, and shared a room with another family, an architect, his wife and son. Their time was surely coming and Romek was sent to the Wilks' house. They in turn had arranged for him to stay temporarily with a Catholic family on the outskirts of Krakow. Within a few days, however, the family decided they could not keep him because neighbours had become suspicious of this boy who had suddenly arrived in the household.

For a time, Romek returned to the ghetto, but once again was taken back to the Wilks by his mother as more and more of the ghetto streets were emptied. Soon after Bula returned home, the Nazis arrived at her door. She was dragged from the house, put aboard a truck with a dozen or more other women and driven away. Her daughter Annette was also taken, and so was Romek's grandmother. No one knew then that their destination would be Auschwitz.

Ryszard Polanski managed to bribe a guard to let him slip away from his labouring job in the city to find Romek and tell him that his mother had gone. Even with the knowledge of the raids, and Bula's constant warnings that she and Ryszard might one day be taken, the arrival of that day was difficult for the boy to accept. He repeatedly asked his father when his mother would be coming back. Ryszard was both distraught and angry. He raged about the Germans and he raged about Romek, as if it was his fault. His uncle explained to the boy that all women in the street where they lived had been taken that day. The men were left behind because they were still required for work in the city.

Days, then weeks, passed and Bula did not come back; there was no word of her. Romek was sent back to the Wilks. Several times he ran away, back to the ghetto to find his father and to try to discover if his mother had returned. There were many narrow escapes as the months passed, with Romek moving back and forth between freedom and the ghetto, until finally, in March 1943, came the discovery that the Jewish quarter was being cleared and every remaining inhabitant moved out to the concentration camps.

Romek had been warned by his father to stay away, but on the very day of the evacuation, he made his way back to the ghetto to try to find his father. The houses were empty, and he saw the column of male prisoners being marched away. He ran and ran until he caught up with them and finally found his father, who told him bluntly to push off.

He was a month from his tenth birthday, and alone. But at least he had the Wilks to care for him.

Chapter Two

*I*n 1992, during a publicity interview for a British magazine, Polanski
reacted fiercely to being questioned about his 'traumatic' childhood.
He is always volatile in interviews and sometimes it is difficult to distin-
guish the actor from the reality, to know whether this is a man seeking
the promotion of his latest work or truly stating his beliefs and feelings.
On this occasion he shot back with a response that challenged the interviewer's audacity in presuming to know whether a child's experiences
could be classed, or dismissed, as 'traumatic'. What was trauma, he
asked, to a boy who did not know where his mother was, or whether
she was alive?

Polanski's childhood was undeniably traumatic. Alone at the age of
ten, intuitively ducking out of sight whenever a German uniform
approached, he became a self-taught expert in the art of survival. He
had no alternative but to face squarely every horror that confronted
him. Naturally, in later years, this period of his life would be revisited
by those seeking explanations for particular elements of both his life and
his work. Freudian theorists would have a field-day.

It was an area which invoked sympathy and certainly provided clues
to Polanski's mentality and thinking. To his contemporaries in Poland,
though, his wartime experiences were not considered especially unusual
and were seldom discussed. There were boys like him in every major
town and city throughout Eastern and Central Europe, whose parents
had been taken, killed, shot or had just vanished. In some respects, he
was more fortunate than many, because of the arrangements his family
had made. It was a bad time, very bad, but his first wife, Basia Kwiatkowska, today agrees that the portrait of his formative years – terrible
though they were – was an inaccurate one, painted by writers who,
during the next thirty or forty years, periodically referred back to his
past in an attempt to prove that his explorations of the darkest corners

of the human psyche on film and the scandals in his private life derived directly from his experiences during the war. Occasionally Polanski even offered some new piece of anecdotal evidence which was seized on by interviewers to back up their claims. His story became exaggerated and distorted, as were many events of his subsequent life.

Time and again, in interviews for this book, his contemporaries dismissed the events in Polanski's childhood as an underlying cause of the dark and macabre elements in his life and work. Basia Kwiatkowska, for example, could not remember him ever referring in their private conversations to his mother's disappearance or his childhood experiences, save for fleeting mentions of a particular event; and as we shall see later, Basia would cite other inspirations for the black humour and 'genius' of his work.

Another of Polanski's contemporaries, Witold Sobocinski, who as a student film-maker formed an 'intense relationship' with Romek, never once heard him talk of his childhood, and did not even know what had happened to him until he read about it much later. Nor did his good friend, actor Henryk Kluba, detect an 'Occupation' complex, as a result of the years of the German occupation of Poland from which many of his age suffered badly after the war. The Polish attitude to self-analysis is somewhat ambiguous at the best of times, and reasons given as to why Polanski did not talk to his contemporaries about his childhood might well be offered by Western psychologists as evidence that he was trying to bury it all in his subconscious – and there was much to bury.

In spite of the down-playing of their importance by the Polish faction, we cannot lightly dismiss the effects these early experiences must have had on the young Polanski. Years of abject hardship lay ahead, at a time when a young mind is normally in its formative stages. After watching his father and the column of Jewish prisoners disappear out of sight, Romek ran back across the city towards the home of the family who had been paid to care for him. It would have been just as easy for them to turn him out into the street or even hand him over to the Germans and pocket the cash. They did neither. He was given shelter, and during the next few months he was billeted with various families, including one whose apartment was now in the middle of a building occupied by German officers, where the family acted as caretakers. The story Romek would tell anyone who asked was that he was the son of a relative who had been killed.

He earned money selling newspapers and spent some of it going to the cinema to watch the German-approved films, usually propaganda movies or German-made dramas. Later on, as he became more street-wise, he joined up with a gang of urchins who scavenged, stole and dealt in black market goods for their existence. They roamed the suburbs of Krakow in small packs, and lived rough in abandoned buildings. That was Romek's story in Krakow during the early part of the war. But he managed to come through relatively unscathed, at least in body.

By the summer of 1943, when the intensity of the Occupation was at its peak, Romek became an increasing worry to his surrogate family who feared that he would be arrested, or that someone would inform on them. They decided that he should be sent away to distant relatives. He was taken on a hundred-mile rail journey to a peasant farming family in the village of Wysoka, which was miles from the nearest rail station. The final part of his journey was on foot, and the descriptions are of a harsh trek, in ill-fitting shoes, under blazing sun. And so on.

But he was alive.

Wysoka was no different from a thousand other Polish villages – just a scattering of white-painted houses surrounding a Catholic church, a hall that doubled as a school, and a shop that sold everything. These rural areas had been relatively undisturbed by the war, apart from the loss of men and the deprivation of supplies. In any event, such deprivations barely affected the family who would offer Romek shelter. They were impoverished peasants who grew their own food and, war or no war, struggled to stay above subsistence level at the best of times. One more mouth to feed was more of a hardship to them than it was to the recipient.

When he was moved to the country, Polanski had visions of a paradise, with rolling fields of corn and wheat, sheep and cattle and a carefree life without Germans. It was like that to a degree, but the countryside is also a culture shock to a city boy. True, it looked charming and picturesque compared with the terrible ghetto of Krakow and the gloomy back-streets where Romek had run with his friends, hiding in cellars and sewers: perhaps what struck him most was the sheer peacefulness of it all.

His recollections of this period of the war, however, were that it was harsh and hard. Home was a peasant hovel, with the family of five – two sons and a daughter, aged between ten and sixteen – sharing two rooms. They were rough and ready people who farmed 3 acres of land from which most of their income was derived, and owned a cow, a few hens and a couple of pigs. The father did other odd jobs around the village and acted as a shoe repairer, though few people came to him because he was not very skilled. They filled their bellies with potatoes and soup, and gritty bread made from hand-ground flour. But Romek never starved.

The wife, a tough and weatherbeaten woman, was the real head of the family. Deeply religious, she ensured that the entire family began each day with a hymn and went to church three times a week. In his guise as a relative from Krakow, Romek had to join in the religious activities of the family, and to all intents and purposes became a practising Catholic while living in Wysoka.

He was assigned sleeping accommodation at the back of a ramshackle barn, where insects were attracted to his tender white skin, and he suffered the permanent consequence of irritation from their bites. Although the youngest child in the family, two years his junior, went to school, Romek was kept at the farm where he was put to work. He had no papers, and the family preferred not to risk the possibility of his Jewish background being discovered. Once, when the German administration decided to carry out a population census of the area, Romek was sent away to another village for two nights until the officials had gone.

The hot summer of 1943 gave way to a bleak winter which was lightened by new and pleasurable experiences. Romek joined other village children on home-made skis and sledges on the snow-covered slopes around the village. With little work to do on the farm, he began to explore the countryside which still seemed a long way off from the war.

As the New Year dawned, however, the threat of Nazi troops heading deeper into the Polish countryside did become a reality, and before long, almost overnight, the roads around the village of Wysoka saw the first signs of the German invaders as they began fortifying a range of hills a few miles away. Apart from the census, there had been little contact with the Germans until then. Even news of the war itself was scant; radios were banned and the few newspapers were produced under German controls.

By word of mouth, news swept through central Poland that the sudden build-up of German military movements in the spring of 1944 was to counteract Russian advances from the east. By the summer, first proof of the rumours of terrible atrocities committed by the Germans against tens of thousands of Polish citizens imprisoned in the concentration camps was revealed when the Russians reached Maidenek, a 670-acre compound surrounded by an electrified barbed-wire fence, interspaced with fourteen machine-gun posts from which would-be escapees were shot. It was estimated that 1.5 million people, of many races and creeds

20

from all over Europe, were gassed here, and their bodies burned in mass crematoria.

Now, with the German front against Russia collapsing, Soviet troops were advancing south and eastward towards Warsaw, and talk of uprisings by the Free Polish Resistance movements brought fierce reprisals by the retreating Germans. Marauding German troops plundered their way across the countryside and Romek had some close encounters as the German presence around Wysoka became more prevalent. One day, while walking along a road to visit a girl he had become friendly with in a neighbouring village, he was spotted by a group of German officers who took pot-shots at him for no apparent reason.

In the village itself, his presence was becoming uncomfortably worrying to his host family, and one day he decided to run away. He had gone only a few miles down the road when he encountered a German road-block and was spotted. One of the soldiers called to him to stop and produce his papers. Romek, who had none, ran off into the forest, ducking a hail of pistol shots as he went, and for two days sheltered in the undergrowth with only berries for food. He returned to the farm cold and hungry.

By the late summer, news had filtered through of the terrible events taking place in Warsaw. A resistance movement of remaining Jews had taken up arms against the Germans and had been virtually wiped out. Then, on 20 August, after continual battles with the Polish Home Army, the German High Command ordered the city to be razed to the ground. The Home Army, the largest resistance movement in Europe after the Yugoslavian partisans, held the city against 30,000 German troops for almost two months. The Polish High Command appealed to the Red Army for help, but got only token and belated assistance from the Communist Polish Army, fighting under Soviet command. They were driven back, allowing the Germans to continue the onslaught, and the Home Army was defeated, suffering terrible casualties. Tiger tanks supported by Luftwaffe bombers moved in to shell the Old City, where the Home Army had established its stronghold, and systematically blew up every building, while ground troops fought house-to-house battles, with heavy losses on both sides. By 2 October, when the fighting ended, 200,000 people lay dead.

In the countryside the Germans were commandeering local labour to join prisoners of war in establishing new garrisons, and their retreat was halted for a time, but the carnage went on all around, as both the Germans and the Russians devastated the landscape with their artillery. The

Nazi troops, with their supply-lines under attack, pillaged all available food, raiding the tiny farms for anything they could lay their hands on.

By the end of the summer, as swarms of Allied bombers began to appear in the skies over Poland, Romek talked with the woman who had been his surrogate mother for these past months, and decided he should try to make his way back to Krakow, where he could lose himself in the city. The war was going the way of the Allies, and perhaps his relatives might return soon. At worst, he could hide away with the family he had lived with before being sent to Wysoka until the German threat had finally gone, as now seemed likely.

Ahead of him lay the long road back to Krakow, and just how he would manage to undertake this journey, without transport, with the roads filled with Germans checking the flood of refugees, with dangers at almost every turn, remained something of a mystery. In his auto-biography, Polanski curiously omitted any mention of what must have been a monumental trek; he merely stated 'that he arrived back in Krakow' in the final days of the German occupation.

Other accounts have placed him with a group of refugees who made it back to the city under the protection of a group of Communist freedom fighters. Krakow was still a dangerous place, not simply because of the war and the air raids which had started again. Romek still faced the threat of being arrested as a Jew. He headed first to the old ghetto area, which was wrecked, and then on to the apartment building to find the family with whom he had been lodged before being sent to Wysoka.

They still lived there, having survived the German Occupation in relative comfort as caretakers and cleaners of the building used by Nazi officers who had just been moved out in retreat from the city. The Occupation was all but over; the Red Army was positioned on the outskirts of Krakow, ready for its final push. Bombing raids on German positions continued day and night, and for Krakow at large, joy as the Germans began to leave was tempered by the fear of what might follow in these final days.

Romek once again moved in with the family who had sheltered him in 1942–43, and during the day began running off into the city, and then towards the old ghetto district, scouring deserted houses trying to find someone who might have news of his parents. For the time being there was no news, but people were pouring back into the city from the hillsides every day.

The streets were filled with Red Army soldiers, bedraggled and exhausted by their rout of the Germans fleeing ahead of them. The

Soviets were welcomed as heroes for the first – and probably the last – time in Polish history, though even heroes were not averse to theft, looting and even rape.

Krakow was in chaos as thousands of homeless refugees flooded into the city, which, compared with Warsaw, had escaped the war lightly in terms of overall damage. To those thousands would soon be added many more who were to be freed from the concentration camps. The snow in the streets turned to filthy sludge as Romek roamed the city, rediscovering a few old friends. The child gangs, like the adult gangs, were soon re-formed now that they could have the run of the city without fear of arrest. Looting and scavenging became the main form of activity for many Polish children who ran wild, Romek among them.

By early 1945, there was still no news of the Polanski family. Concentration camps were being liberated and emptied. On 24 January 1945, the Russians sweeping through Poland and on towards Germany arrived at the now notorious Auschwitz death camp where Romek's mother and sister Annette had been held. Marshal Zukov's tanks battered down the gates to reveal the absolute horror of this shocking death factory in which millions from all over Europe had been slaughtered.

By the time the Russians arrived, however, most of the surviving prisoners had been marched off into Germany under Nazi escort, leaving only 5000 men, women and children, most near to death through disease and starvation and unable to walk, among the mounds of skeletal corpses. It would be months before the detailed identities of the living and the dead of Auschwitz could be assimilated, and for the time being Romek, like many others, was no nearer knowing the fate of his mother, his sister or his father who was in another camp, location unknown. As the weeks rolled by, he continued to be a child of the streets. These were perilous days. Once or twice he fell foul of competing scavengers and was beaten up. He brushed with danger and with death when he came across lethal items of German artillery, and had a particularly narrow escape when he pulled the pin on a hand-grenade and watched it explode just yards away.

Ironically, after the end of the war life did not suddenly become any less traumatic. The beginning of his return to comparative normality was when the threats to his very existence began to disappear with the departure of the Germans. For this boy and for many others not yet in their teens, what now lay ahead was a period of accounting, of accepting that he had come through the worst and of restoration to a true family group, if that were ever possible.

It began one day towards the beginning of the summer of 1945. He was running along the streets in the centre of Krakow when a voice called his name. He stopped dead in his tracks, and turned to discover a familiar face. It was his father's youngest brother, his Uncle Stefan. There were bear-hugs from Stefan, and a tenuous kind of reaction from Romek, who no longer knew how to respond to affection. He was also more interested in discovering whether his uncle had received any news of his parents. He had not.

Stefan himself was gaunt and nervy, having spent most of the war years hidden away in an apartment outside the ghetto. Though both he and his wife Maria were Jewish, she had Aryan looks and had managed to survive on forged papers. They had seldom dared venture into the streets but had come through the war unscathed apart from jangling nerves. Stefan insisted that the boy should go home with him.

Soon another uncle, David, arrived. He too had led a charmed existence, having become a *kapo*, a trusty, in his concentration camp. There were some understandable misgivings over his wartime role when the family learned that the fourth of the brothers, the eldest, had been beaten to death – by a *kapo*.

Romek's relationship with his uncles was difficult. He found it hard to accept the discipline imposed by two men who were strangers to him. Before many weeks had passed, he was moved to live with his Uncle David, who was sure the boy needed taming. One beating, in which the ex-*kapo* drew blood from his nephew's backside, only ended when Romek thanked him for the hiding which had made him realize the wrong he had done – a system which, many surviving Jews would recall, was used in the camps.

Partial family reunion had brought no real happiness for Romek as he celebrated his twelfth birthday in August 1945. The war was over; Poland had suffered 5.5 million human casualties and was second only to Russia in the number of civilians killed.

Bula Polanski, Roman's mother, was among them.

Ryszard Polanski survived. In the summer of 1945 he was released from Mathausen concentration camp and sent to a processing centre before final release back to Krakow. There, waiting for clearing, he came across his step-daughter Annette, who gave him the news that Bula had perished in the gas chambers. Distressed and mentally anguished, Annette decided she did not want to return with Ryszard to Krakow. There was nothing there for her now, and she had no great affection for her

24

step-father. She wanted to leave Poland immediately and head for Paris in search of her real father's family.

Dressed in the fatigues supplied by the liberating Americans, and looking remarkably well considering his ordeal, Ryszard went back to Krakow to find his brothers and the son whom he had last seen twenty-seven months earlier. The reunion was charged with varying emotions, not least the knowledge that Bula would not be coming back, and that Annette – to whom Romek had grown very close until she was taken – had chosen not to return. Romek's grandmother had also gone.

In fact Ryszard's return did little to stabilize his son's life. Both found it difficult to talk to each other, and it was weeks before either spoke about the events of the past years. Some of their experiences were never shared.

The surroundings were difficult, too. They shared a tiny apartment with the Horowitz family whose surviving relatives were also returning from the camps, so that eventually more than a dozen people crammed into a couple of tiny rooms. Mrs Regina Horowitz had been in Mathausen with Ryszard. Her young son, also named Ryszard and now six, had survived Auschwitz, saved from death after being thrown into sludge-filled latrines by his father on the day they were being herded into the gas chambers. Mrs Horowitz, determined to give thanks for their deliverance, restored the rites of her Jewish faith with vigour, and this in itself became a strange and almost intimidating experience for Romek, whose only religious attachment had been his forced attendance at Wysoka's Catholic church.

Everywhere the drama of the surviving Jews and other deported hordes, of relatives seeking relatives, or news of them, of tearful reunions with those returning, or the dread realization that so many had been slaughtered, provided a scenario of such intensity that there are no words which can adequately describe the emotions that surfaced in those terrible days of discovery immediately after the war. Romek identified this time as an emotional turning point, where many uncertainties were cleared up only, in many respects, to be replaced with others, just at a time when he might have expected resumption of what would pass for normality. Barely two weeks passed after Ryszard's return before he left those overcrowded rooms, leaving Romek behind again, and went off in search of work or business opportunities.

He returned a few weeks later with an attractive young woman named Wanda Zajaczkowska on his arm, and converted to Catholicism to marry her. Much later, Wanda and Romek would become friends, and she would treat him like a son. At the time, though, he bitterly resented her attempting to take the place of his own mother. He was angry with his father for bringing this woman to Krakow so soon after learning of Bula's death. Ryszard explained his reasoning, that the only way to obliterate the past was to rebuild for the future. This he was intent on doing and he wanted his son to do the same, to go back to school and begin his education ready to find a trade. Romek wanted that too, but as for the rest of it, the prospect of playing happy families with a new mother simply did not appeal to him. They tried it for a while, however. Ryszard and Wanda married and found a modest house near the old Jewish quarter, and attempted to revive a business run by Wanda's parents before the war. Romek moved in and at last began to attend school. His father paid for extra tuition to help him to catch up on some of the lost years, but he grew intensely bitter, watching his father and Wanda together, so that he could hardly manage to stay in the same room. Wanda found him a disrupting influence on her relationship with Ryszard and she often said that she had tried to gain his confidence but he stubbornly rejected her. He was, said Henryk Kluba, an incredibly obstinate and aggressive boy. Ryszard sometimes resorted to the heavy hand, but after all that he had been through, violence was the least likely way to change Romek's attitude.

They decided that he should be moved out of the house, away from the family once again. In spite of everything, father and son found they could not live under the same roof. 'He was apparently a very aggressive child,' said Zofia Komeda, 'but underneath, he was very sensitive, and talented. His relationship with his father was never very good but he was unbearable, believe me. People just did not like him.' The psychologists and the carers of many survivors of concentration camps, or those who had suffered the trauma of other wartime situations, would discover many cases of shattered, irreparable relationships where love had been lost or hammered out of lives.

Ryszard found Romek lodgings near his school with an elderly widow who had a tiny apartment which she shared with a daughter and a niece, orphaned in the war. Romek's fourteenth birthday found him packing his few belongings into a suitcase, ready to be taken to his new home. He would never again live in his father's house.

Chapter Three

So this slip of a boy had escaped the Nazis, survived those tormented war years and given the Devil a run for his money. He believed he had been pretty hard done by, which he had by any account, although many other boys his age had suffered worse and so he could be thankful for something. The irony of it all was that he and all the others who had come through this experience should become the product of another dictatorial system enslaving the nations of Eastern Europe under the hammer rule of Joseph Stalin.

There were plenty in Poland who did not believe it possible and welcomed the arrival of Stalinism in place of the German Occupation. Communist-controlled administrations were installed in the seat of government and in the districts throughout the land, taking control of everything. Newspapers and the performing arts were special targets as tools of the psychological battle, and thus every film, every script, every play was scrutinized avidly by committees.

The agreements signed at the Yalta conference by the Big Three leaders of the United States, Great Britain and the USSR, which gave Soviet Russia a free hand in Eastern Europe, provided certain conditions in regard to free elections were met, very quickly proved to be a complete sham. The fate and future of Poland and its people were sealed on 31 July 1945 when Winston Churchill made his famous pronouncement that an Iron Curtain was falling over Europe.

The iron rule of Communism, which would soon envelop the whole of Eastern Europe, rapidly brought a regimental life-style into Poland during the recovery period. In the early days, the country was governed as if it was part of Stalin's Russia, and successive Polish administrations and presidents would continue their lamentable and uneasy alliance with the Soviets until 1989, offering it as the only alternative to direct Soviet intervention. The system of social order was reorganized, with collective agriculture and every priority given to industrialization: Krakow was overwhelmed by the enormous Nowa Huta steel plant which became one of the largest and most polluting in Eastern Europe. The Roman Catholic church was remorselessly attacked and looted, and priests persecuted.

Romek stayed at secondary school for the time being, and continued with private tuition. Schoolboys like him had few alternatives in the reorganization of the school system under the new Communist administration. At the age of fifteen, pupils were required to enter a vocational training school or a college for preparation for university. Romek qualified for the former and, pressed by his father to become qualified in electronics, for which he had shown aptitude by building a radio set, he gained entry into the Mining Engineers College at Krakow. He soon realized, however, that this was absolutely not his personal vocation. Coming late to the mysteries of mathematics and chemistry, he found the subjects difficult and boring. There were stirrings of other interests, due in part to the Communist ideal, as decreed by Lenin, that the performing arts embracing radio, film and the theatre should all be used as vehicles for the advancement of Communism.

Cinemas were reopening and showing a wealth of imported films, many of them Russian and consisting of ideological tales of heroes of the system, although in those early post-war years there was also a fair variety of films from the West of a kind which would later be barred by the censors as capitalist material unsuitable for the new society. Some early exceptions included Errol Flynn in *Robin Hood* and Carol Reed's 1946 story of the IRA, *Odd Man Out*, starring James Mason and Robert Newton, both of which Romek saw several times.

There was also a thriving theatrical community in Krakow and among the most notable companies was Teatr Rapsodycyny, or Rhapsodic Theatre, whose pre-war troupe included one Karol Wojtyla, later to become Pope John Paul II, who moved to Krakow in 1938 to study Polish literature at the celebrated Jagiellonian University. The theatre produced a lively collection of actors, writers and poets and survived the war clandestinely, only to be abolished when it fell foul of the authorities in the early stages of the Stalinist era. Only 'approved' actors could remain in work, and they found themselves under the constant scrutiny of the Ministry of Culture.

One of the most popular areas of entertainment was the radio. Russian-made sets were imported into Poland in large numbers, and the transmissions included children's programmes which lightly but surely pursued converts to the Communist cause from an early age. At that time the radio was one of the most vital tools of Communist indoctrination, spreading the message far beyond the cities into the rural areas where communications were difficult.

Recognizing that a great mass of the audience they were attempting to reach consisted of unsophisticated peasants of limited ability and knowledge, the authorities kept plays and broadcasts simple. Local committees read the scripts before they went on the air, and actors diverged from their lines at their peril. They could not even 'act' in the real sense, to heighten the impact.

Romek listened regularly to *The Merry Gang*, a twice-weekly children's programme which he thought was pretty awful, and said as much one afternoon when listeners were invited to the studio in Krakow to watch the programme going out live. His opinions were heard by a producer who asked him if he thought he could do better.

He said he was quite certain he could, and the producer, Maria Billizanka, gave him an audition. Maria was impressed by his reading of the material, though she thought he should be watched because he was a precocious boy, not in the child star sense but as one who was not averse to expressing his views and opinions. She had quite definite rules about allowing children to become stars, and recognized that the young Polanski, though small in stature, possessed a curiously strong personality and a brilliant flair for mimicry.

Romek got a job as a part-time radio actor and soon began appearing in a variety of roles. The committee which ran the radio station came down hard on any actors who tried to ham it up. Listeners were not to be diverted from the message or the cause by some budding Olivier. The opportunity of radio work changed Romek's attitude and his outlook. It was the first time anyone had given him credit for anything. For as long as he could remember, and for as long as it mattered, he had been kicked around, and even now, in the family group and in his early days at school, he was always talked of in uncomplimentary terms as the scheming, half-illiterate little kid.

Actors appealed to him. He recognized them as a breed apart, even if they were forced to become the tools of the state committees in the transmission of propaganda. Most were quietly rebellious and, when off duty, acted their plays and scripts in the way they would like to have done. There was a well-known bunch of actors who established themselves in Krakow after the war, and those who behaved, stayed relatively sober and did not bring disgrace upon the system which employed them could enjoy a fairly advantaged life-style, with enough petrol to keep their cars running and sufficient money in pocket to enjoy the night-life which was beginning to seep back into the social order.

Romek took to acting like a duck to water, though he had learned it by accident. He had been applying the techniques to his own very real situation – pretending, lying, even cheating, and in quieter moments living within his own imagination. 'While his childhood obviously had some bearing on his work, I don't think his experiences were altogether responsible for his forcefulness,' said Basia Kwiatkowska. 'Rather, I think this forcefulness derived from his incredible maturity. This man must have been born with thoughts already formulated in his mind. I know that is not possible, but it seemed like it. His brain moved so quickly, he was impatient with slowness, people who had sluggish reactions. He is also from Krakow, and all his incredible showing off is a local trait which Romek developed brilliantly.'

The talent for 'showing off' was such that Maria Billizanka, who also produced plays for the Young Spectators Theatre in Krakow, cast him in several plays until, finally, he was given the lead role in the Soviet play *The Son of the Regiment* by V. P. Katayev. It was typical post-war Soviet propaganda drama, the story of a peasant boy who is adopted by a Red Army unit and then captured by the Germans. The enemy tortures him to try to get information from him, without success. The boy becomes a hero when he leads his Red Army unit back to defeat the Germans. This was familiar fodder for the theatre and cinema in post-war Eastern Europe.

But the play gave Romek his first opportunity of working with professional actors. It ran at the youth theatre in Krakow, on and off, for two years. It was also chosen to form part of the first Festival of Soviet Plays in Warsaw, which brought Romek local fame. Soon afterwards, he landed another major role, one he knew well, as a street urchin who becomes a clown in a play called *Circus Tarabumba* at the Krakow Puppet Theatre. The role, co-starring with the puppets, was an important one and brought Romek to the wide attention of Krakow theatre-goers.

Now a familiar figure in the theatre, he would venture out into the huge Market Square of Krakow where people gathered daily to chat and stroll and drink coffee in the cafés. In the centre of the square is the Cloth Hall with its parapet of gargoyles. Here, on occasions, street performers gave their performances. Romek began going to the surrounds of the Cloth Hall and giving impromptu mime, sometimes mimicking passers-by, especially those with a style of walk or perhaps deformity that he would imitate and exaggerate, or by staging one of his scary practical jokes when he acted as if he was taken by a fit or seizure, and would milk the situation for all it was worth.

He had another passion which was almost as strong as that for the theatre. He and two of his close friends were interested in cycling, and had joined the Cracovia Sporting Club which had relatively good facilities for the training of young men in the sport. Romek wondered if it would help him put on inches. Photographs of him from his stage performances around that time show him as remarkably small for sixteen, and he had clearly developed an inferiority complex about his height.

With money earned from his theatre work, he decided he was going to buy another bicycle and arranged to meet a man who told him he had one to sell. They went to a spot which Romek knew well, where the bike was supposed to be stored. In fact there was no bike, and before he could run away, the man struck him several times about the head with a stone wrapped in newspaper. Romek slumped to the ground and remained conscious just long enough to realize that the man was stealing his cash and also his watch, given to him by his father. He lapsed into unconsciousness for a moment, and when he woke up he realized that blood was pouring like water down his face from the wounds in his head. The memory of that moment when he realized that what seemed to be water was actually blood stayed with him for years, to the point that he hated showers because the water from the spray reminded him of it.

He crawled out to the street where a woman found him. As he held his hand up towards her, he left a bloody handprint on her dress, another vivid memory. He was taken to hospital where his head was shaved for the numerous stitches that were necessary. The police told him he was lucky to be alive. His assailant was identified as Janusz Dziuba who, it turned out, had already killed three people by the same method. He was subsequently arrested, tried for murder and sentenced to death.

'I think Romek had decided what he wanted to do in his life,' said Henryk Kluba, his future colleague in the Lodz National Film School. 'As a boy he had acted and painted . . . he was readying himself for work in that area.' Romek's father still urged him towards a trade or profession, but his studies had been seriously neglected during his work with theatre groups and had virtually put paid to his father's ambitions for him. And sure enough, Ryszard was disappointed when Romek failed to qualify for a place in Poland's state engineering college.

A contemporary said that Romek had deliberately made sure he did not go to the engineering college. 'In spite of his small build, he was a very aggressive boy who usually got exactly what he wanted, and believe me, he would not do anything he did not wish to; he had a conniving kind of nature and he was very manipulative. He could turn things around, talk himself out of any difficult situation. I suppose it could be said that he considered his experiences during the war made him more deserving of a break in life – but then again, there were many of us who had suffered no less than he, some far worse, but I doubt that he would have considered that possibility.'

There are other clues to his developing character. In 1950, when he finally abandoned his technical studies, he enrolled in an art college. Ryszard hated his son's theatrical sorties, which he considered a waste of time, and was even less taken with the idea of art studies. Romek signed for a three-year course at the Krakow Liceum Sztuk Plastycznych where an old scrapbook from the period still survives, providing an intriguing glimpse of his thoughts which he expressed through his drawings and sketches.

He adopted a pseudonym which he scrawled on most of his drawings – 'Dupa', the Polish word for bottom, also used as an expletive, meaning arse. There are various sketches of nude girls, one of a weeping woman and another of a headless body, rather like something from Greek mythology, with a heavily muscled torso and exaggerated genitalia. A few pages further on is one on which he has written 'autoportrait' – a drawing of his own face but distorted to show a wolf's features. It was not difficult to see the analogy, connected as it was with his adopted name during the war of Romek Wilk, meaning wolf.

The art college was a rewarding experience and it also represented another layer of bricks in the foundations he was building for the future. His skill in art enabled him to sketch scenes, design sets and even draw the faces of his characters when the time came to make movies. There was also a good deal of humour about the art college which was lacking in many other grey state-run institutions in Poland where smiles and cheerfulness were, in some quarters, almost an arrestable offence.

Tutors began to regard Polanski's work with some amusement, and one of them who was asked to recall his impressions came out with a remarkable recollection: 'His art seemed to purvey a curious glee in going against convention – whereas most would paint the classic still-life scenes, such as the fruit bowl or whatever, he would do so but turn them into gruesome, surreal interpretations. He was always coming up with the oddest of ideas which were moving right away from what we were trying to teach, to the point that his work, even his very presence, had the effect of creating a ripple effect in the classroom so that others were disturbed by him.'

There was no question about it, Polanski had talent, but he lacked the discipline and direction that the art school required of its students. Some were convinced that his work showed flashes of brilliance verging on genius; others would describe it as at best selfishly gratifying his own whim and at worst displaying a rather sick undercurrent from which he derived a certain self-gratification by being so different. It was one of the earliest examples of his very serious attempt to be radically different from those around him.

Because of his attitude, Polanski and the art college drifted apart. The split coincided with the moment that Poland sank more deeply under the yoke of Stalinist rule to become the most repressive police state in Eastern Europe. The last remnants of private enterprise – whose exponents included Polanski's father – finally went under when the state changed the national currency overnight, and all those with savings saw them vanish into thin air.

For Ryszard Polanski, this was indeed a blow. In the past he had always relied upon his business acumen to survive; he was a natural trader for whom there was no place in modern Polish society – indeed, to continue in private enterprise merely brought into question the subject's commitment to the state ideals. Romek was also in dire trouble. Every institution had to conform to the rigid requirements of the state, and that included the art college where a branch of the Communist Youth Movement had been formed, and which, it was noted, did not have Polanski, R. among its members.

In Polanski's first months at college, he had been treated with some amusement and tolerance. Under the new order, where students and tutors would be monitored for their performance and their political correctness, the college principals decided there was no place in the system for Polanski's disruptive dissidence. He was expelled before he could complete the course.

Not having documents confirming he had passed his examinations was, in work terms, like not having a passport to leave the country. He had to scour the surrounding towns and cities to find a lesser school that would allow him to complete the final months of his studies as an outside student. He passed his exams, but by then his school report, in which every misdeed was logged along with his lack of devotion to the Communist cause, hardly made the kind of reading that would endear him to the system-oriented selection boards for higher education. He seemed destined to settle for army service, followed by a career in some form of manual labour.

With the added pressure of a rift with his father, whom he barely saw for weeks on end, Polanski was in despair, but this was lightened by a ray of hope when a group of final-year students from the renowned Lodz National Film School arrived in Krakow to make a film on industrial heroism. Entitled *Three Stories*, it had a script written and vetted under the censorship formula of the Ministry of Culture through which all movie-making and performing arts productions passed as a matter of course. Polanski used his acting contacts to obtain a small part in the film, which brought him into touch with some of the future key figures in Polish film, including the cameraman Jerzy Lipman and the student director Andrzej Wadja, who were to become two of Poland's most famous film-makers and would figure prominently in Polanski's own future. Wadja provided him with his first close-hand observation of film-makers at work and he recognized later that this was the moment when he decided that it was a goal he would work towards – to get into films, to be around cameras, actors and technicians.

At the time the only possible route towards achieving his ambition seemed to be through acting, because of his childhood experience in the field. He applied to Krakow Drama School to be considered for entry into their two-year drama course and took a preliminary audition which he passed with flying colours, making it into the final selection of fifty students from the 700 who had applied. They all entered the second stage, which consisted of a week's rehearsal and coaching for a series of readings from classical and modern works. When the final list of successful candidates was published, the entire group he was working with were accepted – with the exception of Polanski himself. When he asked one of the tutors why he had failed, he was told bluntly that there were not many parts in the theatre for people as small as himself.

Dejected and disappointed in the spring of 1953, and now seriously worried that his reputation had preceded him, he was becoming desperate. Unless he could find an academy of some sort to take him, he would be drafted for military service. He made several attempts to find a place, first at Krakow University, applying time and again as one department after another turned him down because of his lack of academic qualifications. He went further afield to Warsaw, then, as a military board was about to consider his application for further deferment from service, he even applied to a circus school.

Deep in gloom, he made plans and drew route maps to travel into East Germany and escape to the West through Berlin. Then a lucky break came out of the blue, just when he most needed it. He had been spending a lot of his time hanging around the theatres and with actors, and heard on the grapevine that director Andrzej Wadja was about to cast for a new film entitled *A Generation*, a dramatic, documentary account of Polish wartime resistance to the Germans. Polanski began canvassing his actor friends, and one of them, who was appearing that summer in a Krakow festival of dramatic arts, agreed to mention him to Wadja next time he saw the director. Weeks went by without any contact. Polanski also spoke with the cameraman Jerzy Lipman, who had befriended him during the making of *Three Stories*, and then finally made direct contact with Wadja in Warsaw, and waited for his reaction.

The call came in due course, one day while Polanski was at his father's apartment – he had left the telephone number with Wadja. Ryszard Polanski did not believe his son at first, but he would soon be forced to accept that Romek now intended to abandon all other ambitions in favour of going into an industry that barely existed in Poland at the time: films.

Although his role in *A Generation* was not a significant one, Polanski attached himself to Wadja's company like a limpet, travelling out and about on location, staying on the film set even when he was not required for his scenes, and acting as a general factotum and errand boy. He was never far from the camera action, which he observed with intense interest.

What he saw and learned was stored up for the future. And among the experiences which he would use when dealing with producers and film censors later in his career was his observation of the way Wadja dealt with the constraints of the Communist vetting committee as he began filming. The strong script had been edited and cut to highlight the ideology and to play down any dissension. The censorship continued as each sequence was shot, to the point of removing a major fight scene involving Polanski because it suggested that there were internecine struggles within the resistance movement.

In spite of the censorship problems, *A Generation* was welcomed as an excellent film of its kind, and brought admiring responses from around the world. Keen observers could spot that Wadja at least showed

35

fire and emotion of a kind which had been lacking in film work in Poland since before the war.

The accolades rubbed off on Polanski, who was earmarked to appear in another movie, *The Enchanted Bicycle*, scheduled for 1954. In the meantime, with the encouragement of his new friends in the 'new wave' of Polish film-making, he became determined to get a place at the Lodz National Film School. He sought support and counsel from as many people as possible, including Professor Antoni Bohdziewicz who had supervised the graduates filming *Three Stories* in Krakow. The professor put Polanski's name down for that year's intake, along with several hundred other hopefuls from which only a small number would be selected. Once again, as in the Krakow examinations, he made the relatively small shortlist of people who would be interviewed at length by the board of selectors and then sit a two-week series of examinations at the school, which included acting tests, the writing of a short script and a presentation on directing. It was a tough test and several candidates dropped out before it was over.

Bohdziewicz became a powerful ally who reassured his contemporaries on the examining board about Polanski's past record, his suspect politics and his wayward background. He was a wild boy, to be sure, and had a natural aggression. But he showed sufficient promise and talent to deserve to be considered. At the end of the assessment period, he was among the eight successful candidates to be offered a place at the school.

Polanski was on the path to fame, and escape from Poland.

Chapter Four

*P*olanski had not been long at Lodz when an incident occurred that hardly augured well for his future. He had a room in a house on the campus where Professor Bohdziewicz lived on the first floor. One night there was the sound of loud footsteps on the uncarpeted stairs. Polanski ran out into the street and called a string of abuse to whoever had made the noise. The window on the first floor opened, and the professor's head appeared: 'It is you, sir, who is the prick, not I!' And the window closed. The relationship between students and tutors at the Lodz National Film School was vastly different from other universities and formal education establishments.

For Polanski, this was a blessing – with his ebullient manner, he might not have lasted a single term otherwise. He was approaching his twenty-first birthday, was ill-read by university standards, and had a good deal of catching up to do. That he was able to do so at Lodz was all the more remarkable considering the thousands of young people from all over Poland who were queuing to get in. The board of selectors had the cream of politically correct Polish youth from which to choose its students. In that respect, Polanski was a total oddity, and a curiosity, and it is worth examining for a moment the environment within which he was now ensconced.

There was certainly no better place in Poland – and possibly the whole of Europe, given his inclinations – for him to repair some of the yawning gaps in his schooling and acquire a greater appreciation and study of the cinema and the arts. In spite of its Communist foundation, which was at the time inescapable in the political make-up of the country, the Lodz National Film School was a magnificent facility which arose in the austere years immediately after the war and developed into one of the foremost centres of its kind.

The students, who were outnumbered by tutors and technicians,

37

benefited from the knowledge of some of the foremost people in the Polish film industry. The government had decided to re-establish a film industry, and designated Lodz as the location for the studios of Film Polski, the state-run film company, and for a national film school project. Developed by the new Polish administration in the late 1940s, this came under strong Russian influence.

The town of Lodz was a most unlikely setting for a Polish Hollywood. It was a model of post-war greyness, overhung by a pall of industrial grime and humdrum existence; it was dull even when the sun was shining. Lodz was chosen to become a film centre because it was relatively undamaged and, with the Warsaw rebuilding programme many years from completion, it was the nearest place that possessed suitable buildings. Most were commandeered for the film school, whose headquarters were in an old mansion built in 1893 and set in acres of superb parkland, which had once been the home of a cloth tycoon. There were no tycoons left in Poland now. Private enterprise had been rapidly eliminated and the former upper and middle classes who once owned large suburban houses in the fashionable districts of the cities found themselves sharing with as many families as could be comfortably accommodated. The rebuilding of the nation was under way.

It may seem a curious order of priorities which put cash into the film school project as if it was one of the most important of all the projects in the reconstruction programme. But in the Communist system it was – and this was emphasized in a quotation which appeared under a portrait of Lenin at the entrance to the school, stating that the cinema was the most important of all art forms. 'Art' was a debatable word to be used in this context, which often had more to do with the quest for moulding public opinion through education, propaganda and even fear, than with the presentation of art to the proletariat. In the early years the film school was run to the strictest of Communist principles.

But given that it was ideologically motivated, the facilities were otherwise as good as anywhere in the Communist bloc. The school was supplied with ample modern equipment covering everything that was required in movie-making, from full-length feature films to animated shorts, and projectors for showing them in private screening halls. Lodz also had access to an extensive international library of films, better than anywhere in Eastern Europe, including a large number from Russia and Italy and dozens of British, French and American-made films which were banned from general viewing but became available for analysis by the students. The curriculum covered every aspect of film-making from script-writing to directing, from lighting and camera work to the higher discussions of advanced cinematography.

When Polanski arrived, the tutors included several who would become famous among a highly respected band of Polish film-makers, including Andrzej Wadja, Polanski's friend and supporter, and Andrzej Munk, renowned for his documentaries. The influence of many eminent Russian pre- and post-war figures in film and theatre was prevalent – not least that of the controversial director Sergi Mikhailovich Eisenstein, who made classics out of propaganda films and then used the realism of his documentaries in his later dramatic works. Another important influence was Constantin Stanislavski, perhaps the most famous of all Russian actors in the Western hemisphere, largely for his invention of the 'Method' style of acting which was spread by his disciples in the West before the war and had rapidly become one of the most controversial elements of American theatre and film. It was all the rage in New York in the late 1940s and early 1950s, and was attracting and producing such famous students as Marlon Brando, Montgomery Clift, James Dean, Marilyn Monroe, Caroll Baker and Paul Newman.

The written word had a wide coverage, and the school possessed a complete inventory of some of the great pre-war Russian novelists and playwrights. There were discussions as to how the acting techniques of Stanislavski could be most successfully translated into film, and Polanski's discussion group were agreed that the technique was best suited to acting the works of the Russian writers, Chekhov, Andreyev and especially Gorki, himself an ardent supporter of the Soviet regime, who sponsored what he termed 'social realism' as the official school of Soviet literature and art. When the Lodz school was first established, the edicts of Gorki were well accommodated, and the material discussed and the films viewed followed a direct correlation with the stringent Communist line being imposed across Poland and maintained under the ever-watchful eyes of the Ministry of Culture.

This straitjacket of conformity also had some real benefits and side-effects. The Polish industry from which the school drew its tutors, and the students themselves, were committed to the belief that they were all public artists, and that there was no room for solipsism. They were also unhindered by the Hollywood syndrome of budgets and profit motives; everything they did was based upon the premise that film was a collaborative art.

Finance was not unlimited, but the philosophy enabled both the established and the new national film-makers to explore and experiment in a fashion more or less unheard of in the West, and this system had a profound bearing on Polanski's future career, when he consistently ran into trouble with producers for filming his way, whatever the cost and however long it took. In Lodz, the art of film-making was paramount, within reason. And by the time Polanski arrived at the school, the supervisory board was able to relax the more restrictive demands of the Communist doctrine, especially as most students were being chosen with supposedly as much emphasis on their political correctness as on their talent and promise.

The big question was how the little wild boy, the wolf of Krakow, was going to fit into this hive of intellectual intensity. Egos were not permitted, certainly not among the freshmen, and temperament and volatility were met with contempt by elders and fellow students alike, all of whom realized that those who came to Lodz had the opportunity of a lifetime to learn a craft which they would also enjoy; it was seen as a privilege.

Polanski recalls his early days at the school in a boastful manner, claiming that because he had prior experience of the film world 'as an actor', he slipped into the environment with ease. He found company and common ground with senior students with whom he could converse on a level of experience unmatched by other first-years, and accompanied them to the fashionable bars and restaurants of Lodz.

Polanski had to knuckle down, though, because there was an intense learning programme, including the oral and written history of the performing arts, literature, music, philosophy and the long and involved fundamentals of Leninism and Marxism, allied with modern Communist beliefs. This part of the curriculum was a challenge in itself to a youth who had never even heard of half the names and places under discussion, and had never been in a situation where he had to rely upon his power of debate, rather than his fists, to make a point.

A former student who was in his class recalled that in the discussion groups which centred around a movie or perhaps a lesson on camera techniques, Polanski was a fast and volatile talker who would try to impose his view upon the rest of the group, especially during informal discussion out of the school environment. But when challenged by the academic side of school life, he would often become silent and sullen for long periods, unable to communicate because of his fundamental lack of knowledge.

The gaps in his education affected his ability to reason a particular argument, and he would experience difficulty in proceeding in a logical way, so that in the end he might have a quite brilliant and original thought, but could not find the words to express it. Teachers would become impatient with him as he stuttered and fumbled for words, and some of his fellow students who had no time for the little runt would taunt him. Gradually, however, as his confidence grew, so his response became more in tune with his own aggressiveness, and if someone could not understand the point he was trying to make he would reverse the situation and blame them for being too dumb to understand.

Students were assessed on their ability and standing within the school at the end of each year; if they did not pass the basic minimum qualifications, which called for a fairly high level of ability, they were unceremoniously kicked out at that stage. Henryk Kluba was already a second-year acting student when Polanski arrived. 'We had seen him earlier because when he first applied for entry, he started coming to look around. It was as if he was testing the ground, getting the atmosphere. He wanted to have a look at the place and the people he would work with.'

The work was fairly mundane in the first year. Courses dealt with the technicalities of still photography, the composition of photographs and the framing of the central subject matter, but Polanski was already moving on in his own mind. 'We got close very quickly,' said Kluba, 'because he saw in me someone who might act in his films. I had prepared myself for the school very solidly, and could compare his knowledge with that which was required. I was impressed by his competence. He already knew everything about normal poetics. In that mix of students, he quickly distinguished himself not only with his talent but the way it was complemented by the solid knowledge he was absorbing.'

Polanski's first year started off uneventfully and was into its second session when political developments again began to arouse heated discussions among students. The death of Stalin in 1953 had brought the first murmurs of rebellion and change, and wherever there are artists, writers and thinkers, there are dissidents; the Lodz school was no exception.

Polanski was low-key about politics, and steered well clear of campus debates. There were too many spies – the 'Ear Police', as they were nicknamed – who might easily interpret his admiration of Western films and his fascination with Hollywood as a liking for the capitalist system. But there were developments that he could not avoid.

The Polish workers' uprising in Poznan in June 1956, where the Polish Army opened fire and thirty-eight people were killed, brought reaction

41

across the country, and Russia began amassing its troops to put down the revolt should it become necessary. Wladislaw Gomulka became president and faced down Khrushchev in the famous October Rebellion by threatening to fight against Soviet domination, though he promised that Poland would remain Communist and loyal to the Warsaw Pact.

It seemed a great victory at the time – though it would prove otherwise – and in the wake of this drama the Hungarians staged their massive revolt that October and were crushed under the boots of the Red Army. Three thousand died on the first day.

At Lodz, one of the students had obtained a copy of Khrushchev's secret speech denouncing Stalin, and a mass student gathering at the local sports stadium was joined by local factory workers. Speakers challenged the totality of Communist control for the first time, among them the diminutive Polanski who ran on to the stage and gave a satirical performance mimicking a less than favourite member of the group who was calling for caution and restraint. It was a rare outburst, however: 'Polanski never did burn bridges,' said Kluba. 'He never played politics and the only political speech he made was that one in the sports stadium in which he attacked another so bitterly that he started to cry. Then we learned the other man was a secret police informer.'

Polanski was reluctantly appointed to a delegation elected to seek an interview with Gomulka at the Central Committee headquarters in Warsaw. They went to the capital the following day but never got to see the new president. An aide merely assured them that they had nothing to fear from the new administration; there would be more freedom in Poland, intellectually and physically. As history would show, however, Gomulka's rule would be scarcely less oppressive.

There were some noticeable innovations in the immediate aftermath that would affect Polanski directly. As the more liberal policy crept into the administration of Lodz, requisitions for movies from the West went pretty well unchallenged. Polanski revelled in a viewing programme that included such fare as Orson Welles's *Citizen Kane* (1941), the screen adaptation of John Steinbeck's *Of Mice and Men* (1939), and a selection of Hitchcock as well as some controversial Continental movies, notably from French directors such as Renoir.

Polanski spent hours in the screening room, absorbing all the films available, then entering into heated discussions with fellow students sitting around the great staircase in the main hall of the school – so heated, in fact, that they occasionally came to blows. 'As a person,' recalled Kluba, 'Polanski was unbearable, irritating, and he still is. First of all, he would talk very loudly; it was part of his character. He always had to be number one, the best singer, the best dancer. He had this need to excel in everything. He was very sure of himself. But that constant quest to be top of the class didn't win him any friends, rather the opposite. Many people couldn't stand him . . . he was always involved in fights. There was one famous battle which he conducted in instalments with the writer Marek Hlasko. They were moving from one bar to the other, fighting. He was always covered in bruises, as if his temperament was tearing him apart.'

Kluba did not put this trait down to his childhood – far from it – although his courage may have emanated from those years; certainly, regardless of the consequences, he would have no qualms about challenging men who were bigger and stronger than himself. 'It was rather a struggle for self-realization,' said Kluba, 'and one that was conducted without regard for the cost. Psychologically, he was always open, able to leave his own self and look at himself. He wanted to test himself in various situations. Yes, it was a programme of total self-realization and I could not see any complexes – maybe he had them, his short posture, for instance. He always wore high-heeled shoes . . .'

The temporary thaw in Communist oppression had one other benefit for Polanski. For years, he had wanted to see his step-sister Annette again, but passports were difficult to come by; to his surprise, however, one arrived through the post a month later. He flashed it around the school and informed everyone that he was leaving for Paris as soon as he could. He timed his trip to coincide with the visit of a Polish delegation to the Cannes Film Festival in May 1957 where his friend and sponsor Andrzej Wadja had been invited to show his second film, *Kanal*, a thoroughly unpleasant but powerful account of the 1944 Warsaw uprising against the Germans, when defeated Polish fighters emerging from the sewers of the city were lined up by the Germans and shot.

Polanski remembered nothing of Paris – it was twenty years since his mother and father had taken him to Krakow – and barely recognized his sister Annette or her husband Marian, even though they had been exchanging family snapshots. They talked for hours and it was only then that Roman learned that his mother had been six months pregnant when she was gassed.

Paris was like a great moving montage, a cosmopolitan extravagance which had been untouched by Hitler's bombs and was now fully restored to a kaleidoscope of colours and styles and modernity. It was everything and more that Polanski had imagined from the film clips he had seen, loud and smart and inviting, filled with great wonders, not least James Dean and Marlon Brando peering down at him from the hoardings advertising *Giant* and *The Teahouse of the August Moon*.

After a guided tour by his sister and brother-in-law, Polanski settled into a routine of travelling into the city on his own on the Métro and going to all the places that tourists in Paris visit. What little money he had he spent catching up on the latest films, and saw Paris by night as a footloose explorer.

He also kept some of his francs back to take the train to the Film Festival at Cannes. Here he found the Polish delegation, some of whom viewed Cannes as a shameless self-indulgence of narcissistic self-exposure, and of abundant self-promotion. But the place was crammed with producers, directors, movie stars, starlets galore posing on every inch of the promenade, plus twenty-four-hour screenings. The Communist system which had sponsored Polanski had also taught him that he could look but he could not touch – and poverty is a great remover of temptation in that respect.

The return to Lodz saw Polanski embark on film-making in his own right. His first film was a three-minute shocker made in 1957, notable only for its violence and voyeurism. Entitled *The Crime*, the film showed a shadowy figure moving through the darkness, wielding a knife. The figure opens the door of a room where a man lies sleeping, and stabs him several times before leaving. There was no dialogue, merely a dark and gloomy setting and the act of murder which had similar impact to the shower scene in Alfred Hitchcock's *Psycho*. Polanski's film was not a copy of that sequence, however. *Psycho* lay three years in the future, and this scene came straight out of his own imagination.

Though only three minutes in length, the film shocked his tutors and contemporaries alike, and there were discussions as to what could have motivated him to choose such a subject. Polanski was known to be tough, prone to fights, quick-tempered and aggressive in arguments. But those analysing his work detected something deeper than a small man trying to impose himself upon his surroundings in the only way he knew how, with a loud voice and shocking actions.

This continued to be a topic of discussion, because violence of an unseemly nature figured in both Polanski's next two major projects. The first came in his third-year session at Lodz when he began his important association with Andrzej Munk, who ran the documentary course at the school. The two became good friends – Polanski would visit his mentor's home socially as well as meeting him on the level of tutor–pupil – and they held long and fruitful discussions. That year, under Munk's guidance, students were expected to produce and direct a short documentary.

Polanski's idea was to film a school dance he was planning to organize specially for his film. On the face of it this seemed a fairly mundane subject, and even Munk thought it was hardly an inspiring topic. Polanski had not revealed his secret element, however, which was to get a local gang of youths to gatecrash the dance and start a fight. He would then film the action and call his piece *Breaking Up the Party*. Though his fellow students and his tutor were aware that he was filming the dance, they had no idea what lay in store, and at the given moment the gang made their entry, fists flew, girls screamed, tables were overturned – and Polanski directed his sole cameraman into the fray. The party collapsed into disarray, dresses were torn and noses were bloodied, and as soon as it became known that Polanski had set the whole thing up, he became the object of his comrades' anger, and the school's disciplinary committee threatened to expel him.

Polanski defended himself by recalling that Munk, his mentor and tutor, also enjoyed practical jokes. He received derisory jibes from his fellows for even daring to compare himself to the director. Munk did not like the film either, but rescued his student by stating that the film represented a genuine documentary, though he found few supporters for this view.

Polanski's documentary was a parody, a complete sham. He had engineered the débâcle from start to finish, from the point of organizing the event to provoking the violence and recording it, and thus it was pure fiction. 'I think our growing up manifested itself in the need to create a constant happening,' said Henryk Kluba. 'There were parodies, little studies of behaviour, actions. But most of all we were reacting against the time. We started reading Beckett. That made us a different generation. We had plays of Ionesco which we would read aloud . . . Romek achieved a strong position. He could initiate ideas, and he knew which ones to accept and which ones to reject.'

That was certainly the case as Polanski set about looking for a new film project. He had his eye on a major international competition for shorts which was to be staged in conjunction with the Brussels World Fair in 1958. In casting his net for a subject, he had read a script written by Jakub Goldberg, one of a small band of admirers who surrounded

Polanski. Goldberg was himself a survivor from a concentration camp and as such witness to horrors which were clearly an influence in his writing, along with the despondency of his hero Samuel Beckett. His work was filled with cold, often surreal and absurd images intermingled with sinister, black humour contemplating the mysteries and cruelty of life.

Goldberg's script portrayed two men who emerge from the sea carrying a giant wardrobe between them and begin a farcical journey. This is really a clever device which would permit the film-maker to explore the various diversions they encounter as they journey on with their burden. Polanski liked the outline, but rewrote the story for his film, building up certain aspects and bringing a more clearly defined story into Goldberg's meandering philosophizing, which he called *Two Men and a Wardrobe*.

He presented his script to the school administrators and announced that he was going to enter it for the World Fair competition; all he needed was the money and permission to take a film crew and actors to Gdansk, since it needed a seaside setting. There was some apprehension among those in authority. The film was another adventure in nonconformity, quite diverse in its appeal and once again littered with indiscriminate violence.

Polanski struck lucky, however. At that time, Poland had ventured into another liberal era, albeit a temporary one, when writers and film people were touching new boundaries in their freedom of expression. Polanski was granted the finance, and permission. He travelled with his unit to Gdansk, where crowds of holidaymakers looked on in wonderment as this troupe of students began their project, attracted not least by the tantrums of the director. Roman Polanski was given to outbreaks of rage and temperament which neared the violence portrayed in his movie. 'Every time he could not achieve the effect he wanted,' said Kluba, who was one of the film's two main actors, 'he would take it out on his surroundings or even people in the crew – he would beat them up. In that wardrobe that we carried, he smashed the mirror with his fist so many times that in the end we had to carry spares. He was unbearable.' He would storm off the set, leaving everyone wondering what would happen next, and then he would return and pick up as if nothing had happened.

There were interruptions from bystanders as well. Polanski himself made an appearance in the film as the leader of a gang of young hoodlums who strikes one of the men for reasons which are not clear. The gang

46

was then filmed hurling stones at a kitten – an act which attracted the attention of a local animal cruelty campaigner who demanded that the scene should be halted, and indeed cut from the film. Her complaint about Polanski's attitude now lies in the archives at Lodz.

Once again, Polanski's own experiences are apparent in the action of the film, especially in another disturbing scene where a young man is beaten to death by an attacker hammering his victim with a rock. His head is held under water, and the camera focuses down on the mingling of the blood, thereby re-enacting the director's earlier fear and fantasy of water and blood on the face.

Polanski was now in control of a fictional situation, portraying it in what might have been some perverse sort of reaction to his past. Only he knows the extent of his intentions, or how deliberate these motivations were, but it is interesting that when he became famous, he studiously avoided linking images from his own memory with the scenes he created for his films. His written recollections make little or no mention of the effects of his past, but the similarities to known incidents are so plain as to be incontrovertible. What remains hazy is whether they were deliberate or subconscious.

When Polanski returned to Lodz, he spent hours alone in the editing suite to compile his masterpiece, for which he needed a musical accompaniment. For this, he went for the best available, seeking out one of Poland's leading modern composers and jazz pianists, Krzystof Komeda, who had emerged from the anonymity of a career as a doctor to become a full-time musician during the recent thaw of official attitudes towards jazz music. It was Komeda's first involvement with Polanski, but he would be called upon again and again during the next few years, until his tragic death in Los Angeles.

The completed film was shown to Polanski's superiors who agreed that it should be entered for the competition at Brussels – one of several Polish entries. Six weeks later, Polanski and his friends listened to the announcement of the results on the radio. At first, it seemed he had got nowhere. The gold medal went to Poland, sure enough – to two graphic artists for their animation film. But Polanski won third place, and a bronze medal.

He was invited to Brussels to receive his award, and the Ministry of Culture, delighted with Poland's success, sponsored his trip. He also obtained permission to make another quick visit to see his step-sister Annette in Paris and then returned to Lodz to a reception at the school which hovered somewhere between disdain and delight. For however much some of his colleagues might have disliked Polanski's little movie, ostensibly his first real attempt as a director, they could not avoid the fact that it was a success, and it became the first Lodz National Film School short to be released commercially into Polish cinemas. His fame, for the moment, was local, and some believed it was carved out of his growing fascination with experimenting on film with the macabre. In that they were right.

Chapter Five

*T*he novelist Jerzy Kosinski once gave a description of Polanski that could be applied throughout his career. He said he had a gift for arrogance. Kosinski himself, though born in the same year as Polanski, was far more intellectually advanced than Roman could ever aspire to be. After studying at the University of Lodz, he became an associate professor at the Polish Academy of Science in Warsaw in 1955, returning to Lodz to teach political science before leaving at the end of 1958 for America where he became spectacularly successful first as an educator, then as a novelist.

His novel, *The Painted Bird*, was a harrowing semi-auto-biographical story of 'The Boy', who is separated from his parents in the war and discovers in his encounters with life thereafter that survival depends not on kindness and religious beliefs but on hatred and the pursuit of vengeance. When it was published in 1965, many took the story to be that of Roman Polanski's life. Kosinski did not object at the time. Polanski had become famous by then, more famous than himself, and it was good publicity for the book. Their lives in the war years had run a similar course – they were just two of many, and few ever talked about their experiences. His fellow student and later cinematographer Witold Sobocinski said that although he was a member of Polanski's group, he never really knew his background. 'No, that never came into it, even though my relationship with him at the time was very intense. He was a very intriguing person, very forceful, which was in an inverse proportion to his height . . . he was a leader, not in the ideological sense, but he always had to be the one who directed our student plays. There couldn't be anyone else. He had to be the one who assigned the roles.'

Kosinski, in sharing common ground in childhood and getting to know Polanski before he left for America, gleaned a more apposite appraisal of Polanski's emerging talents and character than any other person around him. He believed Polanski's arrogance was the exterior shell which he had constructed against a hostile world, which had grown since he faced the appalling conditions of his childhood into a protection against whatever life would throw at him in the future. Beneath it was a layer of insecurity and fear that someone, somewhere, was waiting to slap him down or cast him out once again, and the only way to combat such an act was to strike first.

As with Kosinski, emotion was dispelled at an early age and replaced by ambition and determination which flourished in his latter years at the film school. Roman found female company difficult, even though Lodz had a greater population of attractive females than almost anywhere in Poland. He had numerous girlfriends but few firm relationships. Henryk Kluba believes that this area of Polanski's character provided a more interesting scenario than his childhood. 'If one is really looking for an area in which he might have had complexes, it was certainly women. I don't know whether he had some problem with them, whether he had failed as a man, but there was something about him . . . he was always showing off, playing superman, yet he was curt, almost unkind, to women. Strange to think of it now [interviewed in 1993] but there were almost no women in our circle at school. But our contacts with women were not only of a social nature, but also a way of learning, increasing the knowledge that is so necessary for a director.'

When Polanski later boasted about sexual conquests from an early age, he was less than specific in detail. The stories of prowess came out when the myth and legend surrounding him were first being written and cannot be taken too seriously. Zofia Komeda could remember only one regular girlfriend, called Kika. 'She is still a friend of mine,' said Zofia, 'and now a theatre set designer. Kika was a very intelligent girl, not beautiful but an outstanding athlete, later a member of the national ski team. She really loved him but they were fighting all the time – they often came to blows.'

A new and greater love walked into Polanski's life in the wake of his success with *Two Men and a Wardrobe*, along with the limited fame the film had brought him. Through his success he became involved with two French film-makers. Claude Guillemot, a new director from Paris, arrived to work at Lodz for a few weeks and Polanski was appointed to assist him. Guillemot was followed by a French television director, Jean-Marie Drot, and Polanski spent several weeks touring the country with him as the director prepared his film on Poland's cultural heritage.

It was between these two bouts of assisting foreign film-makers that Polanski met a seventeen-year-old starlet named Basia Kwiatkowska. He first caught sight of her at the Grand Hotel in Lodz while waiting to meet Guillemot. She was staying there too, and wandered through the foyer without giving him a glance. She was a Slovak beauty with a slender but amply contoured body. Later, Polanski learned that Henryk Kluba was working with Basia on a new film and persuaded him to arrange an introduction. This casual encounter was to change his life.

Basia had already achieved an unexpected pinnacle, having been snatched from the jaws of total obscurity when she won a contest in a weekly magazine, which was campaigning to Get Beautiful Girls On Screen. Hers was an unusual rise to instant fame – more akin to the discovery of Lana Turner in Hollywood than the traditional route to acting success in Poland which was through a state school for the performing arts.

Having won the competition, she was brought from her peasant home in the tiny village of Szulechow where she used to wander barefoot as a shepherdess, to Lodz for a screen test, and won a starring role in a comedy entitled *Eve Wants to Sleep*. Director Tadeusz Chmielewski gave her the part more on her looks than her ability, but the role might have been written for her – it was about an innocent country girl who moves into big city life. For a girl of seventeen to have become a movie star overnight, while dozens of impeccably trained young actresses toiled away hoping for such a break, caused what was then regarded as quite a sensation.

Basia was completing *Eve Wants to Sleep* and screen-testing for a new film when Polanski first saw her. By the time he had managed to achieve an introduction, two thoughts dominated his mind – first, he wanted to get her into bed as soon as possible, and second, he was determined to cast her in a starring role in the big film he was planning to mark his graduation, and upon which rested his successful acquisition of a diploma of excellence from the Lodz National Film School where he had been studying for the past five years.

Basia was naïve and unaffected by her sudden rise to fame, except that she now wore clothes which looked skin-huggingly Western and walked with a kind of sexy jaunt which comes naturally to all women who know they possess an alluring quality that makes men's heads turn. Polanski was smitten from their first meeting and, perhaps because of her naïvety, she found him a fascinating man. She was impressed by his confidence and amused by his antics and erratic behaviour, qualities which occasionally drove his more familiar circle of associates to distraction. She recalled the moment she first met him: 'I went to the Honoratka, a coffee bar in Lodz which was a well-known hang for artists. I didn't know that it had been pre-arranged. Romek had recently returned from Paris and I remember he had red socks. I was very impressed. He kept saying, "Do you know how they dance in Paris?" I said I didn't but I would like to learn, so we made a date. For about a year after that, he was springing traps for me . . . I was seventeen years old then, and getting intimate with men for me, a peasant girl, was a big problem. It was not unpleasant, and to be honest even with my plain peasant wisdom, I could see his genius and talent.'

Henryk Kluba and others in the circle believed that Polanski was motivated for other reasons than just sexual desire, though that was important. Ambition and advancement were also at stake. In other words, he could use Basia. At last he was being seen around in the company of a very beautiful girl, who was also seven years his junior. More than that, she was a beauty *and* a star – a phoney one, to the Lodz brigade of aspiring actors and actresses, but a star none the less. The kudos was evident.

They were parted by circumstance early on in their friendship. Basia was working on her new film and Polanski was touring the countryside with Jean-Marie Drot. He wrote long love letters to her while he was away, and returned to Lodz whenever possible, just to see her. When his assignment with Drot was concluded, he began pursuing her in earnest. He told people with pride that she was his girl, and that it was serious. But Basia was in no hurry to jump into bed with him, and weeks passed before he achieved that aim.

There were to be no secrets surrounding this milestone in Polanski's life, and in his own kiss-and-tell account later, he would allege that once Basia had agreed to return with him to his shabby little apartment which he shared with a fellow student, she stripped off immediately and got into bed with him, which seemed to surprise him. They made love, he said in his published recollections, time and again, and afterwards he 'feasted' his eyes on her 'flawless' body as she stood naked by the window, staring into the street below. He said he had never seen such 'utter perfection' and was proud 'at having possessed it'.

It sounded like a passage from a cheap novel, and doubtless Basia thought it *was* cheap that he should reveal the detail of their first sexual act in such graphic terms. He would never be a gentleman in that respect

52

and seemed to find it necessary to boast of 'my many relationships'. The encounter obviously had a greater impact on him than it did on Basia and he admitted that he found her reticent in giving her all, and that he 'got more out of it than she did', which was something of an admission from a man who would go on to make a habit of wooing girls much younger than himself.

Having achieved his first ambition, he moved rapidly on to the second and broached the subject of Basia appearing in his film. This was not a foregone conclusion, considering her status compared to his. The film script he had chosen for his final project at Lodz was not especially inviting either. He made two films in his last year, 1959. The first was another short called *The Lamp*, about a dollmaker whose shop burns to the ground through faulty wiring after he installed electricity. It was not a success, and has been rarely mentioned in Polanski's own retrospectives of his work.

The main project was his graduation film, a twenty-minute production and his first in colour, entitled *When Angels Fall*. It is an early exercise in Polanski voyeurism, this time with some crudity. The story centres around an old woman who tends a men's urinal; every day of her life, she sits there watching the men passing by her, and standing virtually in front of her, relieving themselves. Countless men come in, day in, day out, and she is seemingly oblivious to the continual flow of bodily functions and secret assignations that go on around her.

The woman, gnarled and wrinkled, was played by a woman of eighty whom Polanski recruited from an old people's home. She says nothing and sits with a vacant expression on her face because the action is told through flashbacks. Basia plays the woman in her younger years, except in one sequence where the flashback is to a later period in her life, and for this, Polanski in drag makes a cameo appearance as the older woman. It was a kind of signature that he would apply to several of his films.

Although his project was accepted, he was not issued with his graduation certificate because he had failed to write an accompanying thesis, a mandatory part of the final presentation for film direction students. And so, after all, he failed to pass the final muster and left film school under a slight cloud. Later, when Polish film critics began to examine his work, they called him a Lodz drop-out, which caused him immense irritation.

Polanski, now heading for his twenty-sixth birthday, was out on his own for the first time in five years. The possibility of military service was already looming when he was offered work as an actor doubling as an assistant director at a film production unit called Kamera.

It was one of the eight newly sanctioned film units financed and run under the auspices of the Polish Ministry of Culture, and one of the most professional. Polanski had several acquaintances at Kamera. Jerzy Bossack, head of the directors' faculty at Lodz, was also artistic director of Kamera. Andrzej Munk, by now a powerful figure in the Polish film world, was also a director and was on the point of starting a new film for Kamera, a satirical comedy on Poland's suffering called *Bad Luck*. At Bossack's suggestion, he hired Polanski as an assistant.

In the months since they had completed his graduation film, Basia had been busy with her own projects. The release of *Eve Wants to Sleep* and work on new projects and theatre roles kept them apart for weeks, and Polanski continued to write intense, rather pathetic love letters to her, declaring his undying devotion and pleading with her to join him in Lodz as soon as she had the opportunity. In the background, he was also working on a move to make sure they were reunited.

The Munk film called for an attractive young actress to play a nymphomaniac. Polanski suggested to Munk that he should hire Basia. Munk objected. He did not believe the girl possessed the talent. Polanski said he would direct her scenes personally and make sure she came through.

Munk auditioned a few actresses and finally gave way to Polanski's suggestion. Basia was hired and Polanski persuaded her to move into his tiny apartment with him for the duration. Munk mischievously added fuel to this offscreen situation by casting Polanski in the film to play the role of her tutor whom she seduces.

The film, from Basia's point of view, was a difficult experience. To begin with, Munk allowed Polanski to direct her scenes, but there were days when she was reduced to tears by her lover's constant and scornful criticism of her acting and his demands for retakes of her scenes over and over again, until Munk felt he had to intervene. He accused Polanski of unnecessary bullying and insisted that he take over from him. When Polanski continued to interrupt filming with suggestions from the wings, Munk threatened to bar him from the set unless he kept his mouth shut. Back at the apartment after work, Polanski insisted to Basia that he just wanted to make sure she gave her best possible performance; he would bring out her finest attributes and make her a big star.

One other opportunity for togetherness presented itself when Basia was invited to the San Sebastian Film Festival, where *Eve Wants to Sleep* was to be shown. There was also talk of *Two Men and a Wardrobe* going into the fringe cinemas and so Polanski somehow managed to acquire an invitation for himself, financed, like Basia's, by the Ministry of Culture.

Once in Spain, Polanski was faced with the grim prospect that Basia's fame was outstripping his own progress, and that he might soon lose her. In demand by media and PR people, she was whisked away from her insignificant companion and shown the real glamour of the film world that she had never before experienced. This was her first trip outside Poland, and she found herself caught up in an exciting whirl which was capped when a Spanish film company offered her a screen test and the prospect of a contract. Basia was tempted but Polanski fought against it, telling her she would be a fool to accept. 'I owe a lot to him in this area,' she said. 'He would rigorously and brutally put any trash out of my head.' He also could not bear the thought of losing her.

When they arrived back in Poland, however, they were parted almost immediately. Basia had already fixed other work and was also due to appear at the International Youth Festival in Vienna that summer of 1959. When she returned to Poland, she did not go back to Polanski in Lodz and made no effort to get in touch. Rumour had it that she had found another suitor.

Polanski went to Warsaw where Basia was reportedly staying and finally tracked her down, back at the railway station where she was waiting for a train to take her back to Lodz. Yes, it was true that the artist she had met had fallen in love with her, and she was very fond of him. Almost in tears, Polanski said he was sorry that he had been such a bastard to her and that he had tried to teach her to become more worldly rather than accept her for what she was, a warm and simple girl. He knew now that he had been wrong, and overpoweringly domineering.

As the situation ebbed and flowed over the ensuing days, Polanski finally became so desperate that he might lose Basia to her new friend that he proposed marriage, immediately – that week, that day, or just as soon as he could get the licence. Basia, according to friends close to them both at the time, felt sorry for Polanski; his big, baleful eyes and pinched cheeks made him look like a spaniel that knew it was about to be put down. He was very capable of such looks, just as he was capable of turning instantly into a sharp and satirical comic, or a raging bull.

So Basia said yes. They married on 9 September 1959 in a brief ceremony in Lodz. 'It was a terrible rush,' said Zofia Komeda. 'Romek phoned us a day earlier. He had arranged nothing except the ceremony at the register office, and a couple of us had to provide the wedding breakfast for eighty or more people in a matter of hours. He said they would have it at Wadim's [Wadim Berestowski, a director who was widowed and had a large flat]. Wadim agreed and we went over and cooked two big pots of *bortsch* and *bigos*, hunter's stew. I didn't get to the ceremony – just cooking until the guests started to arrive, all those young directors with their attractive wives, and actors and actresses in their finery and perfumes, and me with scalded hands, sweaty and tired. It was only later that I remembered they did not even say thank you.'

It was a good marriage, said Zofia, in difficult circumstances. The Polanskis stayed for a while with the Komedas in Krakow. 'The conditions were terrible, a toilet outside, only cold running water. There were only two beds, one wardrobe and four stools. We were very poor.' Later the couple moved into Polanski's room in a villa in Lodz, and Roman scurried around looking for work with the film units, taking anything from acting to sound-dubbing. Basia was off in more glamorous surroundings: as her career was making increasing demands upon her time, she would travel frequently, leaving Polanski pining and jealous, especially as she was working for some of the top film directors in the country. He was impatient for success of his own, and they had many rows. 'I wasn't capable of joining in his intellectual discussions,' said Basia, 'and he could crush me. So I cried a lot.'

Out of school and with no pattern of work emerging, Polanski had decided he must make another film himself. He formed a writing collaboration with his student friend Jakub Goldberg to start work on the outline of what he hoped would be his first feature-length film. But Goldberg ran out of ideas and failed to produce a completed script. So Polanski teamed up with another budding writer, Jerzy Skolimowski, a thick-set, pugnacious young man who looked every inch the boxer he had tried to be for a time, although he was a poet at heart, and was currently attempting to get a place at the Lodz film school. His background, apart from his boxing days, read like a CV of which any young student in Lodz would have been proud; it undoubtedly attracted Polanski. Skolimowski had made what amounted to a sensational entrance to the Polish literary film world. He worked day and night for months and produced a portfolio of poems which were published in two slender volumes, and attracted a good deal of critical attention.

On the strength of this, he was admitted to the closely guarded membership of the Polish Writers' Guild, and took advantage of his card to spend time at a writers' retreat where he met and conversed daily with some of Poland's famous novelists. He also introduced himself to the film-maker Andrzej Wadja – Polanski's hero – who was working on a new screenplay about post-war youth, and, being a pushy young man who had strong views about everything and a habit of speaking them, soon found himself in regular deep conversation with one of the giants of Polish film culture. Wadja used him to help with the dialogue for his new film, to be called *Innocent Sorcerers*. Then, when casting began, he selected Skolimowski for one of the roles, and it was doubtless on his recommendation that his young protégé applied for entry to the film school at Lodz.

Skolimowski was resident in Lodz for the two-week entrance examination and met Polanski in a jazz club. They talked and talked and Polanski introduced him to Jakub Goldberg. Together they worked on a script which Polanski had started with Goldberg and which would eventually mature into his first major film, *Knife in the Water*. He found Skolimowski a natural talent with a fast mind brimming with ideas and creations, who wrote at speed. He was also, like Polanski, of volatile temperament, and they would argue and rage at each other, almost to the point of coming to blows as they wrote their script.

Night after night, they worked into the early hours, with Goldberg adding his own contribution. After Skolimowski went home to await the call for entry to the film school, Polanski continued polishing their script until he had achieved what he believed was a highly marketable project. He took it to Jerzy Bossack, the artistic director of Kamera, who was sufficiently impressed to dispatch it to the Ministry of Culture for approval. Polanski's hopes were dashed when the screenplay was returned with a rejection slip, on the grounds that it was socially uncommitted. Over the coming months, Polanski and Skolimowski would continue to tinker with their work, but for the time being it lay unwanted.

Towards the end of the year a remarkable coincidence occurred which would have implications for them both. Polanski was at home in his room one day when he received a call from his friend Jean-Marie Drot, the French director, who told him of a curious article in a French film magazine in which there appeared a photograph of Basia, taken at San Sebastian, under a headline 'Who is the mystery girl?' It transpired that a French producer was trying to contact her to put in a film.

Polanski telephoned immediately and reached an aide of the producer, telling him he was the husband of the girl sought. The aide asked if she spoke good French, and if she would be available to come immediately to France if required. Polanski fudged the issue of his wife speaking French but said that it would be necessary for himself to travel with her as her coach. The upshot was that within a couple of weeks, they had obtained a visa to travel to Paris.

Basia, as Polanski well knew, did not speak French, but he gave her a crash course and said she would get by – after all, in the picture itself, a comedy entitled *The Thousandth Window*, Basia was to appear as a Polish au pair girl living and working in the home of a Parisian business-man played by Pierre Fresnay.

News of the Polanskis' good fortune spread like wildfire through the film community at Lodz, although some of Basia's own friends questioned whether she was wise even to consider going to Paris. She had a worthwhile career in Poland – why risk failure in a foreign land whose language she did not know?

Polanski, on the other hand, put up a convincing argument that it could be the making of her (and perhaps him), and anyway, what had they to lose? Wasn't the French producer, Pierre Roustang, paying their fares, and providing them with hotel accommodation – and money? And of course, while in Paris, there could be other opportunities that might open a few doors for himself. He decided that Basia needed a new image and name to fit the part. Kwiatkowska? Who was going to remember that? He chose the name Barbara Lass, after the English word that the dictionary told him meant attractive girl or young woman.

They flew to Paris and found Pierre Roustang, a balding, middle-aged man, waiting for them at the airport ready to drive them to the suite he had reserved in the Hôtel Napoléon. He spoke rapidly in French to Basia, only to receive a blank response. She did not understand a word he had said. Roustang realized this immediately and queried whether Mr Polanski had been asked about his wife's fluency in the French language. There had been a misunderstanding. Polanski said he had told Roustang's representative quite clearly that he would coach his wife to speak French; that was, after all, why he had come along.

Roustang was on the verge of calling off the deal and putting the two of them on the plane back to Warsaw, but he could see that Basia was even more beautiful than her photograph and decided that he would at least try to make the best of a difficult situation. There were clearly going to be problems, however, with a Polish actress, appearing in a French film, being given directions by a Frenchman who did not speak Polish.

Polanski, desperate for the deal not to go wrong at this stage, said he would teach his wife the lines before each day's filming – even if they had to stay up all night. Roustang accepted the position and Basia nervously began to settle into her new acting career in a film which, it turned out, was not anything like as high-profile as Polanski had expected. But Roustang was not an ungenerous man and, eager to impress his voluptuous young star, provided Basia and Roman with very adequate living expenses. He also arranged for them to receive media attention which Polanski felt might aid his own mission, which was to try to sell *Knife in the Water*.

There were hopeful signs, but very soon the Paris trip began to take on an air of disappointment.

Chapter Six

*B*asia's film for Pierre Roustang was completed within a couple of months and the Polanskis' money began to run out, partly through Roman's cavalier attitude to their finances. Basia recalled that once, when they were down to their last 400 francs, Roman spent the lot throwing a banquet for the Bim Bom, an avant-garde Polish theatre group, when they arrived to give a performance in Paris. They were faced with the decision of trying to get more work in France, or heading back for Poland. Polanski had put on a show for the visitors, but so far he had failed miserably in his hopes and expectations. Apart from some translation work for Roustang, he had been unable to secure either work for himself or interest in his script. At first they lived off the charity of Roustang, who gave them a bedroom in his apartment, and later, when the producer's interest in his Polish protégés began to dwindle, they moved into a tiny flat belonging to some Polish exiles who had befriended them.

Basia decided to seek an agent to try to get work and was taken up by Lola Mouloudji. This in itself presented Polanski with a number of humiliations, since he was seldom allowed by the agent to accompany his wife to her meetings with potential employers because he was demanding and quarrelsome. Among the try-outs Lola arranged for Basia was a screen-test for the Italian director Gillo Pontecorvo who was seeking a star for his film *Kapo*, about a French Jewess who survives the horrors of a concentration camp by becoming a trusty. Susan Strasberg, who was also in Paris at the time, had already tested – and it was she who got the part.

However, Basia found herself among the stars at the 1960 Cannes Film Festival where *Bad Luck*, the Andrzej Munk film in which she had played the female lead, was among that year's Polish entries. The Ministry of Culture, which had sponsored the film, did not include Basia in their party because she was already in France, but Lola lent her the money and Basia went along at her own expense, checking in with the rest of the Polish delegation at the Hôtel Martinez. Polanski smuggled himself into her hotel room so that he could stay free of charge.

Cannes was full of the usual hype and razzmatazz, and mixing in such company boosted Basia's confidence. Polanski confided to his friends in the Polish community that he felt they were being driven apart by the situation in which they now found themselves – she on the brink of a break, he with little or nothing in sight.

A touch of this resentment was reflected in one of his earliest interviews, given around that time for a French film journal, *Positif*, which sought Polanski out to discuss his prize-winning *Two Men and a Wardrobe*. At the end of it, he confided that he was working on the plot for a new movie, the story 'of a girl attracted by the mirage of the cinema and who wants at all cost to become a star'. To those close to the couple at the time, it was not difficult to imagine what had inspired such a plot – Roman's own disappointments, plus a touch of jealousy about the interest in Basia.

Cannes helped them both. They made new contacts they could call upon in the future, and back in Paris, they were able to persuade the Polish authorities to extend their visas allowing them to stay in France. With the possibility of work in the offing, the Polish embassy granted them both special passports as cultural students, which gave them the freedom to travel back and forth as and when they wished.

The promise of work arrived not a moment too soon. They had virtually outstayed their welcome with accommodating friends. Although Basia's Polish-made film had made no impact at Cannes, Lola was confident. She arranged an interview with the French director René Clément, who was casting for a new movie starring his recent discovery and new French heart-throb, Alain Delon. The movie, *Quelle Joie de Vivre*, would be going into production in Rome.

Roman took Basia to the appointment at the Hôtel Lutétia and had to wait around outside for more than an hour while Clément interviewed her. When she came out, she was beaming. She had secured the part, and Lola negotiated a fee which to them was substantial – 3000 dollars upfront and more to follow. As they walked away hand in hand, Clément roared off in an expensive sports car, and Polanski said that now they were rich, he would like one too.

Basia, feeling guilty that she and not he had secured their finances, agreed. As soon as Clément's cheque was safely deposited, they paid off their debts, rented an apartment of their own on the Left Bank, and Polanski went to the nearest Mercedes dealer and put a down-payment on a bright red convertible.

Basia left almost immediately for Rome to begin filming, and the change in their fortunes was reaffirmed when Polanski managed to obtain backing for a film, modest though it was. A French Canadian producer who was searching for projects had a series of meetings on the possibility of funding a production of *Knife in the Water* but could not raise sufficient money for a feature film. He did, however, agree to finance a fifteen-minute short, called *The Fat and the Lean*, which Polanski had prepared on the back of a script idea he had worked out back in Lodz with Jakub Goldberg. It was to be made much in the style of *Two Men and a Wardrobe* and would, they hoped, get a showing as a support feature in European cinemas.

Funds were so limited that there was no money to spare to hire professional actors. Polanski himself took the role of 'The Lean' and one of his friends from the Polish community, Andrzej Katelbach, who had never acted in his life, was persuaded to play 'The Fat'. The film opens with Polanski as a slave dancing barefoot, playing a flute and beating a drum to entertain his master, the portly Katelbach. It is a light exercise in a psychological study of slave and master, of power and subservience, which won two prizes in European festivals, but made no money. Even before filming was complete, the minuscule budget that the producer had promised evaporated before all the bills had been paid. He skipped the country, leaving a trail of bouncing cheques, and Polanski had to finish the film in a back-street workshop.

When his little movie was completed, Polanski and a couple of friends piled into the Mercedes and drove off to Italy to find Basia. The cracks in their marriage were already beginning to show. On one level, Basia recalled, Polanski took her success very well, but on another he was angry. 'The worst situation was in Italy, where no one took notice of his genius,' she said. 'It manifested itself in his hostility towards me.' Unable to watch Basia at work, he started writing the script for another short film which he had virtually completed by the time she had finished her picture. They drove on to Krakow for a Christmas reunion with their friends and relatives. The red Mercedes – in which Polanski could barely see over the huge white steering wheel – gave them the appearance of being very successful after their eighteen months in the West.

The illusion was not denied by Polanski when he left his wife with his father and Wanda and drove off to Lodz in search of his old friends, showing off his Mercedes and regaling them with stories of life in Paris and Rome and what wonders there were to behold. Behind this façade of good fortune, however, he was gloomy and despondent.

Without Basia's money Polanski was penniless, and all he had to work on was the script called *Mammals* which he completed in Rome. He showed it to the authorities at Lodz but the project was turned down without so much as an explanation. He had been in regular touch with Jerzy Skolimowski in their continuing efforts to get approval for their script, which would eventually become *Knife in the Water*, but so far they had received nothing but rejections.

Undaunted, Polanski decided he would make *Mammals* anyway, even without the approval of the film censors. Wojtek Frykowski, with whom he had caught up in Lodz, happened to have some money and agreed to help finance the filming privately. Friends were pulled in as actors, including Henryk Kluba, one of the co-stars of *Two Men and a Wardrobe*, and Frykowski himself took a small role.

Mammals, like *The Fat and the Lean*, was yet another variation on the theme of *Two Men and a Wardrobe* – this time, two men with a sledge, who come into shot far in the distance in the snow, are followed in a journey which is used as a device to display one's attempt at dominance over the other. Polanski filmed the fifteen-minute short over a period of a few days in January 1961 and returned to Lodz to discover he could not get his film developed. It would be months before he could even begin editing, and for the time being, *Mammals* lay dormant in the can. By now it was time to return to Paris. Basia was in demand again but Polanski still had nothing, and according to Basia there was a fire burning inside him. 'He has such an amazing impatience that he vibrates, sometimes shaking with anger. He had no tolerance at all for other people's views or ideas. He was always right. The aggressiveness could flare up at any time . . . in Paris once, he managed to have a row with a driver of another car. On the first set of lights, he got out of his car, smacked the other driver in the face and ran off.'

Basia had been offered a new film by an Italian director and was required to be in Rome for the end of the month. Her future looked rosy. Polanski's was less certain, and the troubles in their marriage were all too evident. Basia's glamorous new life had confronted her with the excitement of male attentions which were flattering and tempting, especially when the handsome male torso of her movie co-star was set in comparison against the puny, ill-dressed Polanski who, in her new world, looked a loser.

Not long after Basia's return to Rome, someone sent Roman a newspaper clipping of her in a night-club with the Italian producer Gillo Pontecorvo, which resulted in some long-distance rows by telephone before Polanski turned up in Rome again. 'It was true,' said Basia, 'that Pontecorvo had sussed out the whole situation and thought, "That girl is for taking and it would be easy to make her happy." He wanted to create an image for me, and rented a big apartment – three bedrooms, the works. And I had to give it up because of Romek – do you know, I have never told him that. The trouble with Romek was his bluntness, and before people realized his genius they saw him first as a person. Anyway, Pontecorvo said he did not want Romek to live in the apartment with me, and I had to leave. They kept asking me then how I could have chosen such an inappropriate partner. I never blamed him; his brusqueness was an expression of his pride.'

In spite of his growing number of contacts in Paris, Polanski was still unable to find worthwhile work and, curiously enough, it was the developments back in Lodz that saved him. The word from Poland was encouraging. The Ministry of Culture had reviewed *Knife in the Water* yet again and subject to some amendments was prepared to sanction the movie being made at the state-run production facilities. Furthermore, it approved the appointment of Polanski as director, and a unit from the Kamera production unit would be made available. 'This made Romek very happy,' said Basia. 'He had presented *Knife* to the committee about ten times and they rejected it each time – in the end they had to accept it.'

Polanski was filled with nervous apprehension. His conception of *Knife in the Water* is best compared to a best-selling novel that would cross boundaries, borders and languages. It is a story in which sex and violence rise slowly to the surface and perhaps it was no wonder that the Ministry of Culture took so long giving approval. It contained none of the elements of ideological or social study that the Ministry liked to encourage from its film industry.

Jerzy Bossack, the director of Kamera, gave Polanski his head but kept a supervisory eye on the proceedings as he gathered about him his cast of technicians and actors, mostly friends or people he had worked with previously. Jerzy Lipman, whom he had first encountered when he met the group of graduation students from Lodz in Warsaw eight years earlier, was selected to handle the cinematography. Jerzy Skolimowski and Jakub Goldberg, who had given him varying degrees of collaboration on the scripts, came along as assistant directors, and Wojtek Frykowski, who was a strong swimmer, was hired as life-guard since most of the filming would take place in a boat on the Mazurian Lakes.

The script called for a very small cast, basically three actors, for a story in which a young couple pick up a hitch-hiker, ask him to spend a weekend on their yacht, and live to regret it. As in earlier films, Polanski did not place great emphasis on the ability of his actors – nor would he in the future. They were selected for their looks and demeanour, and his friends wondered at the significance of his female lead, a young music student named Jolanta Umecka, whom he discovered quite by accident while looking around for the perfect female body for the role. She was spotted, bikini-clad, by a swimming pool, and Polanski delivered a version of the classic Hollywood line, 'How would you like to be in the movies?'

Jolanta had never acted professionally, and it was no coincidence that she was the absolute image of Basia, who, at the very time Polanski began work on the film, was departing his life for good. This was his first mistake. Jolanta may have been beautiful, but she could neither act nor swim, and could not remember more than a few sentences of her lines at a time. Before the filming was finished there would be screaming matches between herself and Polanski, whose admiration of her body was quickly superseded by his impatience with her lack of passion or fire in the delivery of her lines, for which, in all fairness, she could hardly be blamed. He was asking too much and it could be considered another form of his arrogance that he believed he had the ability to turn someone who had never acted into a star in her very first picture.

For the male lead, in the role of Jolanta's screen husband, Polanski selected Leon Nieczyk, the only professional actor in his film. This left one role vacant, for the student hitch-hiker, and the script calls for a handsome, intriguing young man. Polanski surprised everyone by announcing that he planned to take the part himself – the prospect of love scenes with Jolanta was reason enough. He also believed he was handsome and intriguing and possessed all the qualities that the role required.

Jerzy Bossack thought the idea was ridiculous and summoned Polanski to his office as soon as he heard of it. At first he tried gentle persuasion. In all fairness, he said, Roman would be asking too much of himself to direct the film and play the leading character as well, especially since he would find the movie a difficult project to direct anyway – even without taking one of the roles.

Polanski would not be moved by reason. So Bossack insisted he could not do both. Polanski marched out of his office in a rage and slammed the door behind him. A few minutes later, he returned. He had stripped off all his clothes and stood before Bossack stark naked, asking him if he was not handsome enough to play the role of the student.

Bossack said he did not think so, and that Roman was being very vain and rather stupid. Much rested on the success of this film, and if he could not see that he might ruin it, then he might as well call the whole thing off. If he did not drop the idea of starring in the movie, Bossack would ensure that the project was dropped from his list of immediate productions and delayed for a year or two.

Polanski gave way and hired a drama student from the Lodz film school, Zygmunt Malanowicz. He was handsome and striking, but, according to Polanski, not striking enough. He gave the boy a bottle of peroxide and told him to dye his hair blond. Even then, Polanski was not satisfied, having not given up on his claim to the role – when filming was completed he ruled that Zygmunt's physical presence may have been right, but his acting voice was not. He recorded the entire part himself and dubbed his own voice over that of his young actor's.

The row with Bossack over casting, and the subsequent troubles with Jolanta, were but two of a string of misfortunes. Not least of these were early rumours of a controversial script and of sex orgies out on location. The editor of the Polish movie magazine *Ekran* had heard that the production went against the grain of films normally produced in a Communist society, and sent a writer to investigate.

The visitor was pleasantly entertained and given the run of the set; he interviewed each member of the cast, and even Polanski was cooperative, believing that the article would be good publicity for himself and the movie. However, when the article appeared, an explosion of outrage could be heard for hours. The reporter proceeded to attack Polanski and his crew for lavish extravagance, for drinking and generally enjoying themselves at the expense of the Polish government and taxpayers, and, worst of all, for using a fleet of Mercedes for their transport.

Jerzy Bossack was sent immediately by Kamera to the Mazurian Lakes. He discovered there had been two Mercedes, one belonging to Polanski (or to his wife Basia, to be more precise), the other had been hired as a car to be used in the film. This in itself was a breach of form. In Poland, as in most Communist countries, such cars were available only to the upper ranks of the hierarchy, certainly not for the class of people making a film. Bossack ordered the Mercedes to be returned at once and replaced by a small Peugeot. Once again Polanski argued, screaming that Bossack was intent on ruining his picture; he could not see that the man was actually trying to save it from being scrapped altogether.

Word was out: Polanski was bad news. He was directing the movie as if it were his own, without regard to the Communist guidelines of social and political exploration. He was going solo, giving precedence to his personal feelings and compulsions. The people at the Ministry already had misgivings about the film which, in Polanski's usual brand of voyeurism, forced each of the three characters to reveal their inner selves to each other and to the audience in a rising climax of violent and sexual overtones. The doubts of the Communist hierarchy were becoming threatening.

Meanwhile, other unfortunate, tragic distractions came one after the other. First Andrzej Munk, Polanski's mentor and tutor of both Goldberg and Skolimowski, was killed in a car accident. On the night it happened, when drink was taken during the drowning of sorrows and the toasting of a good man, Goldberg and Polanski made some insulting remarks to a passing policeman and were thrown into the cells for the night.

Next, Polanski received a letter from Basia confirming that she wanted formally to end their marriage. She was involved with another man, not named at the time, but who turned out to be the German actor Karl Heinz Boehm, the star of Polanski's favourite film, *Peeping Tom*. Basia said she realized what love really felt like. She wanted a husband she could rely on, she wanted to build her career and she wanted to start a family.

Polanski felt bitter and resentful, above all because he believed he would be humiliated in front of his friends once the news broke, even though they were expecting it. He stormed around in a rage for days after receiving the news, but with all the other pressures surrounding him, he decided to keep his personal problems from his colleagues.

Yet more troubles lay ahead. After the setbacks described so far, production on the film began to slip behind schedule, a situation which was further exacerbated one night in late September when cameraman Jerzy Lipman was driving Polanski and Goldberg back to the houseboat on which they had lived for the duration of the film. The company Peugeot skidded on leaves and ran off the road, coming to rest wrapped round a tree. Lipman and Goldberg were shaken but unhurt. Polanski was out cold – at the hospital it was discovered he had a fractured skull

– and remained unconscious for three days. He was in hospital for two weeks until he discharged himself against doctors' wishes, fearful that his film project might be taken out of his hands if he did not return. Wanda, his step-mother, became a friend and aided his recovery, taking a room near the hospital for the time he was there and bringing him freshly cooked food every day.

When he came out there were still a number of interior scenes to film, and editing and music to be taken care of – weeks of intense work. He also used the facilities to develop and edit his film *Mammals*, which had been lying in the can since its completion almost a year earlier.

There was one major problem remaining before *Knife in the Water* could finally be completed. In spite of Polanski's confidence that he could turn Jolanta into a competent actress, good enough for the movie, he was now proved wrong. Her speech was slow and uninspired, and he had to get her speaking lines dubbed over by a professional actress, just as he had dubbed his own voice over that of the hitch-hiker.

The music was provided by Polanski's old friend Krzys Komeda, who had by now risen to become one of Poland's foremost jazz composers. This was the finishing touch. Now all they had to do was wait for the reaction of the critics, which was not slow in arriving.

Komeda's wry score provided a then modern background influence to the movie, shot in black and white. Polanski used the ingenious combination of a confined psychodrama, in which his two male characters compete for the girl, and the setting of the vast landscape of the Mazurian Lakes. It remains to this day one of his most compelling achievements. And though it would immediately be applauded in the West, reaction in Poland was rigidly in accord with the party line.

A hint of the trouble that lay ahead had already emerged in a number of hostile newspaper articles. When the film opened for a limited premiere showing in Warsaw, the reviewers showed no great enthusiasm. One openly ridiculed the story, the characters and Polanski's direction, and made it clear they were not interested in the film as art. The official youth journal, *Youth Flag*, said that Polanski had nothing interesting to say about contemporary man and that the youth of Poland would not identify with any of the three characters the film portrayed.

But most astoundingly of all came proof that Polanski had annoyed the Party hierarchy – *Knife in the Water* was officially attacked by the leader of the Polish Communist Party, president Wladislaw Gomulka. His hard-line speech to the Thirteenth Plenary Session of the Party singled out two films which 'displayed the kind of thinking for which there is no place anywhere in the Communist world' – one was Andrzej Wadja's *Innocent Sorcerers*, to which Skolimowski had made some small contribution, and the other was Polanski's own film, *Knife in the Water*, which Gomulka described as being neither typical of nor relevant to Polish society as a whole.

Gomulka, banging his clenched fist on the lectern, said that such films had no place in the Polish cinema. The two directors had shown a selfish expression of their art, which consisted of a personal focus rather than a socialistic study, and were thus an anathema to the principles of Communism. Naturally, the state-run production unit, Kamera, immediately cancelled plans for a series of gala presentations. Publicity was scrapped and *Knife in the Water* received only a limited showing in Poland.

Polanski's career in Poland looked dead in the water. The moment Gomulka began criticizing him, he knew that he might as well pack his things and get out. His reaction was no less aggressive in rebuttal than his friends had come to expect of him – he said he was very proud indeed to have been categorized with one of Poland's greatest film-makers, Andrzej Wadja.

Polanski had made no money out of *Knife in the Water*. He had been paid a small directorial fee but the bulk of his earnings was to have come from royalties on a nationwide showing. Now there would be none, and what little money he had left was not legally convertible into any Western currency, so he had to cash in his limited savings on the black market to finance his trip out of the country.

He was not planning to defect, nor was he even rejecting Poland. He was still reliant in some ways on maintaining the status quo in regard to his relationship with the immigration department which allowed him freedom to come and go as he pleased. The Ministry of Culture, through Film Polski, would put *Knife in the Water* and his short, *Mammals*, into their overseas catalogue despite the criticism levelled at Polanski.

But there was no point in hanging around. Roman packed his two suits and other meagre belongings, said goodbye to Wanda and his father, climbed behind the wheel of his car and pointed it in the direction of Berlin and then on to Paris. If the news behind him was bad, it looked no better ahead. Basia was filing divorce papers and their one meeting resolved nothing. 'In fact,' said Basia, 'Romek started to woo me again. We met and we went for dinner, together with my agent. It was very nice and at the end we said goodbye, tenderly. I thought that was the end of it. Going home by taxi, I had to stop at my local drug-store at Place de l'Etoile to buy something. And there was Romek waiting by the Mercedes. He called me over, asked me to get into the car, and I agreed. Lord, what a night that was! We were battling inside the car for hours on end. He was trying to impose his will upon me again – I shall never forget it. It was all a question of dominance. From the moment I became a public figure, I held an advantage over him. Probably, he had a creative crisis as a result and he was very obviously suffering . . . I ran away from Romek. I was too proud to say it then, but I was afraid of him.'

They came to no amicable arrangement for a divorce and Polanski would learn soon afterwards that Basia had gone back to Poland, taking her lover Karl Heinz Boehm with her for all to see. Polanski's friends were now to learn for the first time of the broken marriage he had been keeping secret from them. Basia and her handsome German lover looked every inch the pair of Continental movie stars they had both become. Friends in Lodz and Warsaw soon learned that Polanski was trying to stop the divorce, but eventually he gave up, and Basia married Boehm. Polanski confessed to suffering the greatest humiliation of his life to date, worse even than the attacks on his film. Basia was his proudest 'possession', along with the Mercedes, and now both were gone.

'Polanski blamed me for leaving him on the streets and hungry,' said Basia, 'but I had to get away from him and I think then that when I left him, he began to think of revenge.' For months afterwards he was deep in poverty, often in debt, and knocking on any door that might give him work, money, lodging and hopefully all three. He looked up Pierre Roustang who pointed him in the direction of a few parties which would at least provide free food and drink, and at one of these he met an equally struggling young screenwriter named Gerard Brach, who, also like Polanski, was a small man. They shared similar thoughts and desires and had both been recently discarded by their respective women, a situation for which – as Basia forecast and Polanski admitted – they would exact some revenge on the female species through their writing, especially in scenes which attacked the dignity and rights of women.

They became inseparable, sharing their poverty, their disappointments and their hunger. They lived in low-down dives, seedy hotels and squalid rooms, being chased for the rent and by other sundry creditors. They co-wrote a script in somewhat tortuous circumstances, goading each other through each scene in what was an ultimately perplexing black comedy provisionally entitled *If Kastelbach Comes* (this eventually became *Cul-de-Sac*). They spent weeks honing and improving and months trying to get a producer interested, but no one took it up.

There were moments of renewed hope. First, *Mammals* had been sent by the Polish film board to an exhibition of shorts at the Tours Film Festival where it won first prize, an accolade which brought Polanski a statue by Max Ernst but little else. Next, he heard that *Knife in the Water* had been selected for the 1962 Venice Film Festival where it won the Critics' Prize – and Film Polski sold the distribution rights to a French producer for the smallest of fortunes.

Polanski believed this was a breakthrough and that this time, he would surely make a name for himself. For the moment, however, it proved to be another false dawn. *Knife in the Water* was given a limited showing in Paris, received virtually no publicity, and faded quickly from view – at least as far as the French public was concerned.

Polanski went back to join Gerard Brach in scribbling away on new ideas, bolstering a threadbare existence with occasional writing and directing. One commission, which came from Pierre Roustang, earned them what was then a massive fee of $5000, but this was virtually offset by loans Roustang had already made to them. They were to write an episode for an omnibus film called *The Most Beautiful Swindles in the World*. Their section, about a jewellery swindle in Amsterdam, was entitled *River of Diamonds*. Other sections of the film were to be prepared by well-known directors including Jean-Luc Godard, Claude Chabrol and Ugo Gregoretti. Filming was to be on location in Amsterdam and Polanski persuaded Roustang to hire two of his friends from Lodz for the work – cameraman Jerzy Lipman and, for the musical score, Krzys Komeda. For a brief interlude, they lived like kings.

New Wave film-makers, notably Godard and François Truffaut, were all the rage in Paris. Like Polanski, Godard had started by making short films and established himself as one of the leaders of the New Wave with *À Bout de Souffle* (*Breathless*) in 1959. His elliptical narrative techniques and other devices such as freeze-frame pauses won him a good deal of attention in France but he was less successful in America. Thereafter, he began what he termed as his era of revolutionary anti-capitalist films.

Similarly, Truffaut was a founder member of the French New Wave, making his feature-film debut with *Les Quatre Cents Coups* (*The Four Hundred Blows*), and winning international applause for his compassionate studies of human behaviour. Polanski may have admired their work, but his own techniques were very different. His style, learned from Lodz, was remarkably traditional for a young director whose work was based upon artistic approach. He drew detailed sketches of his scenes, and demanded that his cinematographers followed these directions closely, whereas the French school of Godard and Truffaut required spontaneity and the improvisation allowed by the freedom of the new hand-held cameras. In the snobbish avant-garde world of French movie-making, Polanski's approach was viewed as more akin to painting by numbers, and after a long year verging on starvation, he was without a patron, a sponsor or money.

Outside France, however, in a less precocious atmosphere, there were those who believed he merited a closer look. Unknown to him at the time, a first-class ticket to Hollywood was in the offing.

Chapter Seven

O utside Poland, *Knife in the Water* was slowly crossing the international boundaries, but the benefits for Polanski as yet remained hidden. His story continues to be one populated with people who would become important in his development. Sometimes luckily, sometimes accidentally, sometimes by devious scheming, he met and stored up contacts because past experience had shown that he might one day be able to use them. One such figure towered on his current horizon. 'May I buy you a drink?' said an American voice at a neighbouring table on the terrace of the Carlton Hotel at Cannes, where people who could afford the prices hung out to be noticed during the week of the Film Festival in the early summer of 1963.

Polanski was in his best clothes but still looked something of a waif among the mohair suits and the silver lamé dresses with protruding busts and the dyed blonde hair and 6-inch-high heels. He nodded to the voice, assuming, although he had no knowledge of the English language, that the man was striking up a conversation, an opportunity he would never let pass. The voice might be important – this one, as it turned out, was.

It belonged to Victor Lownes, tall, thirtysomething and darkly handsome, who was a collector of people and stars. He had had good training. His boss Hugh Hefner was the president and founder of the Playboy organization whose magazine and Bunny Club enterprises were on the brink of its most virulent and successful era as the social, cultural and sexual revolutions swept through the West. Lownes had been put in charge of launching what would become the Playboy base in Park Lane, London, and had come down to Cannes to put himself around, mix with his Hollywood and European film friends arriving for the Festival, buy dinner for the occasional stray starlet and do whatever business he could for the benefit of his organization.

It seemed barely conceivable that day in May 1963 that Polanski would before long become one of the most notable frequenters of the Playboy clubs, in both London and Los Angeles, or that Lownes and he would become the closest of friends. Certainly, when Lownes said, 'If you are ever in London . . .' as they parted, neither imagined they might see each other again.

The glamour of Cannes had the lure of contacts for Polanski, people who might one day do him some good or buy one of his ideas for a film. Unable to converse with the Americans, however, he came away with nothing more substantial in view than low-budget movies for small-time French producers, and even that kind of work was not sufficient to support him.

Not long after returning from Cannes, the first flicker of interest emerged when he received an invitation to attend the Montreal Film Festival, where *Knife in the Water* was being shown. Since the adventure was an all-expenses-paid junket, staying at a five-star hotel and in the company of Jean-Luc Godard, among others, from France and a fair smattering of VIPs from North America, he gladly accepted. Canada was intrigued by the little Pole who was about to celebrate his thirtieth birthday and still looked a teenager. He felt sufficiently relaxed in the French-speaking city to be able to give interviews and converse with his contemporaries in a confident manner.

The visit aroused the interest of the organizers of a new film festival being staged in New York the following month, and the good news was that Kanawa Films, a small independent distribution company, had bought the American rights for *Knife in the Water*. It would be premiered at the festival, to be staged at the magnificent new Lincoln Center which had rapidly become the cultural hub of the New York performing arts. The organizers were prepared to pay for Polanski's return air flight to New York and had reserved him accommodation at a hotel in the heart of mid-town Manhattan where he would be fêted as the boy from behind the Iron Curtain.

He arrived in the heartland of the American performing arts on 8 September, in time for the screening of *Knife in the Water*. He was nervous and filled with the wonderment of what the capitalist centre of the universe might hold for him. He imagined the streets of New York to be paved with gold, lined with clean and shiny buildings, and the Great White Way – Broadway – as pristine as its name suggests. Instead, he discovered a run-down and daunting urban sprawl, with pot-holed roads, that was distinctly unappealing. Then came the culture-shock of the oppressive, neck-bending skyscrapers, the swirling steam from the subway, the noise and smell of the traffic and the pavement crowds who all seemed to be going in the opposite direction.

Worse, the Great White Way was a gaudy mélange of hoardings which overshadowed the historic theatres. The biggest of the billboards was in Times Square, advertising *Cleopatra*, and the square itself was surrounded by discount stores and girlie bars. Forty-second Street was in the process of giving itself over entirely to the soft-porn trade. And although a stroll through Central Park was still possible without the certainty of being mugged, off to the east of it Harlem, the home of some of Polanski's musical heroes, was a smoking slum.

But New York was also exciting. The theatres, the bars, the nightspots, the jazz clubs were as available and stimulating as ever, and Greenwich Village was still a beating heart. The people, despite New York's harsh reputation, were also friendly, and everyone called Roman by his first name and jabbered on at speed, so that he had no hope of understanding.

There was a welcome mat for cultural émigrés from behind the Iron Curtain and Polanski received a warm reception. The unfamiliarly opulent limousine he boarded at the airport, where he was met by Archer King, marketing director of Kanawa Films, carried him to a reception at the Hilton Hotel and then on to the Lincoln Center. Polanski was a minnow in every respect, but at the time it may not have seemed that way to him. He also came on board the US movie-go-round at the very time that old Hollywood was disintegrating. The studio system was finally dead, a new band of movie-makers was waiting in the wings, and the glamorous icons of old Hollywood, bejewelled and adored, were about to go out of fashion.

At the time, it seemed barely possible that this boyish-looking Pole in the tight suit would, in two or three years' time, be among the new wave of movie-makers who were shaping up to take over towards the end of the decade. At any rate, the highbrow talk, there in New York in 1963, which compared his work to that of another of his heroes, Federico Fellini, was a breathtaking experience. Polanski's own film, *Knife in the Water*, was screened on 11 September. He was asked to introduce it from the stage, for which he had rehearsed a single sentence in English, stating that he was not good at making speeches and that was why he made films. This was his one and only attempt at the English language; thereafter he spoke in Polish or French, with an interpreter by his side.

After the screening, Polanski was asked to join a discussion group

75

and found himself surrounded by an enthusiastic crowd who fired meaningful questions about the film's message, about his intentions, and wasn't the knife really used as a phallic symbol? That he should be taken so seriously came as a shock, both for him and, for that matter, for a number of his hosts at the festival.

The greatest shock of all – and the greatest accolade – came the following week when *Time* magazine, that bastion of the American establishment, featured a still from *Knife in the Water* on its front cover, describing it as an excellent example of the cinema as an international art. The magazine was received with great enthusiasm in Poland, especially by Polanski's former colleagues at Lodz – it was an important recognition for an unknown film-maker to make the most coveted front cover in the world.

Media interviewers were amused and confused by Polanski. The language barrier enabled him to stage the act of an enigmatic man, quoting old fables from Eastern Europe which he often made up on the spur of the moment. Archer Winsten, in the *New York Post*, was baffled: 'Polanski is cherubic in looks yet he tells me he feels very old. He said, "I am the combination of an old man and a baby . . ." and he mentioned a man who was afraid to shave for fear he might see an old man in the mirror. He mentioned an actor who had played young boys all his life and suddenly, without having any manhood at all, he played the role of old men.' Polanski was describing himself, but no one knew it then.

Interest in him was brief and to the point, and when he had completed his commitments for the festival and it was time to go, he flew back to Paris still no nearer a deal for anything than when he had left. Hopes that an American producer would snap up his talents remained forlorn optimism, and weeks later he had to accept that Paris had not been moved by his recent accolades either.

Yet more were to come. In January 1964, he was invited to Munich for a showing of his work during an exhibition dealing exclusively with Polish films. Then, at the end of that month, he heard the most sensational news of his career – the American Academy of Motion Picture Arts and Sciences had nominated *Knife in the Water* for an Oscar in the Best Foreign Film category, along with Federico Fellini's *8½*.

The news was shattering and was received ecstatically in Poland. *Knife in the Water*, Polanski's only feature film to date, had now garnered a healthy clutch of prizes and honours, but had brought absolutely no benefit other than his attendance at a succession of junkets at which he had met fast-talking producers, half of whom he did not understand, and a few pretty girls whose interest in him waned rather quickly. It was an important time. 'One has to stress,' said Henryk Kluba, 'that in Poland his position was high even before his full-length debut with *Knife in the Water*. His short films had received prizes at festivals. But now, with this kind of debut for *Knife in the Water*, he did not have anything to be afraid of – not the critics, state authorities in Poland – no one.'

And now Hollywood was calling. The Oscars award ceremony was three months away and in the meantime Polanski redoubled his efforts to get something moving. News of his flirtation with the North American cinema made little or no impact in Paris where he and Gerard Brach continued their foot-slogging efforts to sell their script, *If Katelbach Comes*, but ended up meeting a long line of chancers and financial no-hopers who were always trying to put together the big deal but never managed it.

Gene Gutowski was another struggling would-be big-dealer but an honest one who, in his career as a movie producer, had so far managed to put together some television dramas and something not very big in Munich. He was a Polish-American who had a little money and lived in a pleasant apartment in a fashionable part of London. Ten years older than Polanski, he had escaped from Poland in the last weeks of the war, and because he spoke fluent German was able to make his way into Allied-held territory where he offered his services as an interpreter to an American army unit. Later, he was transferred to the OSS as an interrogations officer and when his war was over, emigrated to America. There he had married, had two children, divorced and came to London alone, married a model named Judy Wilson and lived in a flat near Montpellier Square.

He had seen *Knife in the Water* and did not think much of it, but after reading a couple of articles about Roman Polanski, he decided that here was a talent to be helped, and perhaps a way to make money. Polanski was, said Gutowski, living in Paris with virtually no work and no money, and Western producers who might have been interested in his work had no idea who or where he was. Gutowski tracked down his fellow-countryman to Paris and, over the telephone, analysed his problem: he needed representation, an agent, and a good English teacher as soon as possible – if he wanted to pursue his career as a movie director, he should move to London immediately and allow him, Gutowski, to assist him. He would even send him his plane fare.

77

Gutowski was right. London was on the brink of its sixties' extravaganza. All the major Hollywood studios at that time maintained a London staff which included talent-spotters and buyers, and numerous films originating from the Los Angeles offices were being made in the UK or Europe to take advantage of tax loopholes. The British film industry was also enjoying one of its periodic revivals and a number of major films produced in Britain had become international hits.

Polanski had not realized that London was far more cosmopolitan than Paris in that respect; certainly the elite of the business were less ring-fenced than the French film community. He had no idea, either, that at that particular moment in time all the musicians and writers, the photographers and directors, the designers and models, the singers and poets were already gathering, ready to become international celebrities come the revolution.

That he should be one of them was the result of one of those incidents of pure chance – that one man should decide to make a particular telephone call at a particular time. If the line had been busy, or if there had been no reply, he might never have called again and perhaps Polanski would not have come to London when he did. But all the above elements fell into place. Gutowski rang. Polanski answered. They had their chat, and Polanski caught the shuttle to London forthwith with a dog-eared copy of *If Katelbach Comes* for the perusal of anyone who might be interested.

Unfortunately, no one was – not the William Morris Agency who he asked to represent him, not the script departments of MGM, Paramount and Warner Brothers whose offices he visited, nor the two or three British independents they contacted. Gutowski gave Polanski a room in his apartment and he and Judy began showing their protégé the sights.

Polanski was bowled over by London. Paris was good, but London in 1964 was the place to be: the restaurants, the girls, the music, the writers and artists were all getting into position to make the most of what *Time* magazine would describe as the city of the decade, eventually renamed the city of decadence.

Once again, Polanski was thrilled by the experience, but another adventure beckoned. By then, it was time to prepare for his Los Angeles trip, and his nerve ends were jangling. The film magazines and show-business columns in London were full of the details of the Oscar awards and Gutowski would translate them for him, reading aloud the stories that he could not read for himself.

The papers were full of the Oscars because Britain, for once, had a larger than usual contingent of nominations, almost entirely due to Tony Richardson's movie *Tom Jones* which was nominated for nine awards. Also in the British party that year were Margaret Rutherford, nominated for Best Supporting Actress in *The VIPs* with Taylor and Burton, Richard Harris and Rachel Roberts for their roles in another British film, *This Sporting Life*, and Leslie Caron for her performance in Bryan Forbes's *The L-Shaped Room*. It was a vintage year for Britain, the likes of which would seldom be seen again.

Like all recipients of nominations, Polanski was given a first-class air ticket to Los Angeles and would be accommodated for three nights at the Beverly Hills Hotel, the hosts merely providing his transport and accommodation. Polanski had very little money, most of which was borrowed from Gutowski, and that very soon ran out. The Academy, aware that Polanski spoke no English, had arranged for him to be hosted by another Pole, the composer Bronislaw Kaper, who showed him the sights and arranged for him to visit Disneyland.

The presentation of the awards was at the Santa Monica Civic Auditorium on 13 April 1964, when Jack Lemmon was master of ceremonies for the evening. Polanski was brought to the auditorium by limousine and was given the pre-awards briefing about what to do in the event of winning. He was shown to his table where, to his absolute delight, he discovered he had been placed next to Federico Fellini and his wife Giulietta. Then came the announcement of the Oscars, and the winning selection from the Best Foreign Film category in which Polanski and Fellini were competitors, along with three others.

And the winner is . . . Federico Fellini, *8½*. Pangs of disappointment were unavoidable for Polanski who had come this far, only to go unrewarded. His consolation prize was being among the world's largest collection of movie people gathered under one roof at any one time and being mentioned in the same breath as Federico Fellini.

Polanski returned to Europe, and in London Gutowski continued to try to find a buyer for his script, hoping now to cash in on the Academy exposure. Gutowski also formed a company called Cadre Films in which he and Polanski were to be partners, and once again began hawking the script of *If Katelbach Comes* around the various studios and London representatives of European and American film companies, though without success. Finally, he managed to arouse the interest of a small independent production company called Compton Films. Polanski was disappointed when he learned of their background – up to then they had produced soft porn for the cinema club trade.

Compton also ran a club of its own in London's Soho and its movies so far included such titles as *The Yellow Teddy Bears*, *Saturday Night Out*, *London in the Raw*, *Naked as Nature Intended* and *My Bare Lady*. The two leading lights of the company, Tony Tenser and Michael Klinger, young Jewish men from London's East End, were pushing to make a name for themselves, and some money, and wore suits and spoke like businessmen rather than porn merchants. Klinger, who wore horn-rimmed spectacles and chomped on a big cigar, was also of Polish origin, which formed an immediate bond between himself and Polanski when they first met.

Tenser and Klinger were exploring other possibilities in the film business and were intrigued at the prospect of a director who had just been nominated for an Oscar working for them. Polanski was hardly jumping for joy – Klinger seemed a decent enough guy, but Compton was a low-budget, cheap-thrill outfit – but as Klinger himself had realized – otherwise Polanski would not be there talking to them – no one else was even offering to buy him lunch.

His screenplay for *If Katelbach Comes* had been rejected by everyone who had seen it and even Compton did not want it – not yet, anyway. Klinger explained that he was more interested in Polanski himself, and in finding a suitable project, preferably a horror story. There was money in horror, my boy.

He had obviously explored the market. The Hammer House of Horrors had been doing good business with a string of low-budget British films, as had Roger Corman's cheaply made movies in America where among his contract players was a young unknown named Jack Nicholson who had recently appeared in *The Raven* with Vincent Price and Boris Karloff.

Polanski, in his usual boastful manner, said he could write anything. Klinger told him to bring him a horror script, and he would back it. Polanski returned immediately to Paris and began writing with his collaborator, Gerard Brach. They worked day and night for almost three weeks and produced their new outline for Klinger. Considering the speed with which it was written, the screenplay had a remarkable depth and psychological intensity which seemed to come naturally to both men.

Their story, entitled *Repulsion*, was sparsely populated, like most of Polanski's work to date, and concerns a Belgian manicurist named Carol Ledoux who is living in London with her sister. Carol is a beautiful young woman whose apparent innocence masks extremes of reaction to sex, in that she is both attracted and repelled by it.

When her sister goes away on holiday, a young Englishman calls to see her; Carol imagines he has come to rape her and clubs him to death with a candlestick. Now driven to insanity by her action, she murders her landlord who makes advances to her, slashing him with a razor. By the time the sister returns from holiday with her boyfriend, Carol is hiding under the bed surrounded by the bloody carnage.

Polanski and Brach, aware of the language problems they might encounter, had given the screenplay very little dialogue, and it relied entirely on the visual, another of Polanski's specialities. It was not so much a horror story as a dramatic and macabre study of a damaged mind, but written simply and without sophistication so that it appealed to the commercial instincts of Michael Klinger who had but one thought – to make a movie that made money. Klinger liked the sound of the outline and flew immediately to Paris to get Polanski's signature on a contract.

Gutowski was there too. He would be the producer and, with Polanski, take a share of the profits. It was not in Klinger's nature to risk a fortune and the scale of the venture he was planning is best illustrated by the amount he was spending. The most he would offer as a fee for the combined writing, directing and producing of the film was £2500, which had to be split three ways between Polanski, Brach and Gutowski. There would also be a strict budget, over which Polanski should not step.

The door was open at last. It was not the big time by any means but by then, Polanski was ready to clutch at any straw.

Chapter Eight

*L*ondon was just beginning to swing when Roman Polanski arrived. Anyone could become an overnight star, and since Polanski had immodestly described himself as 'an exotic new talent', he seemed to fit exactly into the era. He did not quite know how or why people were so much more friendly than in Paris, but he liked it very much. London was like that then: newcomers were welcomed in a way never before experienced; people came from nowhere and made a crowd. Everyone who became anyone in the sixties was doing it in London with a kind of boundless, infectious camaraderie that enveloped a range of new styles and attitudes which eventually cut across the whole pattern of British life, and beyond.

Polanski was soon to be mixing with the best of them but it took a little time; there were one or two basics he had to learn, including how to speak English. He stayed with the Gutowskis for the time being, while he began work on the final draft of *Repulsion*, and Gene's wife Judy began to give him English lessons. For several weeks, while he was rewriting parts of his script, she would read and write with him, cook for him and even do his laundry. Mike Klinger had hired a British writer, David Stone, to prepare an English translation and inject some Western nuance. Gutowski arranged for a fashionable tailor to kit Roman out, and on the strength of this burgeoning activity he found an apartment in a large Georgian house close to the Gutowskis which he rented at a ridiculously cheap sum but which, to him, was luxury itself. As soon as he was settled, he sent for Gerard Brach to share in this good fortune.

The rewriting and the schooling continued all that summer of 1964, and at night Polanski began to venture out into Soho and the night-spots of London where he was seen as something of a novelty figure – this small young man with a cherubic face that could contort to devil-like proportions when roused, who spoke in a mixture of Polish and French interspersed with his rapidly growing English vocabulary, liberally punctuated by the fuck-word which, for a man of limited powers of expression, seemed to fit a multitude of situations.

Victor Lownes, whom he had met in Cannes, was all over the social diaries as Playboy Enterprises began its publicity build-up for the launch of its London operation. Lownes was seeking and receiving plenty of attention and, if the gossip columnists were to be believed, had a small harem of lovers – enough, indeed to share with a small Polish person who called him one day and said, 'Remember me?'

Lownes did, and Polanski was instantly placed on a fast-track entry into London social life as led by the new elite in all the fashionable new high-spots. The language he was learning via Judy Gutowski would be coloured by the new 'in' phraseology that came with the Beatles and the Stones and the modern Cockney spivs. And women were around at last, and in plentiful numbers.

For all his Jewish carefulness, Michael Klinger turned out to be exceedingly accommodating as Polanski began to prepare his list of potential technicians and actors for the filming of *Repulsion*, though it was more an act of surrender than deliberate expansiveness. Polanski just kept on and on until he got his way.

Klinger found that he possessed a total lack of sentimentality and seemed devoid of feelings about his past, which he talked of in a matter-of-fact way. He hated hypocrisy, and the lack of it in himself actually boosted the impression of arrogance: he appeared to have no regard for the feelings of others. They had set a budget of £40,000 to make the movie, a figure which rather put the whole project into perspective when judged against the lavish spending of the American studios, and even the cheapest of the British. Polanski, though poverty-stricken himself, had little regard for money, and the artistic instincts which were the basis of what many believed was a conceited haughtiness more likely to be found in a director way beyond his current station, were always placed ahead of all else.

Basia Kwiatkowska provided a very succinct appraisal of Polanski's view of money and movies which resounds down the years, film by film, producer by producer, and remains ultimately so very true: 'His biggest fault as a film-maker is the discrepancy between his poetic vision and his showing-off. If he earns a million, he will spend a million and a half. His films are always over budget and he leaves his producer broke.'

83

In the months to come, as he filmed *Repulsion*, he would have a running battle with Compton over costs, because – according to them – he was taking too long, filming too many takes, using too many costly technical tricks. From a personal point of view, money apparently meant nothing, at that time, anyway. If he had sufficient to eat, drink and live in his new apartment he was already richer by far than his starving days in Paris. And so, for the time being, he could reject money as a driving force in his life – as Darryl F. Zanuck, head of 20th Century-Fox, very soon discovered. Zanuck was trying to woo Elizabeth Taylor and Richard Burton back to the fold after the *Cleopatra* fiasco and planned to offer them a million dollars apiece – which was now their going rate – to star in a remake of Polanski's *Knife in the Water*, with Warren Beatty cast as the young hitch-hiker who comes between them. Beatty's fee alone would have been ten times the budget for Polanski's new picture, plus a share of the profits.

Fox made the approach through Gutowski and protracted negotiations began in what was another remarkable episode. Polanski could not understand why they wanted to remake his movie; it seemed to him a ridiculous proposition, particularly so soon after he had won an Academy nomination for his first effort. In his mind, it was like asking van Gogh to repaint the sunflowers, using a different variety of flower.

Furthermore, he would not have artistic control over the new version, because Fox felt that his difficulties with the English language might cause some problems in trying to direct three of the most volatile stars in international cinema. He would merely be an associate director. He was so angered by these Hollywood notions which were alien to him that he threw his hands up and asked, 'Why? Why remake a perfectly good film?' Fox's argument was that though Polanski's film had been shown at festivals around the world and had been run in art cinemas it had not exactly set the world on fire.

Joe Lebworth, one of Zanuck's men in charge of negotiations, said it was difficult getting their reasoning through to Polanski. He kept asking the same question over and over. He said he had a thousand other good ideas that they could film. Lebworth said they wanted that one and were prepared to pay him a large sum for the rights, even if he had nothing to do with it. Eventually the whole project was dropped. It did, however, bring Polanski into indirect contact with Warren Beatty, who was soon to become one of his closest friends.

Polanski's attention focused back on to *Repulsion* and he began making the kind of demands to which successive movie producers would become accustomed, summed up as: The best of everything. Klinger listened patiently. They argued a lot but he gave way most of the time. Polanski had selected photographer Gilbert Taylor who had recently filmed Stanley Kubrick's *Dr Strangelove* and had just finished the Beatles' movie, *Hard Day's Night*, for Richard Lester.

Polanski had already made up his mind that he wanted Catherine Deneuve as his leading lady and would not budge from that. The French actress, who was as famous for her liaisons as her film roles, had a high profile at the time. She had recently given birth to the love-child of her Svengali, Roger Vadim, the French director who discovered her soon after his marriage to Brigitte Bardot had ended. Polanski was better placed than Klinger and Gutowski to know that Deneuve was hot. The publicity surrounding her in Paris had been immense during the past few years, and such notoriety in a young actress of classic beauty was not long in spreading world-wide through the voyeuristic columns of the tabloids and glossy magazines. Polanski's choice was essentially made with an eye on the potential for attracting attention – to himself, his film and his star.

It was a brilliant move. Catherine Deneuve, born in Paris in 1943 into a highly respectable theatrical family, had been appearing in French movies since her early teens, though her debut as an actress really occurred in 1960, in *Les Portes Claquent*, when an actress was required to play Françoise Dorléac's younger sister – since Catherine was that very thing in real life, she was a natural choice. Françoise, who had kept their parents' name – Deneuve was their mother's maiden name – had become a minor star through a series of French movies, and although the sisters were close, Catherine had never shown any inclination towards acting until then.

Catherine was shy, fragile-looking and in the shadow of her more vivacious sister – until the age of seventeen when she was 'discovered' by Roger Vadim, former husband and Pygmalion to Brigitte Bardot, Annette Stroyberg and – after Deneuve – Jane Fonda. Vadim changed the colour of Catherine's hair from brunette to blonde, so that she resembled Bardot, and cast her in two films. *Le Vice et la Vertu* was a screen adaptation of a story by the Marquis de Sade in which Deneuve was victim of some erotic sado-masochism. Next, she caused a sensation in *Et Satan Conduit le Bal*. She was soon being talked of as the sex kitten of France, the new Bardot, her successor to the affections of Vadim with whom she began living. A new round of headlines began when she and Vadim called off their wedding on the eve of the ceremony, saying mysteriously that 'it was something within his family'. She refused to say what, because 'I knew his reasons were being dictated by society', and she left him to have the baby, a son named Christian, alone.

So Deneuve's sheer determination to reject social convention had already assured Polanski's movie of the media attention he wanted. The other major attraction of Deneuve, apart from her stunning looks and publicity value, was that Polanski could direct her in French, and since she was playing the leading role, and would be on screen virtually throughout, it was a vital consideration. He also knew exactly who he wanted for the role of her elder sister. This was the actress Yvonne Furneaux, who made her name in Italy in Fellini's *La Dolce Vita*, playing opposite Marcello Mastroianni.

Klinger and his partner Tenser would have preferred a British actress, and mentioned Francesca Annis as their own choice for the starring role. She had already appeared in one of their frolicking movies and her services could be obtained rather more cheaply than Deneuve's. Annis gave what Klinger described as a 'beautiful audition', but while she was still in the room Polanski made an insulting remark about her nose. 'Michael,' he asked Klinger within her hearing, 'why do you want to cast this Cyrano de Bergerac?' Later he denied saying such a thing but he did. She obviously made an impression upon him, however, because he called her up some years later to cast her in *Macbeth*.

The budget for *Repulsion* was already exceeding values set aside for these two key appointments. The small supporting cast were no slouches, either. Polanski had done his homework and selected three of Britain's best character actors of the day, Ian Hendry, Patrick Wymark and John Fraser, who were talked into joining the production for less than their normal fee for the privilege of working with this great new director who had won an Oscar nomination.

Some years later, Hendry described the way Polanski operated during the making of *Repulsion*, which was filmed entirely at Twickenham Studios. He marvelled at the way Polanski had mastered the English language in such a short space of time. Though he spoke French all the time to Deneuve, he tried to direct the English crew and actors in their own language.

The key was the way he built up tension among actors. Every director has his own system. Polanski's was to get his actors angry, both at him and with each other, and it was carefully planned. His collaborator Gerard Brach reckoned he underlined the parts of his script where he needed to inject fire and fury into his cast to achieve the perfection he was looking for, and he would never let go until it was delivered. 'He was an absolute stickler for planning his scene – every scene and every set sketched out on a pad, even down to the facial features of the actors and their positions,' said Brach.

Polanski taunted Deneuve in a stream of French vitriol that few on the set could understand, but a translation wasn't really necessary. He hurled abuse and obscenities, after which she would explode with anger in response.

If her performance in a particular scene was not exactly how he wanted it, he would order retake after retake to the point where they were screaming at each other. He also insisted that she kept well away from men during the whole eight weeks of filming – he wanted her sexual passions aroused, unsated by offscreen romance.

One scene was particularly important, where she was writhing about on the floor, naked to the black roots of her blonde hair. Normally a shy person, Deneuve hated even opening her own handbag in public, let alone taking her clothes off. 'It was an incredible deal to undress her,' Polanski told an interviewer later. 'I had to convince her it was art.'

Tension between Polanski and the actors grew to such a pitch that one day Yvonne Furneaux went down on her knees pleading with Klinger, 'Tell that little bastard to leave me alone.' Furneaux accused Polanski of psychological torture. Klinger also had some spectacular arguments with him, especially as Polanski's perfectionist traits seemed to be verging on the manic. One scene, the filming of a hand in close-up which was being done on location in a London hairdressing salon, was shot twenty-seven times. Polanski did not give up easily, and would argue with anyone that films were remembered by scenes, and by the characters in them. 'Think of the last movie you saw,' he would say, 'and you'll think of a particular scene in it.' So his method of working was straightforward, at least to himself, in that each scene was the module of which his film was composed and must be conceived as an entity and composed for its memorability. The audience would go away remembering the film's high points, and they would be able to recall them for years to come. In virtually all his major scenes, his technique amounted to shock tactics aimed at bringing his audiences to the edge of their seats or covering their eyes with fear.

By now, news of Polanski's film had reached the media, and several writers in what were then described as 'top people's magazines' were impressed by the man who was talked of as a potential movie genius and a celebrity in the making. In *Queen* magazine, Mark Shivas reported prophetically that 'Twickenham, Middlesex, has suddenly become a Mecca of film journalists all because of a minuscule Pole . . . [who] looks like a pixie, who is thirty and will probably seem much the same age for the next thirty years'. Shivas talked to Polanski to try to uncover his influences, which he claimed were Beckett, Kafka and Hemingway, complaining that art in the film world was restricted by the censors. 'Everyone can read a scene from Hemingway or whoever and say "Ah! Great" – but you cannot portray it on film. Everyone is disgusted and it is cut.'

Polanski said that he would keep pushing the boundaries until such scenes were permissible. In *Repulsion*, there was a very real question of bad taste, and there was some doubt as to whether the British Board of Film Censors would pass the violence and sexual content. Carol, the Deneuve character, is the subject of wide-ranging psychological scrutiny by Polanski's camera, from her loneliness through to her involuntary voyeurism, listening to her sister and boyfriend making love in the next room. There are cloudy visions in which Carol's own tormented hallucinations are of violent sexual acts and anal rape by the shadowy figure of a man, with the cameras bearing down on her own face showing the horror and repulsion until it boils up into violence.

One scene which was cut from the finished print even before it was shown to the censors involved an additional murder – of a woman who inadvertently discovered the first of the killings carried out by Carol. In the scene, she was to be drowned by Deneuve holding her head under the bloody water in a bath-tub. The actress playing the scene refused to put her head in the water, so Polanski found a wig, dressed in the woman's clothes and acted the scene himself. Later, Chico Hamilton, the jazz musician who was writing the music score, complained to Polanski that the scene was horrific, completely wrong and out of context with the rest of the drama. Carol murdered the men through her sexual arousal and repulsion; she would not have killed a woman for the same reason. Klinger had made the same point, when the scene was being filmed, but hearing it afresh from Hamilton, Polanski cut the scene completely.

The final version of *Repulsion* was not at all what Klinger and Tenser expected. First, in spite of all Polanski's goading of the two women, they were outstanding. Deneuve gave a haunted, haunting performance, with her face burned into the memory of all who saw the film. She had played her role as the catatonic murderess to absolute perfection.

Klinger and Tenser had wanted a horror film, straight and simple; this was nothing like it and they now realized that Polanski had known all along that it was never going to be just that. What he delivered to the Compton partners was a psychological study of a disintegrating mind, full of technical devices, tricky camerawork and intriguing images which began right from the opening when the screen was filled with the vision of a single eye, giving the hint that the audience was about to be taken upon a journey into the unknown fantasies of the human psyche which could be traced back into the subject's childhood. And indeed, Polanski's pursuit of that aim was relentless.

Compton were apprehensive, but not unhappy. The film had gone way over budget, almost double the original figure, and it had been a traumatic experience for all concerned. But Polanski had managed to find a balance between the artistic and the commercial and he had a trump card still to play. He talked Victor Lownes into suggesting a spread on his film to Hugh Hefner for *Playboy* magazine. That was fine, said Hefner, but they would have to have some nude pictures of Catherine Deneuve who by then had returned to Paris. Polanski called up and she refused, point-blank.

He pleaded, and assured her that the photographs would be taken on a closed set by Britain's foremost fashion photographer, a young man named David Bailey. She had heard of him – who hadn't? 'I tried to make her see that she is beautiful and that the body is part of art,' Polanski boasted afterwards. 'It was a very difficult thing to do but it turned out to be a great experience because she later married the photographer.'

Deneuve did not see it like that. The hype for *Repulsion* would eventually be built around her, and in a sensational manner which brought Compton a publicity bonus for their film which they could never have imagined possible. The pictures of her, and stills from the film, were used in the *Playboy* spread under the headline 'Queen of the Parisian Cinema'. It was the beginning of a lifelong enmity towards the media on Deneuve's part. 'It was a terrible mistake,' she said, 'and I would never do anything like it again.'

Polanski virtually tricked her into going naked, and added loquaciously in interviews words that added to the promotion of the whole scenario: that she was a 'professional virgin, an angel with a slightly soiled halo' . . . 'not overtly like Monroe, or bitchy like Bardot' . . . she was 'a man's niece whom he would bounce on his knee . . . and all those dirty magazines in France played up to her because they thought she was ripe for exploitation, and had had a kid out of wedlock. She hated that . . .' Polanski's handling of the whole scenario was exploitative and manipulative, as it had been from the beginning. 'He would not care who he uses,' said Basia Kwiatkowska. 'If it was not me, then it would be someone else – that's the way it was.'

Repulsion immediately attracted all the attention Polanski had desired, along with a diverse critical response – not all good, but no review was dismissive of the work. The *Christian Science Monitor* applauded Polanski's technical achievements but found the movie a depressing psychological study which would leave the audience feeling bruised and soiled. Similarly, a reviewer for *Sight and Sound* stated boldly that the effect it might have on any member of the audience going through a period of stress or crisis 'doesn't bear thinking about'. The *Daily Mail* described it as an unashamedly ugly film, 'but as a lynx-eyed view of a crumbling mind, it is a masterpiece of the macabre'.

In Britain, it was passed by the censors pretty well without comment, but some heady reservations were expressed elsewhere in Europe. In Austria, birthplace of the founder of modern psychoanalysis, Sigmund Freud, officials referred *Repulsion* to a panel of psychiatrists for their observations. Far from decrying the film, however, they simply asked where Polanski had studied to get his material to create the character of Carol who was, in their view, a classic schizophrenic.

The Germans enjoyed it. Polanski was invited to the Berlin Film Festival to show his movie and give a short explanation of its intentions, and it won the coveted Silver Bear award. The French were less enthusiastic and the organizers of the Cannes Film Festival rejected it as an official entry. Klinger and Gutowski took a print of the film to Cannes anyway, and gave private viewings.

Those from Polanski's past who knew his history and his childhood experiences, which were as yet of little or no interest to a wider public, would well recognize certain events from his own life upon which he had drawn, such as blows to the head, which he had himself experienced, and the blending of blood with water, which would become a recurring theme.

This is an appropriate moment at which to establish some views on whether all that Roman Polanski went through as a child was now beginning to emerge in his films, in those dark and disturbing explorations of human behaviour. Henryk Kluba, who studied his work closely, said: 'Most Poles instinctively reject Freud. Psychoanalysis is something that never was as influential in Poland as it is in the West.

Romek wouldn't fit Freudian perspectives. He would laugh at it himself. From the conversations I had with him, I could never detect a complex, or that he missed his mother. Maybe I didn't notice it, but if he didn't speak about it, if he did not complain about being wronged, it means he went through that and emerged without any scars.'

However, a pattern was already emerging in the limited exposure of his work to the public which showed that in the mind's eye of Roman Polanski, there were devious and deviant pictures which he wished to explore and pursue with relentless morbidity. Basia Kwiatkowska had definite theories about these images, agreeing in part with Kluba that they were not so much drawn from personal experience as from invention and the creation of events in his mind. 'I personally don't think his films relate entirely to his childhood experiences,' she said. 'I think they are the result of visions which came into his head when he was wandering from village to village as a boy. It was these visions which he retained. I could understand it very well because I, as a child, used to walk long distances [as a shepherdess] and you have such a wide horizon, that the visions you have . . . you reach them in the end. He carried all those things in his head, and all the nightmares that tormented him came to effect in his films. There are some very horrible things in *Two Men and a Wardrobe*; it is cruel despite its poetry . . . I believe that is how he conducted his therapy, through his films. But in his daily life I detected no neuroses, absolutely none.'

The portrayal of the women in Polanski's stories was also distinctly and deliberately controversial and cruel, for which, as we have seen, Basia blamed herself, as an after-effect of her leaving him. This was to be reaffirmed in his next film, the story of an effeminate, transvestite husband and his voluptuous young nymphomaniac wife who are terrorized by two gangsters seeking refuge in their home: this, in a nutshell, was the much-touted story of *If Katelbach Comes* which he had at last sold to Compton Films. After the Berlin award, they were positively raring to go, in spite of all the difficulties they had experienced with Polanski on *Repulsion*. The *Katelbach* script, which they had previously rejected, was now seen in a new light, retitled as *Cul-de-Sac*. Compton agreed a budget of £135,000, and this set Polanski loose on an unsuspecting group of people who would end up wondering why they ever got involved with him in the first place.

Chapter Nine

C*ul-de-Sac* was a story riddled with autobiographical elements and hang-ups, written in anger at a time when Roman Polanski and Gerard Brach were trying to get over being deserted by their respective women. The central theme is an absurd marriage between a nymphomaniac wife and an ageing transvestite husband whose life becomes even more disturbed by the entry of a third person into the triangle – an escaped convict. It was a surreal masterpiece of a story, and although the eventual film did not match up to that description, this was another tale in which Polanski and Brach searched the dark corners of the human psyche, seeking out the macabre and the taboo and stirring up mental disturbances, especially those of women.

According to his friends, Polanski had written *Cul-de-Sac* as a kind of therapeutic revenge after the collapse of his marriage to Basia, and even Gerard Brach was shocked when he learned of Polanski's ultimate intention – to offer Basia the starring role in the film. It was, said one of his former colleagues, a grotesque release of his feelings towards Basia who was certainly no more nymphomaniac than he was transvestite, notwithstanding the fact that dressing up in drag for various roles in his pictures obviously intrigued him: he would do it often. The character he had written specially for Basia was clearly identifiable in the original screenplay. Zofia Komeda confirmed: 'Yes, in the initial version of the script the main female character was a Polish student. Because Romek wanted Basia to play her, he devised a character who spoke poor English, with a foreign accent – just like Basia. She comes to Paris and refused to go back, partly through pride and partly through apprehension with the Communists. So she has gone wrong, and is sliding . . . until this rich idiot falls in love with her. He sells everything and buys an island where a Polish writer wrote his best work . . .'

When they were ready to cast, Polanski sent the script to Basia, by now married to Karl Heinz Boehm and living in Holland at the time. Despite the content, Basia might well have agreed, had it not been for her husband. 'Karl Heinz would not allow it,' she said. 'I had only been married to him a few months and he, and I, both knew the dangers. Romek would try to get me back.' But it was not just the threat of Polanski's romantic intentions that upset Karl Heinz. He did not like the screenplay, with its nasty undercurrents, either. Zofia Komeda and her husband were in Holland when the script arrived. 'Because of Karl's refusal to let Basia take the part, a whole layer of the film was lost – all the nostalgia for a country [Poland] where the character wanted to go but for some reason was unwilling, all the Polish homesickness was lost because Basia wasn't in it.'

So apart from rewriting a huge section of the screenplay, Polanski also had to find a female lead, but with Basia so firmly fixed in his mind, he could see no other. He interviewed or screen tested more than 150 girls, some of them not even actresses but models who might look the part, and who Polanski believed he might turn into actresses, as he had done before. None suited, not even the up-and-coming young star Jacqueline Bisset, although he was so fascinated by her innate beauty that he offered her a small walk-on part. Intrigued by Polanski, she stayed around for almost the duration of making the movie, and he would later make allusions to an affair at this time.

The location was as elusive as the star. Michael Klinger was going for economy, and Yugoslavia was suggested as it was really cheap there. They all flew out and travelled the Dalmatian coastline looking for a small island with a castle-like building. They found nothing suitable, and anyway Polanski was nervous about filming in a Communist-bloc country, then still under the iron grip of Tito.

They repeated their search along the east coast of Britain in a light aircraft which bounced around in the late winter turbulence as they headed north. Polanski insisted that the location was almost as important as the cast, because the setting is an integral part of the story. *Cul-de-Sac* is a tense black comedy which draws its action from the three main characters whose neuroses pour out as they are trapped on an island in a warped threesome relationship. Eventually, the perfect spot was found – Holy Island, off the Northumberland coast near Berwick-on-Tweed, which possessed all the required attributes – isolation, a castle and a certain built-in eeriness.

Next, he pursued his actors, three men who were to be cast exactly to the vision he and Brach had of them when writing the screenplay, and of whom Polanski had drawn sketches long before they began their search. An inspired choice for the key role of the husband was Donald Pleasence, who had a reputation for being single-mindedly creative in his work, superbly sinister and darkly comic, and was established as one of Britain's finest, if slightly off-beat, character actors. He was also a man who would not be pushed around.

Nor, for that matter, would the brash American Lionel Stander, his opposite number in the triangle. He too was an important casting as the gangster, and the search had been fruitless until Gene Gutowski saw him on a television chat show and suggested Polanski should take a look. Tough, pugnacious, loud and flashy, Stander came to London after running into trouble with the Committee on UnAmerican Activities during Senator Joe McCarthy's purge of alleged Communists in Hollywood, and dined out on the experience for ever after. Later famous for his television role as Robert Wagner's side-kick in *Hart to Hart*, the gravel-voiced Stander was then sharp and rebellious, given to wearing pink suits and, in common with Polanski, liked to be the centre of attention.

Jack MacGowran was the third of the male actors, though less important since he was the gangster who died soon after arriving on the island with Stander. A leading lady still eluded Polanski until one day, he found himself talking to Catherine Deneuve. Since making *Repulsion*, Deneuve was in great demand among leading French directors, and a string of successful roles lay ahead. She remained a regular on the London social scene, too, largely through the company she kept: she was the close companion of David Bailey, the man whom Polanski had brought to photograph her nude, and whom she would shortly marry.

Listening to Polanski's tale of woe as they sipped their drinks in the fashionable Ad Lib Club behind Leicester Square, where stars like the Beatles could go without getting mobbed, Deneuve suddenly suggested her sister, Françoise Dorléac. Polanski called her the next day and arranged a screen-test. Michael Klinger was not happy. Françoise was a star in her own country, but virtually unknown in Britain, except as Deneuve's sister. Polanski insisted that she was right for the part and the nearest he had come to finding a replacement for Basia.

Episode two of the story of the making of *Cul-de-Sac* is set on location at Holy Island, where Polanski imposed upon his little throng the same kind of perfectionist discipline that Françoise's sister had experienced in *Repulsion*. A certain air of tense expectancy developed almost from the beginning. Donald Pleasence arrived in his big American Lincoln, the like of which had never been seen by the island community. Polanski discovered that the balding actor had shaved his head, and made it clear that he would have preferred to have been consulted about this decision. 'It was something I did instinctively,' said Pleasence. 'When I read the script, I visualized how this character would look and that was my perception of him as I would play him, given the limitations of my own physical attributes.'

Polanski put Pleasence's back up straight away. He shrugged and walked away, imagining that it was going to be 'one of those films'. In the end, the head-shaving was something Pleasence believed added to his characterization, and one he retained the following year for his brilliant portrayal of the evil Blofeld in the James Bond movie, *You Only Live Twice*.

Françoise Dorléac's arrival was even more spectacular. She came bearing seventeen pieces of luggage and a tiny, hairless chihuahua dog which she had smuggled through British Customs in her hand-luggage to avoid the six-month quarantine regulations. She took up residence at a local inn but filming had barely begun before she made a hasty retreat to Paris for attention to a broken tooth, which at least brought some relief to her colleagues, who were already fed up with the damned dog snapping at the ankles of anyone who approached its mistress. When she returned, bringing the animal back with her, it snapped at a Customs' officer examining her bags, and was confiscated and placed in quarantine kennels until she was ready to return.

Michael Klinger was much in evidence, having assigned himself the task of ensuring Polanski kept up to schedule. Heated discussions on this aspect of the proceedings were evident from the beginning and continued through to the final day of shooting when Klinger himself would call a halt. Perfectionism was one thing, he would tell Polanski, but what was the point of making a perfect film that had gone over budget and lost money? The crew were all on contracts which put them into overtime for every hour that filming continued after a specified time, and Klinger was upset that after the first week, Polanski had filmed no more than half a dozen pages of the script.

As Polanski contrived to fill every scene with the incidents he believed audiences remember a film for, a taut atmosphere developed which threatened to halt production entirely. The story was progressing slowly on film . . . Dorléac and Pleasence are established in their isolated home on the island, and the sexual and psychological intricacies of their relationship are beginning to unfold when the two escaped gangsters arrive, waiting to be rescued by boat and carried to safety. One of them, the MacGowran character, dies, leaving Stander, as Dicky, alone with the couple. His relationship with them now develops into a triangle into which Polanski has woven his stock-in-trade voyeurism, allowing the tensions, the sex and the violence to develop at their own pace.

Tensions existed already, between Polanski and Pleasence, between Polanski and Dorléac, and between Dorléac and Stander to whom she took an instant personal dislike. Divisions between them in the script were easily matched by those offscreen. Hostility flared up in the filming of one scene, where Stander was to chase Dorléac across a cobblestone yard, throw her to the ground and beat her with his belt. It was a violent scene which never seemed to match Polanski's expectations: five or six times he ordered, 'Again, please.'

On the last take, Stander accidentally hit Dorléac with the buckle end of the belt, and she was visibly hurt and struck back. Stander called out an obscenity, and accused her of making him hurt his knee. He was walking with a limp and demanded a walking stick to help him. Filming was delayed while the set doctor was called. Then he began complaining of chest pains which Klinger feared might be the onset of a heart attack. By then, so much of the film had been completed that had Stander been forced to pull out on medical grounds, Compton would have scrapped the movie and claimed on their insurance. Days passed until eventually Stander declared himself fit and they continued, though not without further disharmony.

But perhaps the biggest upset occurred over Polanski's treatment of Françoise Dorléac as he strove to get her to do her scenes in the way he wished. One in particular left her exhausted. It called for her to be bathing naked in the sea while Pleasence and Stander acted out an alcohol-induced discussion about her on the beach. She was reluctant in any case about appearing naked and had to be persuaded to strip, first in a bedroom scene with Pleasence and then for this scene at the beach.

The North Sea was cold and rough, but Dorléac eventually agreed to go in; in any event, there were no stand-ins, so she had little alternative. Polanski insisted on doing the scene in one take because at a given moment an aircraft was to fly into shot. It was a long scene, eight minutes of filming. Twice Françoise went into the water and swam around in her position, and both times Polanski wanted it done again. The aircraft was called back for a third run, and Pleasence and Stander took up their marks.

Michael Klinger, who had arrived to jostle Polanski along, walked over and suggested that the last take was good enough, and that Françoise

Roman Polanski, twenty-six but passing for eighteen, photographed while filming at the National Film School at Lodz in 1959. (*Film Polski*)

Polanski's film school collaborator and close friend was the pugilistic Jerzy Skolimowski, who co-wrote *Knife in the Water*. (*New Yorker Films*)

Stunning was, for once, an apt description of the former shepherdess Basia Kwiatkowska, Polanski's first wife, who starred in numerous continental films under her screen name of Barbara Lass. (*Courtesy British Film Institute*)

Seat of learning: the former Polish tycoon's residence which was turned into the National Film School at Lodz in Poland's post-war Stalinist cultural revival. (*Courtesy British Film Institute*)

A scene from the award-winning *Mammals*, the last of Polanski's short films in Poland, which he shot illegally with the help of his ill-fated friend, Wojtek Frykowski. The film starred Henryk Kluba (*right*) and Michal Zolznierkiewicz. (*Courtesy British Film Institute*)

From the film that made him famous: a passionate scene from *Knife in the Water*, which starred the unknown Jolanta Umecka, whom Polanski picked up at a swimming pool, and Leon Niemczyk. (*Kanawha Films*)

From the low-budget French production *The Most Beautiful Swindles in the World*. Polanski directed one of the segments, entitled 'The Diamond Necklace', which featured an unknown model/air hostess with acting aspirations, Nicole Hilartain. (*Yardley Collection*)

Paris 1961: lean times, literally, in a short film which he wrote, directed and acted in. Entitled *The Fat and the Lean*, it again demonstrated Polanski's early fascination with the psychological power play between individuals. (*Courtesy British Film Institute*)

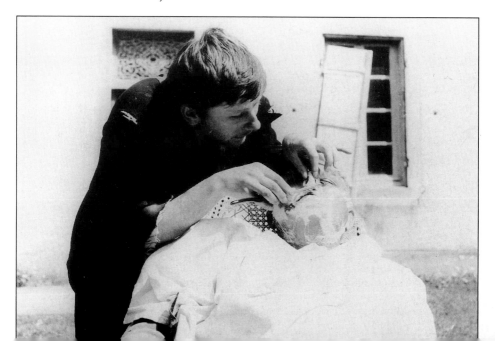

Brought to England after an American Oscar nomination for his first feature film, *Knife in the Water*, Polanski enjoyed the media attention in London in the early summer of 1964 – the young émigré from a communist regime in that most decadent of swinging sixties cities. (*Pictorial Press*)

Polanski at work – on location, finally, for his first major film in the West, *Repulsion*, with his star, Catherine Deneuve. (*Yardley Collection*)

Lionel Stander *(left)*, Catherine Deneuve's sister Françoise Dorléac and Donald Pleasence starred in Polanski's next film, *Cul-de-Sac*, another distinctive and original screenplay from his partnership with Gerard Brach. (*Yardley Collection*)

A spoof on horror movies, *Dance of the Vampires* attracted the interest of Hollywood; and the producers had a young and virtually unknown actress whom they wanted to promote – Sharon Tate. During the making of the film, she and Polanski became lovers. Here they are pictured in a London restaurant after filming. As well as co-writing and directing the picture, Polanski also took a starring role. (*Pictorial Press/Yardley Collection*)

Polanski married Sharon Tate in London in January 1968, and their 'wedding brunch', arranged by London's Playboy chief Victor Lownes, was attended by many stars from Britain and the US. (*Courtesy Sunday Mirror*)

Mia Farrow, looking heavily pregnant with the Devil's child for her role in *Rosemary's Baby*, directed by Polanski in 1968. (*Yardley Collection*)

The cameo role of the Devil in *Rosemary's Baby* was played by a man who claimed to be the Devil's representative on earth, Anton LaVey, otherwise known as the Black Pope and head of the Church of Satan. One of LaVey's own former disciples would eventually be accused of the murder of Sharon Tate. This real-life at LaVey's black altar was taken during the initiation of his daughter into his satanic order. (*Yardley Collection*)

was suffering from the effects of the icy water. Polanski ignored him and ordered the scene to be done again. Françoise took off her towelling robe once more and walked to the water's edge, where she collapsed into a dead faint. By now, Klinger was to be joined in his concern by the British technicians who protested at the way Polanski was treating the actress, and threatened to walk off if he continued in this way. Donald Pleasence was appointed spokesman and relayed the disquiet of all concerned. 'It had to be done,' said Pleasence. 'The director was driving her, and others, too hard. Polanski was the only prima donna on that film, and we had put up with it long enough. I told him and the producers that he should show a little more respect for the workers, and certainly more dignity for Françoise who was receiving bad treatment all round. It was all too much.'

Polanski went off in a sulk, but was forced to moderate his demands on the actress, although there were times when it seemed he had no compassion for her at all. 'Françoise', he said when excusing his behaviour later, 'recovered remarkably quickly, and anyway she bore me no hard feelings.'

Klinger had travelled to Holy Island intermittently to examine the rushes and check progress. Gutowski wisely stayed out of the way for much of the time, and Polanski's allies were now reduced to one, his partner Gerard Brach, who himself was suffering from island fever and could not wait to get away. Klinger's check on the situation brought a further slanging match between himself and the director over the time the film was taking to complete, at which point Polanski said, 'Well, fuck you!', clambered into his Mini-Cooper and drove off at high speed.

Klinger threatened to complete the film without him. When Polanski returned, tail between his legs, Klinger ordered the film to be wrapped up immediately; any retakes would have to be done back in the studios in London. As far as he was concerned, it was over – as, indeed, was his business association with Polanski.

In Klinger's view, Gutowski could not control his young director whose artistic ambitions and egotistical style made it virtually impossible for a small company such as Compton to work with him. Polanski and Brach were to have written a third screenplay for them, but that prospect became more distant in the aftermath of *Cul-de-Sac*, when the relationship between the two parties deteriorated into bitter rows. Accusations from Klinger of overspending were met with hints of massaged profit figures from the other side.

*   *   *

Polanski went home to rest, saying he was exhausted, shattered and disillusioned. For more than two weeks he remained holed-up in his apartment, refusing to come out or take telephone calls. When he did eventually emerge, he went on a twenty-four-hour drink and LSD binge with a showgirl he picked up at a party after a West End show. They took so much of the drug that they scared themselves half to death with the hallucinations, and the girl passed out. Polanski became so worried that he managed to get her into his Mini and drove to Gutowski's house, where Judy put them to bed and cared for them until the effects of the drugs had passed. The dancer left later that morning; he never saw her again.

Polanski's return to London also marked his revival of interest in the social scene at large, and he became a familiar, if somewhat enigmatically observed, figure among the beautiful people who populated a great explosion of trendy night-spots. His list of friends and companions reads, in hindsight, like a *Who's Who* of London's swinging society. The two key centres of his social life were the Ad Lib Club and the Playboy Club in Park Lane which had a kind of compelling attraction for all manner of stars of stage, screen and politics. Victor Lownes's stewardship of Playboy International in London had created a massive profit-machine for the parent body, and along the way he had acquired the friendship and patronage of a vast celebrity cast list, knowing that the club offered facilities of seclusion and privacy, away from the crowds.

Polanski, on the expectation of profits from the foreign rights from *Repulsion* and *Cul-de-Sac*, had also bought himself a house off Eaton Square, one of the most desirable of London's residential districts. He and Lownes had become the closest of friends, the little and large of the Playboy Club social set, with Lownes a good head and shoulders above Polanski. They dined together often, and became fierce competitors in the pursuit of women, of whom there was an ample population around the Playboy honeypot.

Sex and fun, fun and sex were interrupted only by the demands of work. Otherwise, the two of them were the epitome of London swingers. Polanski's personal attitudes in this period were to be found documented in the files of the Los Angeles Police Department, in a transcription of a lie-detector test he was to take in August 1969. 'All I was interested in', he told the interviewing police lieutenant, 'was to fuck a girl and move on. I had a bad marriage, you know, years before, so I was feeling great because I was a success with women again and I just liked fucking around. I was a swinger, uh?'

Here we are reminded perhaps of Henryk Kluba's assessment that Polanski's relations with women was the one key area where he might have complexes. 'It made you think something was not right,' said Kluba, 'I remember thinking that I was not sure this man was able to fall in love. He was so narcissistic that he loved primarily himself. With women, it seemed to be only the physical side which attracted him – the sex.'

But women now abounded in Polanski's life, and because he was part of a social scene and a competitive pairing, there were never difficulties in that area. He and Lownes were virtually fighting them off. Another whose sexual prowess more than his films had hit the headlines in the early sixties was Warren Beatty, currently living with Leslie Caron across the Brompton Road from Polanski's place. Coincidentally, they were making a film together at Shepperton Studios where Polanski had completed *Cul-de-Sac*.

The Beatty movie title, *Promise Her Anything*, was cynically used by the gossip writers in their jibes over Caron's split from her husband, Peter Hall, the strongly establishment figure who was director of the Royal Shakespeare Company. Their separation was about to hit the divorce courts as they battled over custody of their two children. The judge hammered Beatty for stealing Hall's wife and ordered him to pay substantial costs. 'Seduction was his most positive attribute,' Leslie told the present author.

Polanski was an amusing companion for Beatty and Caron, although he had his own worries about the future and the direction he should take in his career. He and Beatty began long and meaningful discussions about movies which would run on for years, and result in both of them respectively producing two of the most controversial films of the sixties: *Rosemary's Baby* and *Bonnie and Clyde*. That lay in the future, but the start of it, the exploration of boundary-breaking movies with alleged artistic use of sex and violence, began there in London and was to have a profound affect on the way they both developed.

Over dinner one night with Beatty and Caron, Polanski talked at length about the French directors, François Truffaut, Jean-Luc Godard and others. Polanski was not a fan of the French New Wave, but he liked to consider himself in the league of creative thought. He told Beatty he had heard Truffaut was casting for a new film, *Fahrenheit 451*, which he believed would be an ideal 'vehicle' for Beatty and Caron who were looking for something more substantial to do together.

Leslie Caron knew Truffaut, and Beatty thought it would be a good idea if they flew to Paris to see him. This they did, and Caron arranged a lunch at which Beatty came in when coffee was being served because he did not speak French. 'It turned out that Truffaut had already cast Oskar Werner and Julie Christie for his film,' said Caron, 'but he had another script that he thought might interest Warren and I . . . it was a screenplay entitled *Bonnie and Clyde*. Warren read it and went like an arrow to New York to buy the rights.'

So Beatty was on the move, heading towards the production and starring role in a movie that saved him from oblivion and turned him into a multi-millionaire. Beatty and Polanski, at the time, were a couple of like-minded revolutionaries. Leslie Caron said Beatty had turned down dozens of major roles, because he was always looking for the intellectual material which seemed constantly either to fail or elude him. *Bonnie and Clyde* took him off at a completely new tangent – as a film-maker rather than just as actor. Polanski similarly looked to film his own writings (mostly in collaboration with Gerard Brach) rather than other people's scripts, and this he would manage to do throughout his career, diverting only twice when he needed money.

Polanski's fame was spreading. Post-production work on *Cul-de-Sac* was interspersed with promotion work for *Repulsion* which had been bought for the European circuit and North America. Polanski was in demand for a whirlwind tour of film festivals. 'The success of *Repulsion*', said Zophia Komeda, 'meant he could work in London without threat from the unions. He had wanted my husband Krzys to write the score for *Repulsion*, but the British craft unions refused to allow it. But now, after the good reviews for *Repulsion*, his position was strengthened and he could argue with them. He wanted Krzys to write the music for *Cul-de-Sac*, but even then he had to make a formal request, with written reasons several pages long, stating why he wanted to employ a Pole and not an English composer. This time they agreed, but he did not like the British unions very much afterwards.'

Cul-de-Sac was ready for its first screening in the spring of 1966. As with *Knife in the Water*, Polanski had again used the form of the chamber drama, investigating the extreme psychological states of the three principal characters against a starkly desolate location – hence the importance of the site for filming. In spite of Polanski's autocratic stance, which had caused so much strife, he produced from his actors some remarkably effective work. It did not rank among his best films, but it bolstered his reputation for the eccentric and the macabre. The movie was destined for the Berlin Festival where Polanski once again took a major honour, this time the Golden Bear. Michael Klinger arranged a series of private screenings at Cannes where Polanski arrived amidst a great deal of curiosity about his latest work. He also discovered that his old friend and collaborator on *Knife in the Water*, Jerzy Skolimowski, now a director in his own right, was displaying his latest film, which was attracting little interest.

Observing this, Polanski gatecrashed a media party, jumped on to a table and said he would like to introduce this picture as he was an old friend of Skolimowski. He added, to the amazement of those gathered, that they might have heard rumours that Skolimowski was homosexual. They should not believe them, because he certainly was not. Having stirred up some phoney interest in his old friend, Polanski then left.

Elsewhere, *Cul-de-Sac* received mixed reviews and many felt that the 'brilliant' young director had pursued his fascination with sex, violence and the almost obsessional study of humiliation as a central theme, to the extent that his film had become more perplexing than entertaining. But there was one important spin-off.

The American distribution rights for *Cul-de-Sac* were bought by one of the new, aspiring independent American companies, Filmways, which brought Polanski into contact with the producers of his next film, the script for which Gerard Brach had been busily researching for the past few weeks. In spite of European acclaim for Polanski's work, there had been no great interest in him from Hollywood until Filmways bought *Cul-de-Sac* and expressed interest in Polanski's next venture. Filmways was in a bigger league altogether to Compton, with its hand-to-mouth ways. In conjunction with MGM, its most recent production, *The Sandpiper*, cost them a $1.75-million fee and a percentage of profits for the joint services of Elizabeth Taylor and Richard Burton. Polanski's association with such film-makers, according to Gene Gutowski, was seen as an encouraging step up.

John Calley, producer of *The Sandpiper*, and his partner in Filmways, Marty Ransohoff, who had brought the long-running series *The Beverly Hillbillies* to television, came to London in 1966 for their latest movie, a star-studded horror film called *Eye of the Devil*, with David Niven, Deborah Kerr, Donald Pleasence, David Hemmings and an up-and-coming young starlet named Sharon Tate. Ransohoff had signed her on an exclusive seven-year contract when she was nineteen and said he was deliberately keeping her 'under wraps' until she had gained experience as an actress.

When he put her into *The Beverly Hillbillies*, she wore a black wig so that she would not be noticed. Now, she had progressed into a stunning beauty and her producers reckoned she would be the next Kim Novak with a hint of Harlow. Ransohoff had even picked out her clothes in a Beverly Hills shopping spree, selecting dresses which were tight and designed to exaggerate her breasts. But Sharon was no dumb blonde.

The daughter of a middle-class military family, she had lived in various parts of the world before her father was posted to Los Angeles where Sharon fell in love with the dream of Hollywood and, against her father's wishes, began touring the film studios in the hope of securing work. Eventually she secured an agent, managed to get some bit parts and was finally spotted by Ransohoff.

Sharon's appearance in *Eye of the Devil* was planned to be her last before being launched by Filmways in her first starring role; this was a smaller part playing a girl who is a practising witch in a dark and gloomy tale of black magic and diabolical happenings in a spooky castle. By coincidence, Polanski was working on something similar himself at the time, though in jokey vein.

The idea for a spoof horror film developed during the filming of *Cul-de-Sac* on Holy Island. Gerard Brach thought the castle there would be an ideal setting. They wrote their story with one actor in mind as the leading man, Jack MacGowran, who had only a small part in *Cul-de-Sac* but had impressed Polanski by his loyalty and friendship. This was another constant in his work – to take someone from real life and turn him into an exaggerated character, sometimes like a grotesque cartoon. 'It went back to our days at Lodz,' said Henryk Kluba. 'He always saw people as potential actors or characters for his films. As an actor, I was being called upon by my colleagues all the time – they could not afford to hire professional people for their films. When Polanski started writing scripts for his first short films, his characters were always identified to such a degree that he even used my name, "Kluba".'

Brach had been writing the screenplay virtually since they finished filming on Holy Island. Jack MacGowran had seen a copy and said he would very much like to play the lead part of the professor on the trail of vampires – a spoof of Dracula, written on the basis that audiences at horror movies often laugh in the wrong places. Brach's notion was that the audience should laugh with the movie, and not at it.

Polanski wanted to engage Jill St John whom he had met the previous year in London and again when he went to Los Angeles. They had become good friends and he considered her to be his ideal for the role of Sarah, a girl who was to become a target of the vampires. He planned to cast himself to play opposite her as Alfie, a buffoon of a student who was to protect her.

The screenplay was laid before Filmways and budgeted at a cost far exceeding anything Polanski had ever tackled: Gene Gutowski had assessed it would cost in excess of $1.5 million. Ransohoff and Calley pondered, studied the figures and took the whole package to MGM who would have to put up most of the funds. Finally word came back that they had agreed, and the movie would be made under the joint presentation credit of a MGM/Filmways/Cadre production, with Gene Gutowski named as producer.

There was one proviso to all of this, however. Throughout the negotiations, Ransohoff had been pressing the name of Sharon Tate upon Polanski, and they finally met at a party at the Dorchester where Ransohoff and Calley were staying for the launch of the *Eye of the Devil*. They did not hit it off, but nevertheless soon afterwards, and in accord with Ransohoff's wishes, Sharon was cast for the vampire movie. Those who believed in fate would mark this meeting down as a tragic turn of events.

Chapter Ten

Sharon Tate very quickly became the object of Roman Polanski's desires, professionally and personally, though there was a distinct coolness on her part at the beginning. As her director, he would naturally be close to her, closer than anyone, and within a matter of days, his natural dominance in that role, which had been experienced by all who worked for and with him, began to have its effect.

As it happened, Sharon needed a strong personality in her life. For one who had spent her adolescence in the tricky circus of Los Angeles, she was remarkably naïve. She tended to take people at face value and was consequently an easy target for anyone who wished to take advantage. Before her affair with Jay Sebring began, she was living with a French actor who raped her and injured her so badly that she needed hospital attention. Sebring was kinder, but had a kinky side for which he was well known; he introduced Sharon to his drug parties, occasional group sex and bondage. She was not an unwilling participant, but there were times when she wished she was out of it.

Sebring was a curious character, and one who would figure strongly in the life of Polanski in coming months. He was born Thomas John Kommer in Detroit, Michigan, and had been a street waif in his early youth, literally living on the streets before he went to Los Angeles. There, he worked at menial tasks while training to become a hairdresser, and in the mid-sixties had become one of Hollywood's most sought-after crimpers. He was close friends with many of his star clients, who included Steve McQueen, Peter Lawford, Paul Newman and George Peppard. Peppard once had him flown out to a filming location to cut his hair, at a cost of $25,000.

Sharon was still in her teens when she met Sebring at a Hollywood party and joined him and Steve McQueen on holiday. She and Sebring subsequently decided to live together and rented a house next-door to

Judy Garland. They became well-known party people on the hallucino-genic scene of Los Angeles in the mad sixties. It was exciting and fun, and there was an element of danger in the now commonplace experiments with mind-expanding drugs, top-quality Mexican grass and cocaine that had become the norm amongst the wild set.

Polanski's own description of the beginning of his relationship with Sharon was best summarized in the transcription of the lie-detector test he took soon after the murder of Sharon and her friends in August 1969. The reasons for the test will be examined in a later chapter, but the recollections set out his early involvement with her and provide an intriguing insight to his own feelings at the time.

'I first met Sharon at some kind of party Marty Ransohoff, a terrible Hollywood producer, had given – the guy who makes *Beverly Hillbillies* and all kinds of shit. But he seduced me with his talk about art and I contracted with him to do this film.

'I met Sharon at the party. She was doing another film for him in London, staying alone. Ransohoff said, "Wait until you see our leading lady Sharon Tate." I thought she was quite pretty but I wasn't at that time very impressed. But then I saw her again. I took her out. We talked a lot, you know. At that time, I was really swinging. All I was interested in was to fuck a girl and move on . . .

'I met Sharon a couple more times. I knew she was with Jay. They wanted me to use her in the film and I made tests with her. Once before, I wanted to take her out, she was being difficult, wanting to go, not wanting to go, so I said "Fuck you" and I hung up. Probably that was the beginning of everything.

'She got me intrigued and I really played it cool. It took me a long dating before I started seeing that she liked me. I remember I spent a night . . . I lost my key . . . I spent a night in her house, in the same bed, you know. And I knew there was no question of making love with her. That's the type of girl she was. I mean, that rarely happens to me. And then we went on location, shooting the film, I asked her, "Would you like to make love to me?" and she said sweetly, "Yes." And for the first time, I touched her, you know. And we started sleeping together. And she was so sweet, so lovely that I didn't believe it. I'd had bad experiences and I didn't believe people like that existed. She was beautiful without the phoniness. She was fantastic. She loved me. I was living at a house, and she would say, "I don't want to smother you. I only want to be with you." I said, "You know how I am. I screw around . . ." and she said, "I don't want to change you." She was ready to do everything, just to be with me. She was a fucking angel. She was a unique character.'

Polanski told how he had first met Jay Sebring, when he came to London to visit Sharon. As past and present lover together, they circled each other, but Polanski later got to know him well. 'I started liking Jay very much,' he said into the police microphone. 'Oh, I know he had his hang-ups. He liked to whip-tie girls. Sharon told me he tied her to the bed once. And she told me about it and was making fun of him . . . very funny, but sad. I knew he was into drugs . . . sniffing cocaine. I thought it was an occasional kick, but Sharon said, "Are you kidding? He's been doing it for two years." Sharon took LSD before we met . . . many times. And when we met, we discussed it. I took it when it was legal. Sharon had been tripping fifteen or sixteen times. It had begun well enough, but then come morning, she started flipping out and screaming, half-scared to death . . .'

On their very first date, they took an LSD trip, with Sharon as the more experienced guide, which lasted until dawn. Polanski brought some foundation into her life which had been missing, especially when they began to work together in a routine which was no less strict than on previous productions.

From the early stages, when they were doing readings and rehearsals in London prior to location filming, Sharon responded to Polanski's regimental discipline with a willingness that eventually moved towards subservience. There were no tantrums and not many fights; at last she had found someone who was telling her what to do for specific reasons from which she felt she could only benefit – as opposed to being given instructions which would ultimately lead to some kind of sexual event, which might be degrading.

Polanski was manipulating her on two levels, as a director wishing to extract from his leading lady the best possible performance, and as a man who wanted to get her into bed as soon as possible. While the former may have been his overriding aim, the latter became a more absolute objective.

Sharon was also, like Polanski, exceedingly youthful in her looks, best noted when Jerzy Kosinski first met her; he thought she was a teenager. This was also important to the film, and because of it, Polanski even heightened the 'little girl' undercurrents that ran through her role, when he introduced a spanking scene. Her father, played by the British comedy actor Alfie Bass, has to spank her for being naughty.

Polanski's brief was to produce a picture which would be commercially viable, and the prospect of bringing any kind of art to the movie very quickly diminished. Though supposedly a tongue-in-cheek horror film, *The Fearless Vampire Killers* contained numerous written-in elements for which Polanski had become noted: the voyeurism, when he himself playing Alfred spies on Sharon through a keyhole in her bathroom door; the nudity of the leading lady; the exploration of psychological traits in his characters, like homosexuality, sado-masochism and other dark, primeval possibilities, such as vampirism itself, for which he and Gerard Brach had researched the occult folklore. To that he added an overstatement in terms of the horror content which mimicked the more commonplace of the genre, notably from the Hammer stable, by using twenty-three gallons of fake blood in a story set in a traditional spooky castle set in snow-covered countryside, in which weirdos abounded.

With the benefit of a $1.75-million budget, Polanski decided they must find a suitable location, hopefully in countryside similar to that in the classic vampire tale, Bram Stoker's *Dracula*. Gene Gutowski went on a scouting mission and discovered the ideal setting in Austria, but by the time they were ready to move out, the snow had melted. It was the first of Polanski's running battles with Filmways and MGM over costs, and the rows and memos flourished between producers and director as the picture took shape. MGM viewed Polanski's demand for exotic locations, transporting his cast and crew across Europe – and in expensive Panavision – with disdain.

Familiar words and phrases like 'upstart' and 'who does he think he is?' began to pepper the discussions. So they finally settled on a location in the Italian Alps where carpenters in the villages all around thought their ship had come in when the production managers began ordering up the coffins and props. No suitable castle was ever found in the Italian mountains, however, and Polanski ordered a mock set to be purpose-built in MGM's London studios. The producers eyed the cost apprehensively and at one point Filmways was talking of having Polanski fired.

Weeks of expensive filming with all the technical problems inherent in the script were suddenly brought to a halt by the melting snow, and the whole unit moved back to London to complete filming on fake studio snow and man-made sets. Throughout, Polanski's attention to the scenes involving Sharon had, according to observers close at hand, become obsessive, and as their offscreen relationship grew more intense, so did Polanski's attentiveness while at work. Take after take of Sharon's scenes drove her fellow actors and the technicians alike to the point of heavy-eyed boredom.

Filming was resumed on the sets of the London studios. Delays and difficulties with the sets, the daily time-consuming need to make up sixty vampires, which took virtually a whole morning, together with Polanski's own insistence on 'getting it right', meant he was falling well behind schedule. Pre-booked space in the MGM studios also meant he had to move to Pinewood, and then on to Elstree for additional filming before Filmways gave him an ultimatum: the movie had to be completed within five days, come what may. By then the budget was heavily overspent, and would finally cost MGM more than $2 million.

Filmways' memos to Gene Gutowski had become more vicious, and MGM, aware of some of the film's built-in bawdiness, had already expressed concern that Sharon Tate was 'unduly exposed' and there was too much unnecessary nudity. They were also concerned about some of the language and 'excessive gruesomeness' in some of the blood-letting scenes. Although the Hollywood code of conduct and the U, A and X rating system which had never allowed Rock Hudson and Doris Day to sleep in a double bed or go into love scenes without one foot on the floor, was on the verge of being scrapped, the mainstream studios still adhered to it with remarkable rigidity, ever afraid that their audience would be restricted by an X rating.

Sharon Tate moved into Polanski's house for a while, and their affair grew ever stronger. It was interrupted first by Jay Sebring's arrival from Los Angeles and then by Filmways, who sent Sharon back to Hollywood almost as soon as she had completed her work on *The Fearless Vampire Killers*, to appear in a new MGM/Filmways production, a lightweight comedy entitled *Don't Make Waves*, with Tony Curtis.

Before she left, Polanski arranged a still-photo session with her, in which he himself took nude photographs of Sharon – just as David Bailey had done with Catherine Deneuve for *Repulsion* – and in May 1967 his contact with Victor Lownes was utilized once more when *Playboy* ran a spread of the pictures, along with stills from the new movie. It was the kind of publicity for which some studio PR men would gladly sacrifice a piece of their anatomy, but in this case MGM eyed the spread with increasing concern.

It was a rather squalid-looking array of photographs, published over three pages under the headline of 'The Tate Gallery', and with captions which portrayed Sharon 'as a very tasty dish indeed'. She was naked except for a scant covering of her pubic areas, thus offering the millions of *Playboy* readers the obligatory titillation with the added dimension that the pictures were taken by her lover, though that was left unsaid.

The publicity value for the movie was immense, and Polanski's preparedness to exploit a woman who had assumed such an importance in his life seemed not to enter the equation. Certainly the way the spread was gleefully pawed over by his associates at the Playboy Club and elsewhere merely improved his image among this macho-dominated group without thought for the other more dubious implications in this pre-feminist era. Did he have no shame? That was certainly the thought of his ex-wife, Basia.

With Sharon heading for Los Angeles, Polanski locked himself away in the MGM editing suite and began to prepare his rough-cut version of the movie. Ransohoff was pressing for a print, for reasons which would only become apparent when Polanski eventually delivered it. It had been an unhappy experience, this first step into the so-called big league, with pressures raining down on him from all sides, but even greater disappointment lay ahead.

In the final stages of post-production, Polanski turned to his former Polish comrades once again, and invited Krzys Komeda to fly to London to write the musical score for *Vampires*. Zofia Komeda remembered: 'There was quite a gathering of us. We rented a flat in the Edgware Road and Skolim [Jerzy Skolimowski, Polanski's co-writer of *Knife in the Water*] came over and stayed with us. Then Fryko [Wojtek Frykowski] rang me from Lodz. We were never friends, even though his second wife, a well-known Polish song-writer, tried to convince me of his qualities. He told me he was about to fly to London and asked for Romek's address. So I told him we would meet him there, too. We were seeing Romek almost daily . . . he invited us and Skolim to dinner. He used to cook it himself. During the conversation, I asked him if Fryko was coming and he said, "I did not invite him. What do I need him for? Iain [the actor Iain Quarrier who appeared in *Vampires*] gets me chicks if I want them."'

Zofia said Polanski was decorating his mews house at the time and asked for her help. 'But it turned out our tastes were not the same. I wanted to make it macho: leather and fur covers, mirrors everywhere. So he did it himself, with crystal handles, and the bath was black, sunk into the floor – it was the first time I had seen anything like it in my life. But in those days, Romek was tender and warm. Some people were afraid of him, of his aggressiveness, but we knew he had other virtues. He changed when he went to America.'

In the summer of 1967 Polanski flew to Los Angeles, convinced that he had made a very funny film, and waited with bated anticipation as Ransohoff and his associates sat through their private screening. At the end, Ransohoff stood up and said he had to admit that he was disappointed with the end-result; in fact, he did not like it at all.

He said it was too long, too arty, too complicated, and he would have to cut it. The title would have to be changed to give some indication of its content, and he eventually suggested *Pardon Me, Your Teeth Are in My Neck*. By now Polanski was making hissing noises and cursing Ransohoff in Polish. But the producer hadn't finished: there was a problem with some of the actors' voices which would be unintelligible to an American audience, not least Polanski's own, and especially that of Terry Downes, the Cockney ex-boxer whom Polanski had hired as the hunchback. He therefore thought it might be necessary to re-dub the entire film with the voices of American actors.

Polanski boiled over. He said he was not going to let them massacre his film. If there was any trimming to be done, he would do it himself, and no one was going to screw around with his work. Ransohoff reminded him that his contract gave him the right to the final edit, which meant that once he had delivered the print, they could pretty much do as they pleased with it. And anyway, said Ransohoff, there were some scenes that would send MGM into apoplexy. Polanski would be given the chance to make his own adjustments, but Ransohoff made it clear that he would personally handle the final edit. Polanski screamed his protests and said he wanted his name taken off the credits. Ransohoff said he had no grounds for such a request and repeated the terms of the contract. Polanski was mortified.

When *The Fearless Vampire Killers* was finally released months later, it was treated with critical disdain and often derision. The consensus branded it a worthless picture that belied the director's early promise. Polanski was badly stung by the reaction and instead of going off to hide, he instinctively fought back. He gave press interviews critical of Ransohoff, who he claimed had butchered his movie beyond recognition by cutting twenty minutes out of his final version. 'It was a very funny and inventive film,' he told all who would listen. 'But Ransohoff turned it into a Transylvanian *Beverly Hillbillies* – he even changed the music. I will never work for the man again.'

This was so. His contract with Filmways for two more pictures was cancelled, and when Sharon Tate completed *Don't Make Waves*, she too was released from the remaining eighteen months of her contract with Ransohoff and returned to join Polanski in London.

The Fearless Vampire Killers was a box office flop and quickly disappeared from the circuit. It re-emerged in its original form years later and became something of a cult movie, but Polanski's first major film had bombed. That might have been it . . . except for a remarkable stroke of good fortune.

Long before the débâcle with Ransohoff moved into the public arena, Polanski was invited to Los Angeles for talks with Paramount Studios, which turned out to be another of those life-changing coincidences that have occurred at various points in his career.

The new vice-president in charge of production at Paramount studios, Robert Evans, was to figure in Polanski's life and career for the coming decade. In 1967, he was himself on the brink of launching some of Hollywood's major new writers, directors and actors in a string of successful films like *Love Story*, *The Godfather* and, importantly for Polanski, *Rosemary's Baby* and *Chinatown*.

Evans was an ambitious and glamorous self-made opportunist, whom Jack Nicholson would eventually call 'The Mogul' because of his string of successes and his opulent life-style. He started life as an actor, discovered by Norma Shearer who thought he was the living image of her former husband Irving Thalberg, and on the strength of that, Evans played him in *The Man of A Thousand Faces*. He followed up with a part in *The Sun Also Rises*, but after these early successes, faded into obscurity and returned penniless to the family clothing business in New York.

In 1964, the business was sold for $2 million and with his share, Evans set himself up as an independent film producer. One day, out of the blue, he received a call from Charlie Bludhorn, head of the Gulf Western conglomerate, which had inherited the virtually bankrupt Paramount Studios in a takeover deal.

Bludhorn, having read a newspaper profile of Evans, gave him complete charge of the creative side of the studio, and in the autumn of 1967, Evans took over his mogul's office, with a pile of scripts, money to spend and ideas to explore. Just as Bludhorn had read about Evans, so Evans read about Polanski. He had also heard on the grapevine that the man had the aura of genius about him, if only he was given a chance.

Sitting on the top of Evans's ideas pile were the proofs of a book called *Rosemary's Baby*, a horror story if ever there was one, about a young wife who is impregnated by the Devil. Alfred Hitchcock had been offered the film rights but turned them down; it was too stiff, even for him.

Paramount contract producer Bill Castle, redoubtable producer of horror movies, mostly cheap B-films, had paid $150,000 out of his own funds for the screen rights and was pressing Evans to put up the cash and allow him to produce and direct the movie.

Evans told Castle he could produce it, but he had an idea who might direct. He buzzed through to his bank of secretaries in the outer office and said, 'Get me Roman Polanski.'

'Who's Roman Polanski?'

That night, Polanski was on his way to Los Angeles for talks – something about a script for *Downhill Racer*, a movie about an American skier, which was appealing because Polanski was also a ski fanatic. The script for *Downhill Racer* was just a ploy to get him there. Evans reckoned he might not attract Polanski with the offer of yet another horror movie, unaware that at that moment in time anything might have attracted Roman Polanski.

Polanski's return to Los Angeles jolted him out of his gloomy despondency that the troubles with *The Fearless Vampire Killers* would re-emerge and kill off any possibility of work for a major Hollywood studio. Gutowski told him to come out fighting and get his name on a contract before they lost interest.

His interview with Evans began as a one-sided monologue, with Polanski somewhat riskily recounting his recent woes at the hands of Ransohoff and MGM. Evans impatiently steered the subject to the reason why Polanski had been sent for. They had proofs of Ira Levin's novel, *Rosemary's Baby*, that they would like him to read. If he liked it, they would ask him to write the screenplay and direct. Money? They would talk about that next time. First, Evans wanted his reaction to the book.

Polanski spent the next forty-eight hours reading and re-reading Levin's occult thriller from cover to cover, enthralled by what would become one of the best-selling books of the decade. Captivated by the style, he immediately began to visualize his film.

Charlie Bludhorn, who liked to dabble in the preliminaries, was curiously taken by Evans' promotion of *Rosemary's Baby* as one of Paramount's titles for the coming season, and questioned the fact that they were placing a budget of $2 million in the hands of a director whose

English was still imperfect and who had yet to show a successful bottom line. Bludhorn called in Bill Castle and offered him $250,000 for the rights to the book and for him to act as the film's producer plus a percentage of the gross profits.

Castle also wanted director approval, and a meeting between himself and Polanski was arranged. It was actually an unlikely pairing. Castle was one of the old cigar-chomping showmen of Hollywood, universally known as the promoter of some of the best – and worst – horror movies of the previous two decades. He was the father of various grotesque gimmicks such as his 'Illusion-O' – a spoof of the Todd-AO cinematograph system – for his 1960s' film *Thirteen Ghosts*. He supplied his audiences with a choice of special ghost-viewer spectacles – one set with blue lenses for the sceptics to expunge the resultant 'double images' which would be apparent to those who did not believe in ghosts, and the other set with red lenses for those who did believe. He and his wife used to travel the country promoting his films, and he was known to arrive at the local cinema carrying a clutch of pre-printed disclaimer forms absolving him from responsibility if any member of the audience suffered a heart attack while watching.

Castle's meeting with Polanski did not get off to a good start. Polanski, fresh from the hip, *Blow Up* world of swinging London, kept looking at himself in the large mirror on Bill Castle's wall. He spoke fast, barely taking breath, in a language quite foreign to the veteran producer. Polanski was speaking English all right, but with words that seemed out of context, and Castle was put off by his clipped style and wandering mind, in which ends of words were missing or key words in sentences were missed out as he rattled out his observations.

Even so, Castle was won over. Polanski was offered $150,000 for writing and directing, nowhere near Castle's fee, but a fortune in his terms. For the first time in his life, he had to acquire an agent and have the paperwork vetted by lawyers, as was the rule for all Paramount contractees.

Evans' deal, however, was exclusively for Polanski. Gene Gutowski, his partner in Cadre Films and the man who got him started in London, was excluded because Bill Castle was producing. Polanski explained the relationship, and Bob Evans told him it was possible that if all went well, Cadre Films would be cut into another two films, one of them *Downhill Racer*, which he hoped Polanski would make for Paramount.

Polanski flew back to London, leaving Sharon in Los Angeles to search for a house for them to rent when he returned. He wanted peace and seclusion for the task of writing his screenplay in the little study in the top floor of his mews home, reached by its spiral staircase. There, alone and uninterrupted, he produced a 260-page draft screenplay in a little over three weeks, and after one night of partying at Victor Lownes's place, where he got stoned and took a blonde model to bed for three hours, he drove to Heathrow and climbed into his first-class seat on the flight back to Los Angeles to present his next masterpiece.

Chapter Eleven

Roman Polanski's whole pattern of life changed the moment he set foot back in Los Angeles from London. It was as much as anything to do with the social scene on the west coast of America where hippies were converging on California, and the counter-culture movement which followed on from Swinging London was emerging under the ever-watchful eyes of the FBI and the CIA. It was a curious accident of location that just as Polanski had stepped into the burgeoning London scene three years earlier, so he had arrived in California at that particular moment in the evolution of its freedom-seeking society of wayoutness, when Dr Timothy Leary had just made his famous speech to the youth of the world, urging them to 'tune-in, turn-on, drop out' – his clarion call to an incredible Human Be-In at the Golden Gate Park in San Francisco in that year of 1967. The poet Allen Ginsberg blew on a conch-shell to command the attention of his audience and recommended that every young person over the age of fourteen should try LSD at least once.

Psychedelia had arrived: flower power, painted VWs, Indian gurus and a huge cloud of sweet-smelling smoke, hash cakes, LSD trippers and magic mushroom eaters; make love not war. On the music front, the Flowerpot Men pin-pointed the place of the action in 'Let's Go to San Francisco'; the Beatles' controversial album, *Sergeant Pepper's Lonely Hearts Club Band*, was riddled with references to LSD, while the Rolling Stones produced their own psychedelic essay with 'Their Satanic Majesties Request'. The media and the politicians had joined the bandwagon and lumped Hell's Angels, dope-takers, black militants and hippies together in a crescendo of critical reaction against this upsurge of protest, drugs and free love of which the Beatles' 'Yellow Submarine' became the official anthem. So the Beatles, too, and John Lennon in particular, were put under surveillance by J. Edgar Hoover. The underlying tensions of the youth of the Western world were bursting out in the cause of peace, especially in America where youngsters faced the draft and military service in Vietnam.

That Polanski, along with Jack Nicholson, Dennis Hopper, Peter Fonda and a whole host of pop stars and others of the rebel breed would become the darlings of the west coast cultural revolution lay a year or more in the future. But Roman's growing circle and contact with the beautiful people took in a wide and diverse array of friends; anyone who was anybody in this wild and wonderful scene came into his orbit.

The temptations of Hollywood extravagance were all around him in his work and social life. His very presence in this hothouse of egos and wealth, real and phoney – with much more of the latter – also signified a change in his own attitudes and the final ejection of the caution which had followed him from the rigid strictures of life in Poland and was still hanging by a slender thread as he moved tentatively into the fast lane. 'The thing about Romek,' said Basia Kwiatkowska, 'was that he had a fire burning inside him that always attracted people. He had brilliant ideas and he was always the centre of attention, even if he was sometimes unbearable. His creativity always emanated in a way that he drew people towards him. He had friends, true friends, the ones who are still his friends today [in 1993]. But when he went to America . . . it changed. When I heard later on of Roman's deviant behaviour, I couldn't believe it, and still can't. It was a new and strange thing to me.'

His first venture – somewhat reluctantly in view of the cost – was to rent a house which, in Hollywood terms, symbolized arrival. While he was away in London, Sharon had been scouring the outer residential district of Los Angeles and had selected a small mansion overlooking the Pacific Ocean at Santa Monica, originally built by Cary Grant and currently owned by Brian Aherne, the British-born actor who had gone to Hollywood in the thirties, and stayed.

The house came complete with those grand symbols of Hollywood opulence, a magnificent winding staircase, sumptuous decor and outside in the walled gardens, a swimming pool. It was very over the top in relation to Roman and Sharon's joint status in the Hollywood pecking order, he the director of a film which at that moment was not high on the list of Paramount's great expectations, and she a would-be star who had yet to find a major role.

Sharon began the task of nest-building, albeit in someone else's nest, while Roman set off to Paramount to start work on *Rosemary's Baby*. Sharon was also about to embark on her role in *Valley of the Dolls*, another film of a blockbuster book – Jacqueline Susann's close-to-home epic about the pill-popping, sex-craving womenfolk of Los Angeles.

Robert Evans was eager to see Polanski's script and read it immediately. It was too long, he said, but he felt Roman had performed an excellent writing job and they could begin casting immediately. Evans had some suggestions for the possible male lead, to play the husband, Guy, whose wife is tricked into being impregnated by the Devil and bearing his son. The name of Jack Nicholson was mentioned. He was a friend of Evans, and to date had appeared in fourteen movies since 1959, but outside a small clique of independent film-makers on the fringes of Hollywood, was virtually unknown to the cinema public.

Polanski was unsure. He gave Nicholson a screen test and thought he was too sinister for the role, and definitely too unknown. So he crossed Nicholson off the list. He wanted a major young star, and his personal choice was his friend Warren Beatty to whom he sent a copy of the script. But Beatty, as Leslie Caron confirmed, was turning down pretty well everything. He was in the middle of his personal battle to get recognition for *Bonnie and Clyde*, and, though intrigued by the story, he turned it down. 'I'll play Rosemary,' he quipped to Polanski, but the truth was he did not think that the movie or the role was anywhere near big enough for his status.

Next, Polanski went for Robert Redford who had made it big in the past two or three years and was currently co-starring with Jane Fonda in *Barefoot in the Park*. Evans agreed, and Polanski telephoned Redford direct and arranged to meet him – unaware that Paramount was involved in a tussle with the star after he had pulled out of an arty western called *Blue* in which he was to co-star with Karl Malden. Redford rightly predicted that it would flop and Terence Stamp was hired in his place at the last minute. Paramount was after some form of recompense, and when legal executives heard about his meeting with Polanski, they burst in and handed Redford a writ for breach of contract. So Redford was out.

Meanwhile, the strong-willed John Cassavetes, having read about the forthcoming movie in the trade press, had suggested himself to producer William Castle. Cassavetes was regarded in much the same light as Polanski, as a controversial actor–director whose early claim to fame was his own movie *Shadows*, a 16-mm true-life drama made in 1959 which attracted diverse critical mentions ranging from 'rambling incoherence' to 'startling immediacy and shocking power'. Cassavetes teamed with

Polanski, both being known for their stridency, meant that an explosive confrontation seemed inevitable.

The signing of Cassavetes was merely one of a number of rods that Polanski was unwittingly making for his own back. The next was the selection of his leading lady, the all-important star who would produce the Devil's child. Paramount had put forward dozens of possibilities from their stable of young stars, but Polanski finally settled on Mia Farrow, who had risen to teenage fame in the long-running television soap opera, *Peyton Place*, but who had recently become even more famous as the surprise wife of Frank Sinatra. Polanski had screened several episodes of *Peyton Place* and was taken with Farrow's slight and wistful appearance which he felt was ideal for the role of Rosemary.

Unknown to him, his interjection into the Sinatra–Farrow household would bring discord which would ultimately lead to their divorce. They had been married a year before, in July 1966, in a glitzy Las Vegas ceremony. She was twenty and he forty-nine, an age gap which had already cemented their place in the tabloid headlines. They had recently been living in London where Sinatra was completing filming of *The Naked Runner* followed by Mia's appearance in the spy thriller *A Dandy in Aspic* with Sinatra's good friend Laurence Harvey.

Sinatra apparently had visions of his young bride adopting the role of the little wife at home, with occasional excursions into film-land as a double act with himself, *à la* Taylor and Burton. Otherwise, her life would be confined by his obsessional regard for security which meant that wherever she went, his bodyguards were sure to follow. This was especially apparent because at the time a Federal grand jury was attempting to seek his co-operation in getting answers to a number of pressing questions about his alleged friendship with Mafia boss Sam Giancana whose own possible links to the death of John F. Kennedy were just beginning to emerge.

Sinatra had his schedule mapped out for months ahead. He was booked for concerts at the Fontainebleu Hotel on Miami Beach, two weeks at the Sands Hotel in Las Vegas, a nation-wide concert tour, the movie *Tony Rome* – and he already had a film lined up in which he and Mia would co-star, called *The Detective*. And so Polanski's contact with Farrow at that point in time was not at all welcomed by Sinatra. However, she agreed to do a reading for Polanski and he was certain then that he wanted her for Rosemary. They had similar thoughts and motivations and they were both 'slightly nuts', observed Richard Sylbert, Polanski's friend whom he had hired as production designer for

Rosemary's Baby. The script also appealed to Mia who, in spite of a strict Catholic upbringing, had a more than passing sympathy with the spiritual and paranormal.

Sinatra detested the subject and said he wanted Mia to stand by in readiness for her film with him, an altogether more down-to-earth story of a tough New York cop. Richard Sylbert recalls being present at dinner one night when Sinatra and Mia were arguing about the picture, and about her role in his life. By the end of the evening, Sinatra had virtually laid it on the line that if she accepted the role in *Rosemary's Baby*, it would be tantamount to rejecting his opinions, and he did not much care for that. Mia did accept, and yet another ingredient of fermenting relationships was added to Polanski's scenario. That said, however, Sinatra showed no particular animosity to Polanski for the time being, and he and Sharon spent a couple of weekends at Frank's mansion in Palm Springs.

Polanski progressed with his cast list, gathering around him a selection of top-line supporting players, including Sidney Blackmer and the actress–playwright Ruth Gordon as Rosemary's apparently charming next-door neighbours who are to be revealed as agents of the Devil, and the veteran Ralph Bellamy in the important role as Rosemary's doctor.

There was one more addition to the list that had altogether more sinister dimensions, and brought Polanski unwittingly into direct contact with the most virulent form of occult activity of the moment – Satanism. He wanted an 'expert' to advise him in his quest for precise and accurate direction of *Rosemary's Baby* and was introduced to a man whose physical appearance made such an impression that the director decided he should also make a cameo appearance in the film, portraying the Devil, and would be seen briefly as the hazy figure impregnating Rosemary.

His name was Anton LaVey who, as Polanski knew from his local reputation, was in the throes of expanding his now notorious world-wide order of diabolism, the Church of Satan. Today, he is more commonly known as the Black Pope, and is the author of the infamous Satanic Bible which became the handbook of practitioners of Devil cults around the globe. *Rosemary's Baby* would become an unexpected and unwitting promotional opportunity in his quest for infamy and domination of this brand of occult pursuit.

Even so, LaVey's contribution to the movie in terms of the practical advice which he was called upon to administer, would not be of more than passing interest had the contact not had far wider implications than Polanski could have imagined. In view of these later developments, which will be dealt with chronologically, LaVey's background merits a brief diversion, set as he was in the mysterious world of the sinister, which would ensure that *Rosemary's Baby* became the instant focus of occultists and Devil worshippers the world over.

LaVey's Church of Satan was one of a number of organizations emerging in the sixties' revival of interest in the occult, which was especially buoyant in London and on the west coast of America where one such group, a far more secret and sinister cult, would enrol the as yet unknown Charles Manson. Polanski's film played its part in that revival, a view later to be supported by the British authority on the occult, the Brighton witch Doreen Valiente, who is among the most knowledgeable and prolific authors on the subject. She wrote in her book *Witchcraft Past and Present*, published in 1973, that *Rosemary's Baby* was 'one of the major influences which have brought about the craze for delving into darker regions of the occult . . . and was it more than a cruel coincidence that Roman Polanski lost his wife and unborn child in the horrific murders carried out by a group who called themselves Satan's Slaves?'

The presence of Anton LaVey in the production of *Rosemary's Baby* is seldom mentioned in film circles today and was certainly expunged from Polanski's own published comments about the making of this film. What is curious is how Polanski ever became involved with him in the first place. LaVey courted show-business personalities and pop stars and boasted a number of famous people among his flock, but he was an inveterate name-dropper whose claims were often unsubstantiated. There is no doubt, however, that there were dabblers in the dark arts on the Hollywood fringes, and one of his associates was Kenneth Anger, author of the scandal-mongering book *Hollywood Babylon*. LaVey would also appear in Anger's film, *Invocation of my Demon Brother*.

LaVey had launched his 'Church' in 1966, on 30 April, the day witches and demonic worshippers the world over celebrate the spring equinox. He ritually shaved his head following the tradition of the Yezidi Devil worshippers and declared 1966 as Anno Satanas, the first year of the reign of Satan, and thus began his worship and rituals with his assembled group of what LaVey termed 'like-minded individuals whose purpose was to use their combined forces of energy and magic to call up the dark force of nature that is called Satan'.

He ran his satanic temple from a large Victorian house in San Francisco, where he practised ritual that was as diabolical as anything that could be seen in the movies. He was devoted to smashing the whole concept of what a Church should be in the Christian sense. His was a temple of indulgence and pleasure, defying all forms of abstinence. As his biographer Blanche Barton described, the Church of Satan was outwardly offering a new religion, but behind the closed and guarded doors of the temple itself, the shock factor was high: 'The rituals were largely intended as cathartic blasphemies against Christianity. Many of the elements were consistent with reports of satanic worship taken from the famous writings of diabolists.'

For instance, a naked young woman was always used as the 'altar', accompanying music was a series of corruptions of Church hymns, the cross was turned upside-down, the Lord's Prayer was recited backwards, mock holy wafers were consecrated for insertion (with a phallus) into a naked woman's vagina, seminal fluid in milk was substituted for holy water, the names of infernal deities were invoked instead of the Christian God.

LaVey allowed limited coverage of his activities, and in 1967, around the time of his association with the making of *Rosemary's Baby*, a photograph taken in his temple of a naked girl lying on an altar covered with a leopard skin was shown around the world. His fame was further enhanced by the first public baptism in the new Church of Satan – that of his own three-year-old daughter Zeena, a child who might otherwise be termed as angelic, with her long blonde hair and cherub-like face. She was baptized on the formal living altar of a naked woman from LaVey's community. LaVey, now taken with the idea of appearing as the Devil Incarnate, was dressed accordingly at the baptism, in a black hood complete with two miniature horns, performing the rites in the name of Satan. He claimed that he could call upon the dark forces for the enactment of satanic magic: his speciality was the ritual satanic curse, a bloodcurdling epic of loud incantation and ritual.

If nothing else, Polanski's movie had gone to his head. LaVey was on a massive ego trip which ultimately led to the global expansion of his Church. From the moment news of his association with the Polanski movie leaked out, membership of the Church of Satan doubled, then tripled. Unknown to Paramount and Polanski, LaVey was cashing in at every turn and continued to live off this unexpected bonanza for the next quarter of a century. Today the Church is still flourishing, and it costs $100 simply to join.

In 1967, those who entered LaVey's temple of sin in San Francisco were treated to a shocking, theatrical display of the diabolical, and a brief taste of an actual satanic ceremony in his temple demonstrates the qualifications of LaVey to act as adviser on Polanski's movie.

There were eighteen or more people moving down a dark corridor to the ritual room, a black-painted chapel with a red ceiling, and the door banged shut behind us, and two hooded guards stood to attention; no one could enter, no one could leave. It was pitch-black and there was an uneasy silence. Suddenly their ears were alerted by the sound of curious organ music which was a preamble to a loud cacophony of instruments and sound effects that shattered the consciousness. The music stopped and somewhere a gong was struck three times, and the room was lit by black candles giving sufficient glow to reveal the black-robed figure of the High Priest, Anton LaVey, his eyes peering, scowling down at them. Off to the side of him was another startling feature, a coffin standing upright and lined with black silk and it was just possible to catch sight of an owl, its eyes glinting, perched inside.

The eyes of the congregation wandered back to the High Priest and on the wall behind him it was possible to make out the image of the Baphomet [the head of the Goat of Mendes] of the same design as that supposedly used by the fourteenth-century Knights Templar. Below this, in the half-light of the candles, the body of a naked, nubile young woman came into view.

She moved slightly and, unlike the owl, was not dead. She was also wearing the Sigil of the Baphomet which dangled on a chain and lodged between her breasts; beside her were two naked female acolytes and in front of her was a priestess, covered in a black velvet robe but with her long golden hair flowing over the lowered hood; she was holding her arms outstretched, clasping a sword pointing down in front of her. The organ played again, a Hymn to Satan, and the naked girl lying across a stone mantle representing the living altar in the Church of Satan, stretched full length and became the focal point of all that proceeded.

Over her body they spoke their words, these priests and disciples in their jet-black robes, and drank their foul Elixir of Life from a black chalice . . . *In nomine Dei nostri Satanas Luciferi excelsi* . . . The ritual was about to begin . . .

Back on the Paramount sound stage 12, Polanski progressed with his movie, and LaVey was often around. The picture had attracted a good deal of media attention and Polanski's reputation brought a stream of famous visitors to the set, apparently intrigued by his precision and attention to detail which, as those who had worked with him before well knew, meant retake after retake.

Tony Curtis, whom Roman had met while Sharon was filming *Don't Make Waves*, often called and tried to entice him away for pleasurable interludes. Warren Beatty came by and persuaded him to take a break for dinner, and they all went to Beatty's favourite Italian restaurant with Peter Sellers and his wife Britt Ekland, Peter Lawford and Mia Farrow.

In such company and with so much talk about his movie, Polanski had assumed the reputation of boy genius, with everyone commenting on how young he looked – 'such a charming youth' said Ruth Gordon – although he was then thirty-four. Paramount technicians spoke highly of his expertise and though he and his cameraman argued incessantly, it was done with the respect of two men who knew exactly what they were talking about; word travelled.

Soon, three of America's most famous directors of the day also dropped in specifically to watch Polanski work – Elia Kazan, director of such classics as *On the Waterfront* and *Streetcar Named Desire*, and Mike Nichols, who had just directed Elizabeth Taylor and Richard Burton in *Who's Afraid of Virginia Woolf?*, both stayed for an hour or more. Then Otto Preminger arrived one day, arm-in-arm with Frank Sinatra whom he had directed in the 1955 movie, *The Man With the Golden Arm*.

Polanski was irritated that day; for one thing, whenever Sinatra was in the vicinity, his star became edgy and nervous as if she was suddenly taken by the thought that she had been caught doing something she should not be doing. The other reason was that Bill Castle's office at Paramount had called to tell him he was behind schedule. Robert Evans wanted to see him on the same topic. Sinatra was in no better mood about the picture, and with his own deal for *The Detective* now pressing, he was becoming agitated about the delays. He telephoned the set almost daily, and witnesses in close proximity heard him shouting abuse at Mia down the telephone. She would then need time to compose herself. She found comfort by talking her heart out to Ruth Gordon, who had befriended her, and by giving her best to Polanski and patiently putting up with his demands on set; she thought he was the best director she had ever worked for, and was convinced that the picture would be a winner.

John Cassavetes was less impressed. As a director himself and of a completely different school – in *Shadows*, he drew widely on the improvisation techniques made popular by the French New Wave directors – he found it difficult to respond objectively to the Polanski system of straightforward disciplines, where every detail, every aspect, every movement of a scene would be sketched and noted and performed until it was exactly how he wanted it. Cassavetes wanted more scope for his own creativity and interpretation, there were rows almost daily, and when the film was over, the two of them conducted a slanging match through the newspapers. Cassavetes said he struggled to 'stay alive' under Polanski's oppressive regime. Polanski attacked Cassavetes for 'hassling me and asking questions . . . why this . . . why that . . . he would challenge me about the way I wanted him to walk across the room or open a door. The man's a fucking bore and not a very good director – any fool could have made a film like *Shadows*.'

And so it went on.

By the autumn, *Rosemary's Baby* was over schedule, with important scenes remaining to be filmed or refilmed, and this meant a real crisis for Mia Farrow. She was due to begin filming *The Detective* with Sinatra who was already in New York shooting his own scenes on location. He expected Mia to arrive any day, and the company had shot around her scenes. But, as she kept telling Sinatra in their repeated telephone conversations, there was no way she was going to leave the set of *Rosemary's Baby* until Roman Polanski was ready to release her. Finally, Sinatra delivered her an ultimatum – that she should walk off the Paramount lot now. She had done her stint and Polanski was just pissing around. It was no mere coincidence that the morning Sinatra called, he received reports from the bodyguards posted to look after Mia that she had gone to a disco called The Factory where she was seen dancing with Sinatra's not-very-good-friend Robert Kennedy – this came hot on the heels of other gossip-column fodder that she was dancing at The Daisy with Peter Lawford, who was also out of favour with Sinatra. Such were the jealousies and rages which continued daily until Frank really blew his top.

He personally telephoned Bill Castle in New York and demanded to know how much longer Mia would be required. Castle told him that it would be at least three, possibly four weeks. Sinatra said Polanski was a 'dumb Pollack who did not know what the fuck he was doing'. Castle said he had to agree that they were behind schedule and he had ordered Polanski to speed up the final scenes.

This was not good enough for Sinatra. He sent lawyers to the set of *Rosemary's Baby* bearing papers dismissing her from his own film and saying he was replacing her. Polanski found Mia weeping and said afterwards that it reminded him of a servant being sacked for insubordination.

Polanski pressed on, late and $300,000 over budget. Evans called him in and pleaded for a speedy completion. Polanski said he had to go at his own pace, or he would ruin the picture. Executives in charge of the financial side of the business, however, were less than placated. Was it really necessary, they moaned, to re-create for one scene a replica of Michelangelo's ceiling in the Sistine Chapel, which took studio artists six weeks to copy, down to the cracks and fading?

The ongoing domestic arguments between Sinatra and his wife merely exacerbated the situation. When Polanski, for example, wanted to make the nightmare sequence into his obligatory nude scene, Cassavetes said he felt it incumbent upon himself to remind the director that Mia was married to Frank Sinatra, and no one told *her* to strip. Was he looking for trouble, or what?

So they did not go nude, but instead wore flesh-coloured body stockings. It was also the scene – filmed on a yacht moored at the Playa Del Ray Marina – where Anton LaVey had his big moment as the Devil, where he rapes Rosemary and impregnates her to bear his child. The whole scene was carefully calculated beforehand by Polanski, who had long talks with Sharon in which they drew upon their own experiences with LSD to explore the possibilities of mind-warping fantasia in which the wife would be violated by a monster. In the sequence, Rosemary's husband prepares her for intercourse in front of a coven of witches; she is drugged and tied down and symbols are placed upon her body, and when she is ready, Guy moves away to allow the Devil, portrayed by LaVey, to come forward and rape her. While the rest of the coven chanted and watched, LaVey took up position astride her prostrate form.

It was supposed to have been a misty, dream-like sequence, brought on by the drug administered. But Mia had not taken the drug, and screamed, 'This is really happening!' It was one of the moments of highest drama in the film, and one which shocked its audiences to the core as she cried out at the climax. It was a difficult scene, in which Polanski had given Mia a detailed briefing. He wanted her every emotion to come through, including the orgasm. Throughout, he and his soundsman squatted as close as they could get to her without being in shot, as she fought through the scene with LaVey atop of her. It required eight or nine takes before Polanski was happy. LaVey got up and told Mia it was a pleasure working with her. Mia Farrow looked on astonished and would recount the experience for some time afterwards.

Though Polanski's movie was surrounded by extramural events beyond his control, the Hollywood adage that all publicity is good publicity remained ever applicable. Not least in focus was Polanski's own relationship with Sharon Tate who, in a publicity interview for *Valley of the Dolls*, had said that he was the only man for her, and the Hollywood sob-sisters immediately began to talk of a marriage in prospect.

The flames were merely fanned by an announcement from Paramount that Ms Farrow was taking a month away from her remaining film commitments with Polanski to travel to India for a 'period of meditation' with the pop guru Maharishi Mahesh Yogi, who had recently become famous after the four Beatles attended a meeting introducing Transcendental Meditation at the London Hilton Hotel. Polanski raised his hands to the sky, and wondered what was going to happen next.

Publicity executives at Paramount rubbed their hands with customary glee as Mia arrived in India accompanied by a swarm of reporters and photographers, and pictures of her and the mystic on the banks of the Ganges were flashed around the world. She was refusing to talk about her marriage, saying everything was fine, but continued to give interviews about her new movie. She stayed with the Maharishi for twenty days and the Beatles themselves arrived just as she was preparing to leave India.

Mia returned to America in the midst of a buzz of rumour about her marriage. By then, Polanski was ensconced in the editing suite, working to have his picture ready for release by June 1968. He had also called Krzys Komeda at the beginning of December and told him he wanted him to write the sound-track, as he had for all Polanski's films with the exception of *Repulsion*. Komeda, said Polanski, should come at once. He did, and wrote some haunting music, which would be his last.

Chapter Twelve

*T*he New Year began with a curious mixture of elation and fore-
boding. Polanski and Sharon were planning to fly to London
for a brief visit over Christmas 1967 and reunions with friends
Roman had not seen for months. Final work on *Rosemary's Baby*
had yet to be completed and he said he needed a break. Peter Sellers,
whom Polanski had met the previous year, provided the opportunity.
In his current role of middle-aged hippie, with his worry beads, kaftan
and handrolled joints, Sellers was planning a Christmas Day party in
Cortina.

Before they left, Polanski wanted to celebrate Christmas in Polish
style. Zofia Komeda, who was due to fly to Los Angeles to join her
husband in January, learned about the party from her husband. 'He
wrote me a letter, saying he could not understand what was going on.
Romek had been making a great fuss about him getting to Los Angeles
as soon as possible and when he arrived the film was not even edited,
and he could not start writing anything. All he knew was that they
would need a lullaby, so he had written them plenty – seven in all (two
of which were used in the film). Just before Christmas, Romek took
them all to the mountains – Krzys, Sharon and the hapless hairdresser
[Jay Sebring] who had been Sharon's lover before Polanski and, I suspect, later on. The party was in Polish style, and Polanski prepared it
himself. Krzys was very depressed and he told me later that the atmosphere was very strange . . . well, I won't tell you any more about it
. . . but he did not like it at all.'

They returned to Los Angeles to prepare to fly to London. By then,
Krzys Komeda had been taken ill, though the seriousness of his condition was not known at the time. He had attended another party organized by some Polish friends. Polanski was among the guests and, at the
height of the revelry, had clambered on to a table and recited lines from

'Pan Tadeusz', a Polish lament for the lost homeland, and the party descended into a drunken, emotional scene of reminiscences.

Some time later, Komeda slipped and hit his head. He returned home that night looking ill and had not recovered by the following day. Polanski and Sharon said he had been overdoing the celebrating, and had probably caught a chill. Komeda decided to remain in bed and the others left for Europe.

During their Christmas break Roman and Sharon were discussing marriage and had barely returned to Los Angeles when they decided to go ahead and do it – among all their friends back in London. Polanski checked on the progress of *Rosemary's Baby*, which was now in the hands of Sam O'Steen, one of Paramount's best editors, who was charged with getting Polanski's four-hour rough-cut version down to a cinema-length two hours and thirteen minutes. Then he called Victor Lownes and broke the news of the forthcoming nuptials. Lownes whooped with delight and asked when. Next week, said Polanski – on the 20th. Lownes, now the undisputed leader of their hedonist pack, said he would handle everything, and they selected the most fashionable wedding venue of the day – Chelsea Register Office, in London's King's Road.

With a party to arrange at short notice, Lownes had no time for formal invitations and instead sent out four dozen telegrams to showbiz friends which read: 'You are cordially invited to the Sharon Tate–Roman Polanski wedding reception at the Playboy Club this Saturday, 20 January 1968, at noon. Informal brunch.'

The guest-list was a veritable Who's Who of the moment – headed, of course, by two of Polanski's closest friends, Warren Beatty and Peter Sellers, plus Rudolf Nureyev, Sean Connery, Joan Collins and Anthony Newley, Keith Richard and Brian Jones of the Rolling Stones, John Mills, James Fox, Mike Sarne, David Bailey, Vidal Sassoon and the film critic Kenneth Tynan who was to become a friend and fan of Polanski's work, and, as it turned out, a future collaborator.

Sharon brought with her Barbara Parkins with whom she had become friendly since they worked together on *Valley of the Dolls* and who was to be matron of honour. Gene Gutowski was Polanski's best man and the customary stag night was held at Victor's place where male friends turned up not knowing what to expect, and were standing around talking and drinking and smoking cigars when the doors burst open and a flood of young women literally cascaded through the double doors and grabbed partners.

Sharon chose Victorian taffeta for her wedding dress, but there was nothing traditional in its style, cut high above the knee to conform with the current mini trend, and with a high neckline and ruched shoulders. She was a picture absolutely made for the next day's newspapers, especially alongside the somewhat eccentrically but formally dressed Polanski, who was wearing a tight-fitting Edwardian-style suit with a ruffled ascot about his neck. The small wedding group at the register office included his father Ryszard and step-mother Wanda.

The plush surroundings of the Playboy Club in Park Lane then became the venue for a series of parties, beginning with Lownes's informal brunch which went on through the day, the guests reconvening later without the wedding pair who had adjourned to Roman's mews house prior to their flight to Cortina for a brief honeymoon.

Zofia Komeda heard about the wedding from her husband. 'As I was about to fly from Warsaw to join him in Los Angeles, Krzys sent me a cable suggesting that I break my journey and stop off in London for Polanski's wedding to Sharon. But I decided not to and arrived in California just before their return. We had a problem with what to buy them as a wedding present, since they had a lot more money than we did, and we decided in the end to behave as Europeans and bought them fifty giant fresh roses.'

To the impecunious Komedas, the present meant a great deal, and Zofia's account of the presentation of their gift succinctly summed up the difference between Polanski, the successful émigré, and Komeda, the brilliant but impoverished composer: 'We put the roses in their living room so that they would see them when they entered. Then we watched for their reaction, but there was none. In the evening, they invited us to dinner (we were staying at the time in apartments in the Sunset Marquee Hotel). Then I noticed on the freezer a small plastic basket with plastic blue flowers the colour of a nightshirt. I asked Sharon what this contraption was for, and she said: "Aren't they lovely? This is a gift from my producer, Ransohoff." I asked her, "What will you do with it?" and she said, "Oh, it will just be standing there. They are very practical. If they get dirty I will be able to wash them." I was stunned. It wasn't lack of intelligence – just a difference in the way we see and perceive things.'

Zofia returned to Warsaw in early March, leaving her husband working on the film score for *Rosemary's Baby*. Polanski threw a farewell party for her at an Indonesian restaurant. 'That was the last time I spoke to him,' said Zofia. Before long, she was summoned back. The earlier fall had produced a blood clot on her husband's brain and one day, while visiting Gene Gutowski in hospital, who had fallen and injured his leg, Komeda collapsed. He sank into a coma and needed an emergency operation. 'When I arrived,' said Zofia, 'Krzys was already dying but I did not hear from Polanski, not in the next three months I was there. I did not exchange a single sentence with him. He did not even ring me. Once, when I came to visit Krzys in hospital, there was Romek and his rabble. He was very loud and noisy and I could see it upset Krzys so I asked the hospital to ensure that Mr Polanski should not be let in to see my husband ever again.'

Zofia spent much of the time sitting beside her husband's bed and watched his condition deteriorate. With hospital bills mounting as the weeks went by, and with no improvement in his condition, Zofia decided that he should be flown back to Poland, which she paid for herself out of Krzys's royalties. He never fully regained consciousness and died soon after arriving back in Warsaw. 'Only when Krzys died,' said Zofia, 'did Romek telephone me and uttered one sentence: "How can I help?" I replied, "You cannot do anything now, but I can help you with some advice: join the human race again because you are an animal now."'

To Zofia Komeda, Polanski's life was almost an obscenity in terms of his opulence and all that had come with it. He was, as Krzys Komeda had discovered, involved in a circle which was the epitome of California's free-loving, liberalistic style, and with which those Poles who had come to observe it with a fresh, untainted eye from the enforced morality of their homeland, found it difficult to come to terms. Polanski, on the other hand, made no secret of his enjoyment of everything that life had to offer. On his arm was one of the most beautiful women in the world who apparently loved him madly and spoke longingly to all she encountered at their wedding reception about their desire to start a family.

In his work, Polanski had just directed what he considered would be his most commercially successful film, and his life was being led in the mode of the current buzz word for people of his life-style – jetsetters. The commuting between Los Angeles and Europe, the red Ferrari he had just bought himself when the final tranche of his money came through from Paramount, and the Hollywood-style living to which Sharon had introduced him all fitted a kind of pattern which had evolved among his friends like Sellers and Beatty.

There was a busy schedule ahead. Sharon had followed up her appearance in *Valley of the Dolls* by being signed to appear in *The Wrecking Crew*, one of Dean Martin's Matt Helm pictures, while Polanski was expecting to direct *Downhill Racer* for Paramount. Then came his first setback. Paramount called Gene Gutowski, who was hoping to produce the picture under their Cadre Films partnership, and told him that the movie had been taken off the schedule. Polanski wanted to know why; there had, after all, been a verbal agreement when he signed to do *Rosemary's Baby*, that he would do three pictures for Paramount which would accommodate his arrangement with Gutowski and Cadre. There was no contract to that effect, however, and Evans had been stalling with the news that his financial people were not keen on taking up their options with Polanski.

He had ended up $400,000 over budget, and there had been a good deal of hassle, and memos from Paramount all the way through the picture, especially over the trouble with Frank Sinatra. Paramount, like several other studios in Hollywood at the time, teetered permanently on the edge of financial crisis, and Charlie Bludhorn had recently ordered a programme of redundancies and rationalization of property assets, which meant selling off the main studios and moving into smaller buildings. So they were not going to give Polanski *Downhill Racer* and he gained the impression that the picture had been scrapped. It had not. It resurfaced a few months later, by then assigned to the American director Michael Ritchie and starring Robert Redford whose own feud with Paramount had been miraculously resolved.

There were still some bright spots around, though. Polanski and Gutowski continued to reassure themselves that something was bound to turn up, and if recognition meant being assessed as able to judge the abilities of one's peers, then another indication that this was so had materialized. Polanski was invited to join the judging panel at the 1968 Cannes Film Festival, an invitation which he accepted with considerable pride, and bragging. At last he would be staying at the prestigious Carlton, extravagantly adding his own touch of immodesty by having his Ferrari shipped from Los Angeles to the South of France so that he could flash up and down the Côte with Sharon at his side, waving to his old associates, some of whom had rejected him in the past.

The show-off element did not go down well with François Truffaut and Jean-Luc Godard, giants of Roman's past in whose company he now found himself. Flashily attired in Rodeo Drive gear, Polanski looked the complete Hollywood success story, and Godard, more in tune with the French proletariat in his dress and manner, had little

131

time for him. 'Every goddamned time I opened my mouth,' Polanski complained, 'he interrupted.'

But it was important to Roman to return to Cannes as the conquering hero. It was typical of him, and as Basia would confirm, when he was in Cannes he just wanted to show off. This time he had good reason. He remembered only too well the days when he had been shunned as an unknown Polish director, where once few except those on the arty fringe of the business would even give him the time of day. And now, here he was, driving up in his bright red sports car, ready to vent his opinions on current movie-making and the films on offer. As it turned out, his show of success was ill-judged and ill-timed. 'He just did not appreciate what was going on,' said Truffaut. 'All he could visualize was Roman Polanski turning up to show everyone what a great guy he was – I could use a very apt description but I will not swear over the telephone.'

The Festival coincided with the student riots in Paris, which began in the first week of May and erupted progressively throughout the country during the rest of the month. Thirty thousand students had been locked out of the Sorbonne and fought the tear-gas with barricades, stones and Molotov cocktails. Workers began joining the protest with strikes and mass demonstrations aimed at De Gaulle and registering their anger at poor state salaries, censorship, discrimination and every other kind of social grievance. Down at Cannes in the second week of May, the bad and the beautiful were gathering for their annual exhibition of vanities and they were viewed as an elitist, capitalist crowd who cared nothing for the plight of the French working classes, which was undoubtedly true.

The riots spread to the south and Truffaut and Godard expressed their sympathy with the move to stop Cannes becoming just a gaudy parade of stars. Polanski, for not unselfish reasons, backed the opposite view – that the show should go on. He made his views known to a reporter from *Variety*, stating that he had left Poland to avoid these kinds of controls and that the band of so-called New Wave directors were 'playing at being revolutionaries', not appreciating the seriousness of what they were doing. He had experienced the real horror of working in a rigidly controlled environment, and he did not propose to work in such circumstances ever again.

In the end, there was a stand-up row and Godard told Polanski to fuck off back to Hollywood. The Festival collapsed in disarray and everyone started to leave as the demonstrators' mood looked decidedly

132

uncompromising. So Polanski never had the chance to voice his opinions about the films that would have been exhibited; instead, he and Sharon clambered back into the Ferrari and high-tailed it out of France in convoy with a couple of friends, including the pop singer turned film-maker Mike Sarne in his Rolls Royce.

Polanski returned to Hollywood in time for the opening of *Rosemary's Baby* in June, which brought good critical reaction and had the added benefit of a number of publicity bonuses, including the publishing success of Ira Levin's novel, published by Random House, which stayed in the best-seller charts for forty-one weeks, and was to be followed up with a print order of 1.5 million copies in paperback to be published at the time of the film's release.

Other publicity swung in from such events as the Sinatra–Farrow saga which had been raging in the gossip columns for a month. Soon after the film opened, a formal separation was announced, and Mia Farrow flew down to Mexico for a divorce amidst a mass of headlines and conjecture about infidelities on both sides. Similar troubles had beset Gene Gutowski and his wife Judy, who also parted.

As to the movie itself, in the intervening months since the completion of filming, producer William Castle and the advertising and PR departments at Paramount had devised a publicity campaign which would leave no cliché unturned. It was headed by a single, emotive line which appeared on every piece of promotional material: 'Pray for Rosemary's Baby'.

Castle, the schlockmeister of past publicity campaigns for cheap horror movies, could not resist standing outside cinemas, where queues were stretching around the block, and occasionally warning would-be viewers that they were in for a shock. He also set up a series of private screenings to which press and cinema people were invited, along with representatives of various religious organizations, thus ensuring some controversial and critical hype even before the movie was officially premiered. With this kind of Hollywood razzmatazz and tabloid coverage, there was always the danger that the quality of the film itself would be overshadowed. Polanski extracted from Mia Farrow one of her best-ever performances. As a film of its time, when all matters weird and wonderful were in vogue, it was a minor classic and remains even now one of the few movies of its genre that truly suspended disbelief, leaving its audience in little doubt of the existence of evil.

Reviews were largely favourable, and some reckoned that Polanski had at last returned to the promise he had shown in *Knife in the Water*. Polanski particularly liked the sentence, 'Tension is sustained to a degree surpassing Alfred Hitchcock at his best', in a review in the *Daily Telegraph* in London. He was roundly criticized in some quarters for the shock content of his film, a debate which was joined in *Look* magazine, by his male lead, John Cassavetes, who boldly stated that Polanski was, without doubt, obsessed with the bloody and the gruesome and was 'behaving like a kid in a candy store'. It was a description similar to others voiced in the past, and it would not be the last time Roman would hear it.

The movie's alleged affront to Christian decency did not harm its promotion either. The American Catholic Office gave it a C rating for its explicit content and its 'perverted use and distortion of fundamental Christian beliefs', while the British Board of Film Censors ordered fifteen seconds to be cut from the rape scene because of its 'elements of kinky sex associated with black magic' – all of which, of course, was enough to ensure vast attendances.

Rosemary's Baby was a runaway financial success, with the box office grossing $30 million (in 1968, remember) in America alone, and then as much again around the world.

There were other implications, too, in the dark and mysterious regions of the occult, where *Rosemary's Baby* became the instant focus of very considerable attention – far more significantly than either Polanski or Paramount would have imagined, or even understood, to this day. In spite of the hint of unseemly 'black magic' publicity which had been appearing in some articles about the movie and Polanski's supposed obsession with the supernatural (for which there was no tangible evidence), Paramount and Bill Castle continued to give some prominence to the presence of Anton LaVey in the film. He was invited to attend a number of private screenings and official premieres. And wherever LaVey went, his message carried further to the masses. His line, according to his biographer Blanche Barton, was that *Rosemary's Baby* was 'a metaphorical as well as a very real offshoot of the Church of Satan'. Small black buttons signifying the Church were handed out, carrying a parody of the film's publicity slogan: 'Pray for Anton LaVey'.

LaVey himself told Barton that *Rosemary's Baby* did for the Church of Satan what *The Birth of a Nation* – the great but inflammatory 1915 silent epic on the American Civil War – did for the Ku Klux Klan, 'complete with recruiting posters in the lobby'. Thus Polanski's film became the unwitting stimulus for the promotion of satanism and, to a lesser degree, witchcraft, by those in the business of attracting members and followers to a variety of occult and black magic groups. It was a turning point from which many unexpected developments would follow, in particular the beginning of an explosion of interest in the dark arts. Blanche Barton, in the historical account of the era she gives in her book *The Church of Satan*, quotes LaVey's own assessment of what happened: 'A Christian mind can only see things in black and white . . . or God versus Satan. But Satanists go beyond these rules, because of their peculiar interests and talents. It is healthy for misfits to have a secret life . . . and that is why *Rosemary's Baby* was such a breakthrough in the portrayal of real satanists . . . we could be the nice old lady next door or the valedictorian of the high school. That's why the film was so important to us . . .'

The publicity offshoot for the Church of Satan followed rapidly and the media around the world sent reporters to San Francisco to find out more about LaVey. He received coverage in major American magazines, including *Time*, *Newsweek* and *Cosmopolitan*, and appeared on the front cover of *Look*. He was even on the Johnny Carson show. His message was treated with caution, but there were sensational qualities in the way the photographs of this hooded disciple of the Devil were displayed.

The following year, he published the infamous Satanic Bible which represented a reversal of all that the Holy Bible stood for; it is still on sale in occult bookshops around the world to this day and is widely advertised in occult magazines by the Church of Satan. By early 1969, LaVey's Church was claiming 10,000 paid-up members world-wide, a figure that would grow rapidly over the years. A film company produced a documentary on him and the Church, entitled *Satanis*, which was released as a double bill with Kenneth Anger's *Invocation of My Demon Brother*. Anger planned another film, to be called *Lucifer Rising*, starring a young actor named Bobby Beausoleil, later to be identified as a member of Charles Manson's 'family'.

LaVey, meanwhile, began touring the States, making stage-managed appearances wearing a black cape and mimicking the scene in *Rosemary's Baby* which was an actual newsclip of Pope Paul VI's arrival in New York on 4 November 1965 to address the United Nations. In the more serious areas of the occult, LaVey was branded a buffoon, a media black magician, a showman and a charlatan.

These were the background events occurring in the occult world of which Polanski would have had little knowledge. Among them were other far more dangerous stirrings which would ultimately shatter the seemingly charmed world of Roman and Sharon Polanski . . .

Chapter Thirteen

Although *Rosemary's Baby* had been a runaway success which helped boost the fortunes of Paramount, the studio did not rush to claim Polanski for another project. The response from Robert Evans and Charlie Bludhorn, while congratulatory and pleasant, was decidedly cool on another level. Gene Gutowski, disheartened when *Downhill Racer* was postponed, returned to London with his hopes of a breakthrough in Hollywood for Cadre Films seemingly fading into oblivion.

Scripts were arriving from other quarters for Polanski's consideration, but most were cheap thrillers and horror flicks that did not even begin to stir his imagination. Gutowski himself teamed up with Polanski's former collaborator Jerzy Skolimowski, with whom he had co-written *Knife in the Water* during their brief and tempestuous relationship. Gutowski was interested in producing a new screenplay by Skolimowski called *A Day at the Beach*. He signed Peter Sellers to star and they all went off to Rome to make the picture. Sadly for Skolimowski, the partnership with Gutowski did not bring him the same fortune and recognition as had his collaboration with Polanski. They failed to sell their movie to a distributor and it was never released.

Polanski and Sharon, meanwhile, had moved temporarily into the home of Patti Duke on a short-term lease after Brian Aherne returned to Los Angeles from New York. They were not sure whether the future lay in Los Angeles or London. Either way, apart from Sharon's work on a new film being shot in Rome, they had no firm schedule. So they were taking it easy in the summer of 1968 when Wojtek Frykowski turned up in Los Angeles, barely needing to remind Polanski that had he not found the money for *Mammals* back at Lodz those few short years ago, Roman would not be where he was today, languishing in a small mansion in Hollywood. Zofia Komeda recalled: 'Fryko was following Romek, but had never really become part of his circle. His pursuit of him began earlier when he turned up in London. But Romek wasn't very pleased. Now, Fryko had followed him to America.'

Frykowski landed in New York with very little money. He located another of the old gang from Lodz, Jerzy Kosinski, who was now a famous novelist, having published *The Painted Bird* and *Steps*, which had firmly established him as a powerful writer. He had also 'Americanized' himself, and he believed that was the difference between himself and Polanski, who was never anything other than Polish – whether he was in France, England or the United States, they were just temporary residences, places to visit.

Kosinski's view was also reinforced by his having married a rich American, Mary Hayward Weir, the widow of a steel tycoon who possessed a considerable fortune; Frykowski had been quick to follow his old friend's advice and had found a cushion against hard and inflationary times which were all the more difficult for a Pole whose command of English was somewhat limited at the time.

Abigail (Gibby) Folger, the heiress to a coffee fortune, was in the circle of Kosinski's wife's wealthy friends: 'Fryko was introduced to her as a joke, really,' said Zofia Komeda. But the joke rebounded. Gibby Folger became intrigued by the tough Pole with whom she conversed in French so that she could understand him; his English was not very good. Frykowski, who had still achieved little in his own right, lived off his boasts about producing one of Roman Polanski's best films. Gibby was impressed and wanted to meet Polanski. 'Fryko kept telephoning Romek in Los Angeles asking for a job,' said Zofia, 'so finally he found him one.'

That summer Gibby and Frykowski travelled to Los Angeles. Polanski found Wojtek a job constructing sets in one of the studios. He felt he owed his friend that much, and Frykowski was sure he did. The job lasted only a few days. Zofia said, 'Fryko told them he wasn't going to spend his life knocking nails in the fucking floor and quit.'

So now there was something of an entourage gathering, with Wojtek, Gibby and the ever-present Jay Sebring, Sharon's former lover who continued to come racing round to the house in his black Porsche, in spite of Polanski's reservations about his presence. Polanski and Sharon continued their jetsetting life-style, commuting between Los Angeles and London. Then Sharon had to go to Rome for the preliminaries on a possible new film. While she was away, Roman joined Warren Beatty and others cruising the boulevards and enjoying the night-life at The Daisy or The Factory, and sometimes they would dive into one of the seedy girlie bars that burgeoned on Sunset Boulevard in the late sixties.

To close observers, Polanski's relationship with Sharon was a model of the much talked about 'open' marriage, another sixties invention, which was really just an excuse for screwing around. It was open house, too; the couple's parties would be populated by people neither of them knew, as well as by the rich and famous like the Kirk Douglases, the Yul Brynners and the Mike Nicholses, all of whom became regular companions.

Sharon enjoyed it all at first, but there was a good deal of gossip about there being a *ménage à trois* between herself, her husband and Jay Sebring, and, after a while, she began to get anxious about her marriage. Polanski's appetite for sexual pleasures had not subsided and he had become almost as famous as Warren Beatty for his brief encounters. Sharon was humiliated and hurt. For the first time in ages, she felt neurosis overtaking her.

Nineteen sixty-eight was a fractious year in many ways. The assassinations of Martin Luther King and Bobby Kennedy, the shooting of Andy Warhol, the Paris student riots and the Vietnam peace demonstrations in London and virtually every major city in America, mirrored the agitation and tension of society in general, except of course for the laid-back flower people languishing under their marijuana cloud. There were militants in the peace movement who were all for attacking the establishment, there were militant black groups and militant right-wing groups. Chicago police, under the orders of Mayor Daley, responded to the peace protests by clubbing and tear-gassing the marchers in scenes reminiscent of Berlin in 1938.

Hollywood was also an uneasy place, torn between the need to turn out entertaining movies, yet reflecting society with its increasing violence, sex revolution and drugs craze. This was Hollywood at its most schizophrenic. Many major stars took it upon themselves to comment publicly on the current issues. Warren Beatty had recently immersed himself in the backrooms of Democrat politics. Others lent their support to a variety of campaigns, including the peace movement in which the likes of Jane Fonda became famous for their stance, the legalization of pot, on which Jack Nicholson had some controversial views, and tighter gun laws in the US which were being backed by a galaxy of stars ranging from Elizabeth Taylor to Robert Redford. It was a period when issues such as these split the loyalties of Hollywood stars and film-makers between their work as artists and their stance on the way their films reflected, and affected, developments in society. While Beatty, for example, supported a full-page advertisement in the *New York Times*, organized by Elizabeth Taylor, calling for gun controls, and backed the anti-Vietnam campaigner George McGovern for president, his latest movie, *Bonnie and Clyde*, was one of the most determinedly violent non-western shoot-outs of recent times.

The turmoil was evident in every studio, and the answer seemed to be to go on stretching the boundaries of explicitness. Sex, drugs and violence were the burgeoning topics to be treated not as social commentaries but as the basis for titillating, thrilling, shocking, frightening excitement that would bring audiences back to the cinemas. The only serious consideration in the dream factories was the bottom line. The moguls might pay lip-service to social correctness, but the realities were quite cynically ignored.

Polanski cared as much about politics as he did about religion – so long as he was not affected, he wasn't interested. But he was drawn into the periphery of the current scene when his next project landed on his door-mat. It was to be the film of another book, Robert Merle's *The Day of the Dolphin*, the story of a marine biologist who discovers that dolphins are being used in a plot to blow up the President's yacht – another 'Let's kill the President story', which abounded at the time.

Polanski was not particularly keen on the project, but it came with a personal note from the vice-president of United Artists inviting him to take it on. As he now also needed to replenish funds, he accepted. He decided he would go to his house in London to write the screenplay, a trip planned to coincide with Sharon's commitment to fly to Rome to begin a new film for the Italian director Vittorio Gassman.

London was still swinging. Victor Lownes and the Playboy Club were living up to their joint image of self-indulgence and there were a good many social interludes of varying kinds. Victor Lownes's parties were always aimed at sheer, unadulterated pleasure, but at others Polanski found, as in America, that the discussions on current issues could become heavy, even among the liberally-minded. Kenneth Tynan – renowned as the first man to say 'fuck' on British television – was currently berating the Americans over the 'bloody carnival in Vietnam'.

Polanski, as an émigré from Communist rule, was often dragged into the conversations because of his first-hand knowledge of Communism, and frequently became angry about what he regarded as the fatuous nonsense being spouted by those who he considered knew nothing of the true circumstances. Though Polanski sympathized with the peace protestors, he often became impatient with the political posturing that went on at these soirées, heavily populated by champagne socialists seeking a fashionable cause, where he might find himself facing discussions of solidarity with the French students or lectures from Vanessa Redgrave on the financial plight of young Americans who had fled the draft so as not to fight in Vietnam.

Ken Tynan and his wife Kathleen had an especially mischievous penchant for bringing together lively people whose views might provoke confrontation and argument in the course of the evening. One such occasion was a party for Mike Nichols, who was visiting from Los Angeles. Kathleen recalled that when the Polanskis arrived, John Lennon was sitting on the stairs dreaming up satirical, lewd and shocking sketches that might be introduced into Tynan's forthcoming revue, *Oh! Calcutta!*, which he was preparing for its New York opening in June 1969 and in London the following year, the Lord Chamberlain permitting. Lennon suggested that real male masturbation should be included, and everyone around laughed and went on merrily devouring a large tray of hash cakes which Sharon had just baked and was offering around.

Polanski had already written two three-minute inserts for *Oh! Calcutta!* One he had typically called 'The Voyeur', a little fantasy in true Polanski mould. It was based upon a static camera view through a window of a room where a girl is stripping, though her breasts and pubic areas remain concealed by the furniture. Then another girl appears, also strips, and the two make love; the frustrated voyeur is viewed in blurred fashion on the edges of the shot. The second act is observed through the window of a railway carriage in which a girl is seated; a man enters, sits down opposite her and apparently unzips his fly, an unseen act indicated only by the girl's facial expression. She lifts her skirt and they disappear from view, apparently copulating. Tynan read the scripts and was delighted. He called them typical 'cock-teasing' Polanski shorts.

Polanski was in good company for the Tynan project. As well as Lennon's 'Liverpool Wank' and Tynan's own sketches, Jean-Luc Godard and Federico Fellini had promised short films, and Gore Vidal, Edna O'Brien, Joe Orton and Jules Feiffer had offered to write inserts. In the event, Polanski's contributions were not filmed; he wanted them made for a wide screen and that put them beyond Tynan's budget.

*   *   *

In between the social discourse and the current issues being rammed down his throat, Polanski was struggling with his script about a dolphin and a president. It was heavy going, and he was having difficulty in making it work, so he was tetchy and impatient. He wasn't exactly ecstatic, either, about the news which Sharon delivered in December – she was pregnant. He was moody for several days; a baby did not suit his plans. They were always on the move, mixing with a crowd whose habits were as liberal as the age. His wife had been a regular user of LSD and pot, and somehow a child did not fit their very fluid, flitting life-style. Once they had talked, however, and Sharon had insisted she would take no more drugs from that day on, Roman began to warm to the idea.

The baby would be born in America and they would need a bigger house, so in February 1969, as soon as Sharon had finished filming in Rome, they returned to Los Angeles and began to look for a more permanent home. Roman heard that Terry Melcher, the record-producer son of Doris Day, and his lover Candice Bergen had moved out of their rented house on Cielo Drive, a superb ranch-style property set in its own fenced grounds on a remote hillside off Benedict Canyon. The Polanskis went to view and took the lease straight away. The house was owned by Rudi Altobelli, a show-business agent who in his time had represented numerous high-profile stars, including Henry Fonda, Katharine Hepburn, Sally Kellerman and Samantha Eggar. At the time, though, he was travelling extensively and wanted to lease the property, although when the Polanskis moved in he was temporarily living in a guest cottage in the grounds. The property had all the attributes of modern living for the financially well-endowed – manicured gardens, swimming pool and security gates. The desirability of the house was reflected in the rent – $3000 a month.

Roman and Sharon moved in towards the end of February 1969 and threw a huge housewarming party in early March at which all their friends (and some gatecrashers) turned up. It was an eventful party; one incident in particular would be a topic at dinner tables for some time to come – the moment when Polanski's maid apparently banged on the bathroom door, shouting, 'What's going on in there . . . open the door at once.' What was going on was described by Roger Vadim since it concerned his then wife Jane Fonda. 'There was I,' said Vadim, 'hoping that everything was working out for us when . . . during the party at Polanski's house . . . Jane disappeared for over half an hour with J, a very handsome man. When she reappeared her hair was dishevelled and her skirt slightly crumpled. Interrupted in the middle of their flirtation, Jane and J reluctantly had to leave the bathroom.'

This policing of moral standards in the Polanski household by the maid was such an unlikely event that the story did the rounds for weeks. Polanski was remarkably open about his involvements and his infidelities, with women taken 'and possessed' – his favourite term – at every opportunity. This was especially so while Sharon was growing larger. He could not bear the thought of making love to her, and could not wait for the day when she delivered their child and her body returned to its normal shape.

Towards the end of March, they had to prepare to leave for Europe again. Sharon was required back in Rome for some sound-dubbing on her film, and Polanski had to press on with his screenplay and meet with producer Andy Braunsberg. It was about eight o'clock on Sunday, 23 March that Sharon Tate had a brief but incredible face-to-face encounter with the man who would eventually be charged with the murder of herself and three of her friends – Charles Manson.

Rudi Altobelli was taking a shower in the guest cottage when the doorbell rang. He went to the front door and found Manson standing there. Altobelli recognized him because they had previously met at the home of Dennis Wilson of the Beach Boys, where Manson had been living for a short time in 1968. Altobelli had been invited by Wilson to listen to some of Manson's songs on tape. He was unimpressed and had said he would think about it. He had not seen Manson since.

Now, Manson turned up again at the house in Cielo Drive – he had called four or five times previously – looking for Terry Melcher who had also been supplied with tapes by Manson. Altobelli said, 'When I saw him standing there, I was surprised. He said he was looking for Melcher, and then skilfully turned the conversation around to his tapes. I told him Melcher had moved, and that I had no time to discuss it, because I was preparing to leave for Europe.'

Altobelli sent Manson away, but he did not leave the property. He walked over to the main house and rang the doorbell. He was met by Sharon Tate's personal photographer Shahrokh Hatami, an Iranian who was a close friend of the Polanskis and was visiting Cielo Drive on the night before Sharon left for Rome. Hatami recalled, 'Manson arrived at the door and asked for someone whose name I did not recognize. I don't think it was Melcher. I felt a little protective towards Sharon and I said loudly, "This is the Polanski residence. There is no one here of that name."' Manson repeated the name Polanski and turned to go. Just as he

143

did so, Sharon and the others – Jay Sebring, Wojtek Frykowski and Gibby Folger – came towards the door.

Sharon said, 'Who was that guy?'

Manson turned and looked back, at that moment observing four of the people his 'family' would massacre.

The following day, by coincidence, Altobelli was on the same flight as Sharon to Europe. 'Who was that creepy guy who came round yesterday?' she asked him. 'We sent him away.' Altobelli shrugged and said he did not know.

Before they left, Polanski had arranged for housesitters to take over the property until they returned. Mike Sarne, who was preparing to film Gore Vidal's pornographic novel, *Myra Breckenridge*, a movie for which he was later vilified, was back in Hollywood, and it was originally planned that he should stay at the house. The arrangement was cancelled at the last minute, however, and instead, Wojtek Frykowski and Gibby Folger offered to move in, much to Sharon's annoyance; she had long ago tired of Frykowski's presence. Anyhow, they moved in and the Polanskis left for Europe.

Sharon's misgivings were well founded. In the months preceding the Polanskis' departure, and up to the time Sharon returned in August, Wojtek Frykowski had gone haywire. Though Polanski himself would attempt to make light of it in his own recollections of events, there now seems incontrovertible evidence that Frykowski had become deeply involved in the drug scene, both as a heavy user himself and as a runner. His activities were sufficiently known for a later police report on his activities to conclude: 'Frykowski had no money and no visible means of support. He had lived off Folger's fortune and he used cocaine, mescaline, LSD, marijuana and hashish in large amounts. He was an extrovert character [whose] narcotic parties were the order of the day.' Artist Witold Kaczanowski, another Polish immigrant who, like Frykowski, possessed an expired visitor's visa, recalled that Wojtek once told him he was on the ninth successive day of a mescaline trip and was having difficulty in drawing a straight line.

Some months earlier, Frykowski and Gibby Folger had rented a house on Woodstock Road, opposite the home of Mama Cass Elliott of the Mamas and Papas. Gibby had taken up part-time social work in some of the deprived areas of Los Angeles and now spent much of her time working on a variety of community projects. She had also become a heavy user of drugs, and was lately trying to kick the habit, and at the time of her death was visiting a psychiatrist every day of the week. She was also tiring of Frykowski, horrified by his appalling descent into the rampant subterranean Los Angeles drug culture. Arguments between herself and Frykowski, now constantly debilitated by the effects of his drug-taking, became louder and more frequent. Sharon Tate had grown sick of it before they left and had told Polanski she did not want Frykowski in the house.

While the Polanskis were in London, there were a number of unseemly incidents at the house in Cielo Drive, which Frykowski treated as his own, inviting all and sundry to parties, one of which descended into a street brawl to which the police were called. Jay Sebring also held a party at the house. Some famous names were in attendance but they disappeared when it was gatecrashed by a crowd of drug-seeking hippie types looking for Fryko.

It was a scenario to which Polanski and Sharon barely contributed but which would be used as a backdrop of scandal, sex, drugs and violence when the reporters came looking for the story behind the story – the motives for the murder of Sharon Tate and her friends.

There was another scenario building up elsewhere which can be slotted into the story now, years later, when missing pieces of the jigsaw have fallen into place. Polanski never knew the danger he was personally courting when he made *Rosemary's Baby* and used Anton LaVey as an adviser and actor. He had no way of knowing the immediate background to the growth of occultism, nor of the in-fighting and enmity that existed among satanists and satanic groups after LaVey's involvement in the film.

The chain reaction of underlying events began back in London, and it is necessary to divert momentarily from the chronology of Polanski's activities at this time to explain the unfolding drama that finally led the Manson 'family', dubbed as Satan's Slaves, along the winding path of Cielo Drive.

Polanski always dismissed stories of black magic connections with the death of his wife, but connections there were, as police investigators would later discover. Sharon may have been interested in witchcraft from the days when she met the British witches Alex and Maxine Sanders. And she was undoubtedly fascinated by the activities and charisma of Anton LaVey, although neither she nor her friends were actively concerned in anything more dangerous than a ouija board which they would occasionally sit around, attempting to invoke a spirit or two.

The unknown link, however, began back in London some months earlier. A new 'spiritual' organization called The Process: The Church of the Final Judgment, had been formed. It was an organization whose extremist satanic element made Anton LaVey's Church of Satan look like a Sunday school. The Process, with its swastika-like emblem (which Charles Manson later carved on his forehead) was formed in the mid-sixties by Robert DeGrimston Moore, an old boy of Winchester public school and a former senior member of the Church of Scientology and self-styled pupil of its founder L. Ron Hubbard.

Moore, then thirty-four years old, changed his name to Robert DeGrimston – popularly 'Grim' – and began preaching freedom of choice in line with modern thinking. He pitched his teachings not at society's drop-outs but at a higher level – young middle-class people attracted by his philosophy of 'every person on earth has total freedom of choice'. With twenty-five disciples, he moved into a large Victorian house in fashionable Balfour Place, behind the Playboy Club in Mayfair.

Members could join the Jehovahs, who were puritanical and religious; the Luciferians, who were pleasure-seekers, or the satanists, who were devout followers of blood and sacrificial ritual. DeGrimston also founded a magazine called *The Process* (back copies of which are still widely sold through satanic magazines today). He published three books, and in his second, *Jehovah on War*, he said that the Day of Judgment was near and made the following inflammatory statement: 'My prophecy upon this wasted earth and upon the corrupt creation that squats upon its surface is: Thou Shalt Kill.'

The group had the benefit of a large stock of reading matter on occult practice, notably including the works of the infamous master magician Aleister Crowley whom Lord Beaverbrook once described as the wickedest man in Britain. One of Crowley's books, *Magick in Theory and Practice*, became the handbook of modern sinister occultism, and includes the following passage:

Bloody sacrifice has from time immemorial been considered part of magic. The ethics of the thing did not appear to have concerned anyone – nor need they do so. An animal should be killed within the circle [but] for the highest spiritual working, one must choose that victim which contains the great and purest force; a child of perfect innocence is the most satisfactory and suitable victim . . .

146

Crowley died in 1947, but his following in the late sixties had seen a massive revival, especially on the west coast of America, where his books were in great demand.

DeGrimston Moore was no Crowley and kept a fairly low profile, but he began to attract a large following. In early 1968, he sent a party of thirty of his disciples to set up shop in San Francisco; with them they took issue number four of *The Process* magazine which set out the aims of each of the sects within the Church. Under the heading of 'Satan's Advocate', the following paragraph appears in a long and vitriolic diatribe:

A naked girl, fair-haired and in the very prime of youth lies like a human sacrifice upon the altar . . . Take your choice, leave nothing out and use every means of sharpening your senses. Alcohol to set the blood coursing in your veins, narcotics to heighten your feelings to a peak of sensitivity so that the lowest depths of physical sensation can be plumbed and wallowed in . . . sink down in the decadence of excessive self-indulgence. Let no so-called sin, perversion or depravity escape your searching senses; partake all of them to overflowing . . . there is no dialectic but death . . .

DeGrimston and the Church of Process went to the Height Ashbury District of San Francisco, where the counter-culture movement of America was flourishing. DeGrimston took a lease on a property – 407 Cole Street – which would be his new base, and from there he sent forth his disciples, each group following their own course of pursuit, but all dressed like no one else in San Francisco where they peddled their message and their magazines to the streets full of potential converts in dope-infested Height Ashbury.

They all wore smart black clothes, capes and polo-neck shirts, with the silver swastika emblem on a chain around their necks. Soon after they opened for business, a gaunt, long-haired, slightly built man with staring eyes came through the front door. His name was Charles Milles Manson and he lived just two blocks along the road at 636 Cole Street. He had moved there at the end of March 1967, having just been freed from a long prison sentence for car theft and pimping.

Very soon, Manson was a regular visitor to the headquarters of The Process and was admitted successively into the system of the so-called Church, reaching the fourth of the six levels of initiation, that of 'prophet'. At the end of 1968, he was established as a leader of a group which he called Satan's Slaves.

At the beginning of 1969, The Process Church and its British members moved into Los Angeles. Manson and his 'family' followed in their black-painted bus which doubled as a mobile satanic temple, inside which one of his new members, Bobby Beausoleil, painted the image of the Baphomet, the insignia of satanism which had also hung in Anton LaVey's San Francisco temple.

In the midst of this activity *Rosemary's Baby* had been released, causing a sensation in the occult world. Polanski, with LaVey's help, had unwittingly inspired an upsurge of interest in satanism into the public eye. Doreen Valiente, the Brighton witch–author, claims that the film had angered some satanic groups for revealing secrets they felt should have been kept within the occult movement. She said that the occult grapevine recorded that Polanski had received threats against himself and his family in the film's wake. Some who felt LaVey had betrayed them left his organization to form their own more sinister sect, the Temple of Set, which has since mushroomed into a world-wide order under the leadership of Michael Aquino.

Other groups had been setting up in the wake of the publicity. DeGrimston sent members to several cities to form branches of The Process while he himself moved to New York and opened up new headquarters in Greenwich Village. Manson and his 'family' were extending steadily, recruiting teenage drop-outs and dope addicts. They moved to a deserted old property known as Spahn's Movie Ranch in the Californian desert, which had once been the setting for countless westerns, and there his commune performed orgiastic sex and blood-lust rites.

The final link was established with the coincidence of Manson himself coming face to face with Sharon Tate when he called at Cielo Drive on 23 March 1969, and discovered that Roman Polanski, not Terry Melcher, lived at the secluded residence on the narrow, winding drive in Beverly Hills.

Chapter Fourteen

The Polanskis had lingered too long in London. Roman was still obsessed by his film script for *The Day of the Dolphin*, which was not working out. European premieres of *Rosemary's Baby* meant he was in great demand, and France had surprised him by recognizing the movie – it was shown there uncut. Peter Sellers often went with Polanski to the premiere junkets, just for the party – they might be lunching in London and having dinner in Vienna or some Scandinavian capital, and then back again to London, which was something out of the ordinary even for the late sixties.

Sharon was getting impatient. She had completed sound-dubbing on her film for Gassman and wanted to get back to Los Angeles well ahead of the time her baby was due: they had agreed she would have the child on American soil. At the end of July 1969 she gave Polanski an ultimatum: it was time to go home.

She was by now in the eighth month of her pregnancy and no airline would take her, so Polanski booked her a sea crossing to New York on the *QE2*. Sharon wanted him to join her on the cruise, but he insisted upon staying. He needed a couple of weeks alone to work on the script. Certain parts of the book, in which dolphins were made to communicate by a series of squeaks, were barely transferable to a movie.

So Sharon faced the tiresome journey alone, a heavily pregnant woman with her luggage and a tiny Yorkshire terrier Polanski had bought her in London to replace their pet dog in Los Angeles which Wojtek Frykowski had accidentally run over and killed. Even Roman's closest friends, like Gene Gutowski, were surprised by his insistence on delaying the journey. On the very day Sharon sailed, Polanski went round to Victor Lownes's in the evening for yet another party with the usual scenario of wall-to-wall girls. The draw of the social life was as vigorous as ever. Day after day, he put off his return. There were good playmates around, including Warren Beatty who had just finished filming *The Only Game in Town* in Paris with Elizabeth Taylor. With production delayed by Taylor's recurring back problem, Beatty had been in and out of London and was staying for a short while with his current girlfriend, Julie Christie, before they too headed back to Los Angeles. Richard Sylbert, the production designer, was also in town: he would be one of Polanski's staunchest friends during the traumatic developments to come.

There were some heated telephone conversations between the Polanskis during the first week of August and Sharon said she wondered whether Roman was ever coming back. Polanski told her it would not be long now. He was wrestling with the last pages of script on two areas of the film which he believed would present problems when it came to filming. Andy Braunsberg, who was producing the picture, had brought in a London writer to help with the last scenes.

Even so, on Friday, 8 August, Polanski had still not even bothered to obtain a renewal of his visa for entry into the US, so the likelihood of him returning before the middle of the following week seemed, in reality, an impossibility. However, that day during his last telephone conversation with Sharon, he promised he would return in four days. The conversation was overheard at the Los Angeles end by Winnie Chapman, Sharon's maid and housekeeper, whose evidence later formed part of a police reconstruction of the final twenty-four hours at 10050 Cielo Drive. Chapman said she heard Sharon ask Polanski if he would be back by 18 August, his birthday – she was planning a large party. He assured her he would be home by 12 August. Sharon told him she had enrolled him in a course for expectant fathers and that Frank Guerrero, the decorator, had arrived and was painting the far end of the house which would be the nursery.

At lunch-time in Los Angeles, Sharon entertained two friends, Joanna Pettet and Barbara Lewis, and spent an hour telling them that Roman was a bastard for leaving her alone with Frykowski and Gibby and that if it hadn't been for Jay Sebring, she would have gone out of her mind. Barbara said she and Joanna understood how she felt. The last few weeks of pregnancy were perhaps the most difficult and nerve-racking, as any new mother well knew. 'That's probably why the little rat is still in London,' said Sharon. 'He can't stand the sight of me fat and bloated, and he can't abide having me and my nerves around while he is working.'

After the two women left around 3.30 p.m., Sharon swam in the pool to cool down. Then she went to her bedroom to lie down before dinner. Jay Sebring telephoned very soon afterwards, apparently to say that he would be calling in earlier than expected. His butler Armos Russell would report that around 3.30 p.m. he served Sebring and his current girlfriend coffee in bed. Afterwards, Sebring showered, made some business calls and left his house.

At 4.30 p.m. Gibby Folger visited her analyst. She was coming through an emotional time in both her occupational work and her personal life and saw Dr Marvin Flicker every day of the week, Monday to Friday, at the same time. She was depressed about her work, about her drug habit and about Frykowski. Flicker would tell the police that she was on the verge of breaking with him.

Frykowski arrived back at Cielo Drive around 7 p.m. and he and Gibby Folger went with Sharon and Sebring to dinner at the El Coyote restaurant. Both Frykowski and Gibby had taken a virulent form of speed; traces of it were later found in both their bodies. They argued constantly. A Los Angeles Police Department (LAPD) report on their relationship would conclude that Frykowski lived off Folger, was involved in the Los Angeles drug scene and was a heavy user himself. The four of them returned home and the events between then and the time when their bodies were found would only be discovered from the confession of Susan Atkins, one of those who came into the house on their terrible mission.

It was around midnight when a battered white and yellow Ford drove slowly along the quiet, secluded street and turned into the grounds of the Polanski house. The car carried four 'apostles' of Charles Manson: they were Charlie 'Tex' Watson, Susan Atkins, known in the group as Sadie May Glutz, as she had been 'rechristened' by Manson, Patricia Krenwikle and Linda Kasabian who was to be posted outside as a lookout. Manson had ordered them to kill everyone in the house in a ritualistic fashion, and leave a message.

As they approached, Watson spotted a young man, Steven Parent, in his car. The eighteen-year-old youth had no connection with the Polanski household. He was visiting a friend, William Garretson, who acted as caretaker to the property and lived in a small cottage in the grounds. Watson, a strong twenty-two-year old who had been a former football star in his home town in Texas before he dropped out of college and fell into the drug scene of San Francisco, walked over and shot Parent twice in the chest and once in the head.

151

Watson and two of the women then ran across the lawns to the house. The doors were still open, because Sharon and the others had not finally retired for the evening. Armed with the gun, knives and a bayonet, they went into the sitting room where they found Frykowski fast asleep on a large sofa which had the American flag draped over the back. Watson kicked him and Frykowski awoke to find the nozzle of a .22 Buntline Special pointing up his nose. In reply to Frykowski's dazed questions about what kind of game this was, and had Roman put them up to it, Watson replied, 'I am the Devil. I'm here to do the Devil's business.'

Watson sent the others to check the rest of the house and to bring everyone into the sitting room. They found Gibby Folger in her bedroom. Sharon was in bed, wearing her bra and panties. Jay Sebring was sitting on the side of the bed smoking a marijuana cigarette. They were all ordered into the sitting room, protesting in disbelief that this could be happening. As instructed by Manson, Watson had brought a long rope with him which he flung over one of the exposed beams in the sitting room and linked two of his victims together by putting a noose around their necks.

Jay Sebring was the first to die. He was shot in the back for protesting and mentioning the name of Christ. He was also stabbed seven times. Frykowski managed to break free but was stabbed and then shot as he tried to get out of the house. His battle with the attackers was a ferocious one, to which they replied with apparent frenzy. He was stabbed fifty-one times, was shot twice and was pistol-whipped around the head with such force, causing thirteen separate wounds, that the handle of the gun had broken. He reached the front porch where he was stabbed for the last time, but even then managed to crawl a few yards further across the lawn, where he died.

Gibby Folger also made an attempt to run away and had been cut down with a bayonet. She received twenty-eight stab wounds.

Sharon Tate, who apparently stood transfixed and screaming with the noose around her neck, saw all that went on while Tex Watson taunted her with shouts of 'Piggy'. Now, with the rest dead, it was her turn. Watson thrust his bayonet into Sharon's chest. Atkins pounced upon Sharon as she slumped to the floor. Atkins planned to cut out her unborn baby and carry it back to Manson for ritualistic purposes, but Watson suddenly pronounced it was time to leave. Amazingly, Sharon was still alive when Atkins dabbed a towel into her wounds and scrawled the message 'PIG' on the wall. Then she plunged her knife back into Sharon, a blow which finally killed her. She too had twenty-eight stab wounds. The gang drove off in the Ford back to Manson.

Next morning, Sharon's mother telephoned the house repeatedly and could get no reply. Finally, she called Polanski's agent and family friend Bill Tennant, whose wife Sandy said he was out playing tennis but she would call him and get him to go to Cielo Drive. Sandy also tried telephoning and finally reached her husband who drove to the house still in his tennis clothes. By the time he arrived, Cielo Drive was sealed off by police cars and emergency vehicles. Winifred Chapman, arriving at the house for her duties that morning, had found the terrible scene of massacre and mutilation.

Reporters and television crews, alerted by police radio broadcasts, were all around, beginning what would become a week-long vigil camped outside Polanski's house. Tennant forced his way through and, completely oblivious to what would confront him inside, was physically sick when he saw the bodies. It took fifteen minutes or so before he completed the formalities of identification, as requested of him by the LAPD, and he then had to face the task of telephoning London.

It was mid-evening and Polanski was at the mews house with Andy Braunsberg and writer Michael Braun, discussing final adjustments to the script. He was about to get himself ready to leave the house to meet Victor Lownes for dinner when the telephone rang. Slowly, Tennant broke the news, giving it to him piece by piece, that there had been a terrible disaster, that Sharon was dead, Jay Sebring was dead, and so were Wojtek and Gibby. Polanski collapsed and let the telephone drop. Braunsberg picked it up and got the full story from Tennant.

Braunsberg immediately called Gene Gutowski, then Victor Lownes, who both arrived in double-quick time. By then the news had spread over the news wires and the telephone was ringing constantly. While Gutowski sent for a local doctor to give Polanski a tranquillizing injection, Lownes began to organize for them all to fly to Los Angeles immediately. He called the American consul and managed to get him to issue an emergency visa for Polanski's immediate entry into the USA. Warren Beatty was told and came straight to the house. Lownes and Beatty booked first-class seats on the next PanAm jet and arrangements were made at the other end for an immigration officer to board the plane to give Polanski clear entrance, so that he could be taken from the airport to avoid the gathering horde of media people. Arrangements were made for him to stay in the security of the Paramount compound. Robert

Evans gave him Julie Andrews' recently vacated dressing room and studio doctors kept him sedated for shock.

The reaction to the massacre was astounding, shocking, and cast doubts in the minds of even Roman's closest friends as to just exactly what had been going on in the Polanski household. The police investigation ignored many early leads and, although Manson and his gang would be arrested in connection with another matter, it would be months before they were charged with the Tate murders – and almost two years before they were finally found guilty and sentenced. So the background of Manson's own links to Devil cults and inverted religion was unknown.

The void between the terrible events at Cielo Drive and the point at which Manson was charged created an arena of incredible speculation, gossip and fear in which there was a surprising lack of compassion towards Polanski himself. The media, and Hollywood itself, after an early expression of sympathy, turned upon him with a ferocity best summed up by his friend Jack Nicholson: 'His situation was a very interesting case of what notoriety can do to you. He would be excommunicated by Hollywood because his wife had the very bad taste to be murdered in the newspapers.'

The volatile society of Hollywood was running scared. Doors were being slammed tight. The price of guard dogs doubled. One Beverly Hills gun shop reported sales of 200 weapons in the forty-eight hours after the killings whereas normally it would expect to sell only three or four. Mia Farrow went into hiding because, a relative explained, 'She is afraid that she will be next.' Frank Sinatra doubled his guard. Tony Bennett checked into a hotel. There was hostility, too, in many quarters against Polanski himself. One striking example of this came a little later, when Polanski moved in with Mike Sarne who was renting a house in Malibu while in Hollywood to make a film. Sarne's neighbours got up a petition which they delivered to his front door, requesting that Mr Polanski leave the vicinity because he might attract dangerous elements. Sarne told them to 'fuck off'.

None the less, more than 150 mourners attended Sharon's funeral service at the Holy Cross Cemetery, including Kirk Douglas, Warren Beatty, Steve McQueen, James Cockburn, Yul Brynner, John and Michelle Phillips and Peter Sellers. Several of them also attended the funeral of Sebring, joining a number of his famous-name clients, like Paul Newman, Henry and Peter Fonda and George Hamilton.

Many others, however, began distancing themselves from Polanski.

Indications of how high feelings against him were running were best summed up in a 2000-word article in the *New York Times*. It claimed that the Polanskis were near the centre of a loose group of film-makers who were described with all the current clichés: hip, mod, swinging and trendy. 'Its members,' according to a senior film company executive who did not wish to be named, 'are rootless vagabonds at home in a dozen places and yet belonging nowhere. Their names never appeared on the tourist maps of where to find the stars because they had no homes.' Thus, the senior executive was saying, Polanski 'is not one of us'. According to the article, the Polanskis made money and spent it, like most of their friends, on expensive clothes, flash cars and fast living – the original jetsetters. Their philosophy was 'Eat, drink and be merry, for tomorrow your agent may not call.' They 'exuded a magnetism that people just wanted to be near'.

All that had very quickly changed. With the absence of any arrests, there were some wild stories going around, even suggestions that Roman himself might be implicated in the murders – hence his reluctance to return to Los Angeles. He in turn would begin to suggest his own suspects, who would include a couple of close friends.

The gossip was fed by a strong undercurrent of rumour which painted a colourful scenario at Cielo Drive of sex, drugs, kinky relationships, orgies and ritualistic black magic and witchcraft. All had their part to play in the story in one way or another, but the very presence of each individual element, however tenuous and unproven, was sufficient for even major, respected news magazines to bind them together in a horrific package of fanciful and exaggerated claims which built into a vivid portrayal of unadulterated vice.

There were sufficient pointers which could be used in evidence. The drug histories of Frykowski and Folger would very soon surface, and would be built upon. A rumour went around that Sebring ran a side-line business as a pusher, which, though true to a limited degree, was blown up into major allegations in which he was portrayed as a heavy dealer and a sex fiend who ran bondage parties. It was noticeable, however, that the police did not consider either a significant aspect of the murder inquiry. They interviewed past girlfriends – dozens of them – and discovered that at worst, the kinky sex was mild bondage in which no one got hurt.

Descriptions of the murder itself ran riot. It was reported in a number of places that one of Sharon's breasts was cut off, that she was naked and bonded by rope to Sebring who was wearing only torn boxer shorts, and a black hood over his head, that he had been castrated and his heart cut out. The truth was that Sebring had on a shirt and pants. The hood was a blood-soaked towel that Atkins had flung on him as she left the house, and his body was not mutilated in the manner described, except for the stab wounds.

Sharon, though badly mutilated, had not had one of her breasts removed. Nor was it true that a cross had been carved on her stomach. Though Polanski himself could put an answer to almost every one of what he would regard as inaccuracies – the black magic, the kinky sex, the drug-dealing – there was enough in each strand of the story to add up to an incredibly squalid tale which would leave Hollywood with the belief that, one way or another, the victims had brought this disaster down upon their own heads.

Out of the woodwork crawled numerous people claiming to have knowledge of the past few months of Sharon's life. Associates of Sebring were seemingly all too happy to talk dirty to the press, and this ballooned into an appalling exaggeration of events which were shocking enough even without the elaboration.

There was another factor. Hollywood itself was in the grip of change which was almost frightening to the establishment and less liberal-minded, and that change fuelled a physical fear that violence was blowing up in people's faces. This had in part already been reflected at the beginning of the year, with the débâcle over Warren Beatty's film *Bonnie and Clyde*. *Newsweek*'s Joseph Morgenstern, along with several other leading critics, had branded the film 'the most gruesome carnage since Verdun and for those who find killing less than hilarious, the effect is stomach-churning'. The controversy over its violence had continued to remain a focal point of what *Time* magazine labelled 'The New Cinema: Violence, Sex and Art'. A cabal of new movie-makers, including Beatty, Mike Nichols, Arthur Penn and Polanski himself, were named as the pathfinders, and Polanski's own movie, *Rosemary's Baby*, continued to figure high up in the debate.

Thus when the media were confronted with the Sharon Tate murders, the blurring of the edges between fact and fiction, and the ongoing discussions about sex and violence being pumped out by Hollywood, *Newsweek* and *Time*, forefront opinion-formers in the international news magazine arena, let rip. 'Almost as enchanting as the mystery [of the killings] was the glimpse the murders yielded into the surprising Hollywood sub-culture,' said *Newsweek*, 'in which the cast of characters played . . . Hollywood gossip about the case was of drugs, mysticism and offbeat sex – and for once, there was more truth than fantasy in the flashy talk of the town. The theme of the melodrama was drugs. Some suspect the group was amusing itself with some sort of black magic rites . . .'

This allegation was unfounded. The ritual may well have been present but, as would eventually be discovered, was imported by the Manson gang and had nothing to do with those present in the house at 10050 Cielo Drive that night: there was no party going on.

Time magazine focused on Polanski himself, and compared the scene to 'as grisly as anything depicted in Polanski's film explorations of dark and melancholy corners of the human characters. The theories on sex, drugs and witchcraft cults [were] fed by the fact that Sharon and Polanski circulated in one of the film world's more offbeat crowds.'

Time made mention of the Polanskis' wild and wonderful parties at which it alleged all kinds of unsavoury and often unknown persons were present and concluded that the most likely theory to the mystery was that the murders were related to narcotics. But, again, the topic of drugs itself was under close scrutiny and intense discussion. Only the previous month in Britain, the Wootton Report on Drug Dependency recommended substantially reduced penalties for pot-smoking. Celebrities on both sides of the Atlantic had put their names to various advertisements calling for the legalization of pot.

Drugs certainly featured in Polanski's scene. A number of those in his crowd smoked joints, took LSD, experimented with mescaline and snorted cocaine. Drugs were an integral part of the era. As Richard Sylbert said, 'Toilets are flushing all over Beverly Hills. The entire Los Angeles sewerage system is stoned.' This seemed to be taken as some kind of joke, but Sylbert reflectively pin-pointed this moment in history as 'the end of the fun and games in the sixties – the end of a joke. Everybody became Presbyterian overnight.'

So, as Nicholson later pointed out, Sharon Tate was murdered twice – once by the Manson gang and again by the media. Polanski was alive, but faring badly under the intensity of the spotlight – just when it appeared to be fading a little, some new revelation would emerge.

Dennis Hopper, himself a leading star of the counter-culture movement and avid partaker of every kind of chemical and mind-bending substance available at the time, did not help with his assessment: 'The people at the Tate house were killed because they were into bad shit. What goes around comes around. The people at the Tate house were victims of themselves because they had fallen into sado-masochism and

157

recorded it on video-tape. The LA police told me this. I know that three days before they were killed, twenty-five people were invited to that house to watch the mass whipping of a dealer from Sunset Strip who had given them some bad dope. And Jay Sebring was a friend of mine . . .'

The truth of such colourful tales is beyond reach. Polanski would explain away the video-tape, found by detectives searching the house, as being one he had filmed of himself and Sharon making love – a fact later confirmed by the police who viewed it. No other photographs or videos were found at the house, apart from their wedding pictures and Sharon's film-still gallery, which presumably were the basis for another scurrilous tale about the 'mass of pornographic photographs' featuring a number of famous Hollywood people.

The frantic hysteria heightened ten days after the killings at Cielo Drive, when there was another massacre, also carried out by the gang which killed Sharon and her friends though this was not known at the time. Manson himself headed the second killings. They slaughtered supermarket millionaire Leno LaBianca and his wife Rosemary in similar horrific fashion. The couple had been tortured, half garrotted and stabbed. The word 'PIGS' was scrawled in blood on the wall, thus linking the Tate and LaBianca murders, but as yet there were no suspects in sight.

Now Hollywood was really scared. The film industry itself was taking some of the flak, and the release that summer of *Easy Rider*, the film that made Jack Nicholson a star, gave Hollywood further cause to take a look at itself and what was happening on its own doorstep. *Easy Rider*, co-starring Dennis Hopper and Peter Fonda, became the film of the moment, a marijuana-soaked essay in everything that was wrong with American society.

The wallowing in the death of Sharon Tate and her friends was extensive and unappealing, but the continuation of it came from a surprising source – Roman Polanski himself, as featured in the 29 August issue of *Life* magazine, for which he was strongly criticized. *Life* writer Tommy Thompson, who had met Polanski in London, contacted him and suggested that he might like to 'put the record straight'.

Polanski agreed – and was later at pains to point out it had nothing to do with money, dismissing rumours he was paid $5000 for his cooperation. One hot Sunday afternoon he and Thompson with his cameraman drove to Cielo Drive. Thompson also brought along the 'famed psychic' Peter Hurkos, who had worked with police in the

158

Boston Strangler case, to see if he could make 'contact' and discover some mystic clues. Thompson asked Polanski if he had any objections to Hurkos attempting to 'make some psychic connections' which might help. Polanski agreed, and also allowed Hurkos to take some Polaroid photographs of the scene to help him in his work – which Hurkos promptly sold to a newspaper.

It was the first time Polanski had been to the house since the murders. 'This is the world-famous orgy house,' he said with bitter sarcasm as he drove into the driveway where Jay Sebring's Porsche and Gibby Folger's Ford were still parked. He got out of the car and stopped for a moment to look at the broken fence, which Steven Parent had backed into while frantically trying to escape his executioners. They walked on past the swimming pool; a blue bedsheet which Gibby Folger had used for sun-bathing still lay under the pine trees. The pool was scattered with debris, leaves, floats and airbeds which had remained untouched. There was a large blown-up rubber tyre that Sharon had bought so that she could float around the pool when she was pregnant.

On the front doorstep, a pool of blood where Frykowski had fallen had dried into a dark patch. The word 'PIG' scrawled in blood on the white door to the hall, though fading, was as poignant as ever. They walked through the hall into the living room, a large spacious area with white walls and white beams, with a redwood ladder leading to an open loft above.

Large beige velvet-covered chairs and sofas, a baby grand piano and a mahogany rocking chair were positioned round a huge fireplace, and in the centre was a zebra-skin rug. In front of the sofas were smears of blood where Jay Sebring and Sharon were found. Polanski stood for a moment or two looking around, and kept repeating, 'Why . . . ?'

They walked on through to the master bedroom, where the king-sized double bed looked as if someone had just risen from it. The pillows were just as Sharon had left them, and the lime-green and orange sheets were slung back on one side only. He walked back into the hall and found some blood-spots on the carpet. 'They hit her here,' he said. 'She tried to get out . . . and they dragged her back into the living room . . .'

They wandered back through the rooms, and Polanski posed for photographs, even sitting on the blood-spattered porch where Frykowski's body was found.

'How long had Frykowski been here?' Thompson asked.

'Too long, I guess,' Polanski replied. 'I should have thrown him out when he ran over Sharon's dog.'

Though the article had been designed to 'set the record straight', it was a skilful piece of magazine voyeurism, and did nothing to quell rumours of strange happenings prior to the murders. Thompson reported that 'Roman did not know what was going on at the house while he was away. All he knew was that one of his beloved Poles [Frykowski] was staying there. Sharon probably knew but she was too nice or too dumb to throw him out. If any creeps or weirdos went up there it wasn't on Sharon's invitation.'

By then, the whole business was turning into something of a circus. The presence of the 'famed psychic' Peter Hurkos became a publicity stunt when, the following week, an advertisement appeared in the local *Citizen News*, announcing, 'Peter Hurkos, famed for his consultation in murder cases (including the current Sharon Tate massacre) opens Friday night at the Huntington Hartford, appearing through August 30.'

There were others. Truman Capote, whose chilling, true-life book and film, *In Cold Blood*, had appeared the previous year, went on the Johnny Carson show to give his view of the killings. Millions of viewers clung to his every word as he authoritatively pronounced that the murders were the work of a lone killer who had been at the house earlier, was struck by some form of 'instant paranoia', went home to get a knife and a gun and returned to assassinate everyone in the house.

Capote's colourful theory was as off-beam as anyone's, not least the LAPD who had considered the same theory. They arrested William Garretson, the young caretaker who was the only person in the compound at 10050 Cielo Drive to survive, who said he had seen nothing, heard nothing. He was given a lie-detector test, and subsequently released.

Suspicions grew out of thin air; the police asked Polanski to draw up a list of friends and associates who might be considered as possible suspects or who might have knowledge to be revealed under questioning. It could have been a revenge attack, or drugs-connected, and even Polanski's father-in-law, Colonel Paul Tate, a former Intelligence officer, grew a beard and put on a hippie disguise and began frequenting the bars and discos along Sunset Boulevard where the drug dealers hung out.

Among those on the list of subjects for scrutiny were Polanski's old friend from Lodz, the novelist Jerzy Kosinski, and the singer John Phillips, who was once a target for contact by Robert DeGrimston Moore. Kosinski had given interviews to the press stating that he had

160

been invited to stay at the Polanski house and would have been there on the night of the murders had his luggage not been lost at the airport. Victor Lownes thought it odd that Kosinski should say that, for as far as he and Polanski knew, there had been no invitation to the house to Kosinski.

So, on his way back to London, Lownes read Kosinski's book, *Steps*, which was written in the first person and filled with violent scenes. Back in London, he composed a letter to the Los Angeles Police Department suggesting they should question Kosinski further. 'Is it just remotely possible', he wrote, 'that the author of such weird material might himself be a very weird person indeed? I know the suggestion is extremely far-fetched but surely it is worthwhile to check on the mixed-up luggage story . . . and Kosinski's whereabouts that weekend?'

The idea was indeed far-fetched. Kosinski, as it would eventually be proved, had no connection whatever with the killings. Nor did John Phillips, one of Polanski's closest friends, yet he too fell into the area of suspicion. Polanski never really explained the reasons for his suspicions about Phillips, beyond the fact that Phillips knew that he had had a brief liaison with his wife Michelle (who soon afterwards married Dennis Hopper, left him after eight days, moved in with Jack Nicholson and later still with Warren Beatty). Polanski knew of Phillips's separation from Michelle, and the couple's bitter custody battle over their daughter China. 'In spite of his outward calm, he had the capacity for a deep, burning anger,' said Polanski.

So Phillips was on the list of people who might be investigated by the LAPD and Polanski did some detective work of his own. He went to Phillips's house one night to search the garage and check his cars for bloodstains. Then came a curious incident that, with hindsight, seemed to have greater significance than was admitted at the time.

One day when Phillips was driving Polanski into Los Angeles in his vintage Rolls Royce convertible, they were stopped by a police cruiser. The officers claimed Phillips was wanted for non-payment of traffic fines and asked him to accompany them to the precinct, leaving Polanski to drive the Rolls. Polanski was left alone with the car long enough to make a search, and found a diary which Phillips had left in a bag. He found the entries were all in capital letters, and he believed the writing was remarkably similar to the single word 'PIG' which had been scrawled at Cielo Drive.

Polanski hurriedly got a couple of pages photocopied and sent them off to a handwriting expert to compare with a photograph of the 'PIG'

161

word – but it was all a futile exercise. There was nothing conclusive in the tests, and as time would show, Phillips had nothing to do with the murders.

Few of his friends knew, either, that Polanski agreed to undergo the lie detector test set up by the Los Angeles homicide division. The results of the tests, conducted by Lieutenant Earl Deemer, threw little light on the murder but were revealing in Polanski's attitudes and the details of his relationships, as we have seen from extracts quoted in earlier chapters. It also dismissed any nagging doubts the police investigators might have had on the possibility that Polanski had concealed anything from them.

Deemer wanted to know whether there was a possibility that Sharon and Sebring had ever revived their relationship.

Polanski insisted: 'Not a chance. I am the bad one. I always screw around. That was Sharon's big hang-up, you know. But she was not interested in Jay . . . There was not a chance of any other man getting close to Sharon.'

The final part of Deemer's interview for the polygraph test consisted of brief questions and answers:

'Did you have anything to do with taking the life of Wojtek and the others?'

'No.'

'Do you feel any responsibility for the deaths of Wojtek and the others?'

'Yes. I feel responsible that I wasn't there, that is all.'

'From running this thing through your mind, who have you come up with as the target?'

'I've thought of everything. I thought the target could be myself.'

'Why?'

'Jealousy or a plot or something. It couldn't be Sharon directly. If Sharon were the target, it would mean I was the target. It could be Jay was the target. It could be Wojtek . . . or someone who decided to commit a crime.'

'What would Sebring be doing, for instance, to make him a target?'

'Some money thing, maybe. I've also heard a lot about this drug thing, drug deliveries. It's difficult to believe . . . but the indication to me is that he must have been in serious financial trouble despite the appearances he gave.'

Deemer wanted to know about drug-taking in the Polanski household. '[Sharon] took no drugs at all except for pot and during her pregnancy

162

there was no question, she was so much in love with her pregnancy she would do nothing.'

'Did you receive any hate mail after the film *Rosemary's Baby*?'

'Yes, some. And it's possible this could be some type of witchcraft thing, you know. A maniac or something. This execution, this tragedy, indicates to me it must be some kind of nut . . . I wouldn't be surprised if I were the target. In spite of all this drug thing, I think the police jumped too hastily on this type of lead, you know. Because it is their usual type of lead . . .'

Leads or not, the police at that moment in time were no nearer a breakthrough in the case than they had been from the beginning of the investigation. Hundreds of man-hours had been devoted to the Tate–LaBianca murders, and by mid-September the edginess in Hollywood was reflected through the local media which were, by then, beginning to demand action. None realized at the time that a most vital lead had already been overlooked, the fact that Charles Manson and his 'family' had already been arrested in a raid by detectives investigating a third homicide.

Chapter Fifteen

*P*eter Sellers was on the telephone all morning of 8 September, exactly a month after the murders. The police were no further forward than they had been on day one. Sellers wanted to set up a reward for information leading to the arrest of Sharon's killers but the police were against the idea on the grounds that it would attract a thousand and one cranks, each of whom would come in with a different story that would have to be investigated. The LAPD could quote some daunting statistics so far: fingerprints had been checked against 41,034 samples on file; 18,000 opticians had been contacted over a pair of spectacles found at the scene; 4500 people had been interviewed on a one-to-one basis . . . and so on.

Polanski agreed with Sellers who made a contribution towards a reward fund, as did Warren Beatty and Yul Brynner, along with Polanski himself. On 10 September they placed an advertisement in a Los Angeles newspaper: 'REWARD $25,000 . . . Roman Polanski and friends of the Polanski family offer to pay $25,000 reward to the person or persons who furnish information leading to the arrest and conviction of the murderer or murderers of Sharon Tate, her unborn child and the other four victims. Persons wishing to remain anonymous should provide sufficient means for later identification, one method of which is to tear this newspaper page in half, transmit one half for matching up later. In the event that more than one person is entitled to the reward, the reward will be divided equally between them.'

Peter Sellers gave a press conference to announce the reward and said, 'Someone must have knowledge or even suspicions that they are withholding or are perhaps afraid to reveal. It is inconceivable that the amount of blood on clothing could have gone unnoticed. So where is the blood-soaked clothing, the knife, the gun, the getaway car? . . . Someone must be able to help. Please!'

The reaction to the advertisement was astonishing. Police fears of an overwhelming response from cranks were well founded: Sharon and her friends had been assassinated variously by the Polish Secret Police, a Nazi group from Odessa, the Black Power movement, the Mafia, a Voodoo sect from Jamaica and even by a man who didn't come home that night and refused to account to his wife for his movements. Every kind of hustler, hoaxer and fantasizer came forward with a theory. But eventually, the reward money would have a positive effect in a totally unexpected direction.

Detectives working on the Tate–LaBianca murders completely ignored facts which were brought to their attention by other officers in the LAPD. There had been another murder a few days before the massacre at Cielo Drive – the body of a thirty-four-year-old hippie music teacher named Gary Hinman was found at his Los Angeles home on 31 July. On 6 August police had picked up Bobby Beausoleil, the young man who had played Lucifer in Kenneth Anger's film *Lucifer Rising*. Beausoleil was found in possession of Hinman's car and was in custody as the number one murder suspect in the Hinman case when the Tate massacres took place.

Soon after the Tate murders, detectives working on the Hinman investigation reported one striking similarity to what had happened at Cielo Drive and at the LaBianca house. The words 'POLITICAL PIGGY' had been scrawled in blood on Hinman's wall. The clue, for some reason, was never taken up by the Tate–LaBianca team. Yet another blunder occurred when detectives discovered that Hinman had befriended a group of hippies known as 'the family', whose leader was Charles Manson and who lived in the deserted ramshackle Spahn's Movie Ranch in Chatsworth. Beausoleil was known to be a member of the group.

On 16 August the Hinman team began a series of raids on the ranch and arrested twenty-four members of the group. Most were later freed. Since Beausoleil was in custody at the time of the Tate–LaBianca murders, any connection was apparently ruled out.

The weeks rolled by, with the teams working independently of each other. In the first week of October, police unconnected with either team went to investigate squatters at what was known as the Barker Ranch, an isolated property in rugged countryside in the south of Death Valley, California, and discovered that Manson and his 'family' had moved in. Manson had recently led his flock into the desert, where he proclaimed they would multiply until they reached 144,000 in number. While the police were looking around, two young girls came out of the bushes

165

and asked them for protection. One of them was the seventeen-year-old girlfriend of Bobby Beausoleil and was five months pregnant by him.

The girl was taken into protective custody, and when questioned said she had heard that Manson himself had sent Beausoleil to kill Hinman with a girl named Susan Atkins, a former disciple of Anton LaVey's Church of Satan and, as would soon be discovered, one of the most ruthless of the Tate–LaBianca killers.

What the Hinman team eventually discovered was that Beausoleil and Atkins went to Hinman's house on Friday, 25 July to get money from him, and that later that night Manson turned up at the house and slashed his ear. Hinman was not killed that night, but Atkins and Beausoleil remained at the house, holding him their captive until Sunday, 27 July when Manson and other members of 'the family' returned and killed Hinman. Beausoleil hot-wired Hinman's car, and they all drove off to Spahn's Movie Ranch.

Atkins was arrested after the raid on the Barker Ranch in Death Valley and under questioning talked only of the Hinman killing. Later, however, while in custody, she began to tell two prostitutes with whom she struck up a friendship of the killings at Cielo Drive. The prostitutes did not believe her at first, but subsequently one of them asked to see a detective to tell all she knew. Even then, her request was ignored, and two more weeks elapsed before the realization finally began to dawn upon the police authorities in Los Angeles that the murders of Hinman, the Cielo Drive group and the LaBianca couple were committed by the same people – The Manson 'family' – the all-important word 'PIG' or 'PIGGY' scrawled in the blood of the victims being present at each scene.

With the investigations placed on 18 November under the control of Vincent T. Bugliosi, the thirty-five-year-old deputy District Attorney for Los Angeles, events moved swiftly towards their conclusion, with Manson and other 'family' members finally charged with the Tate–LaBianca murders on 9 December, exactly five months after they had been committed.

In a way, the reward money offered by Polanski and his friends had paid off, certainly from the point of view of the prisoner who listened to Susan Atkins' rambling boasts about the killings, and eventually managed to tell what she had heard to detectives. She shared the $25,000 with a boy who found one of the murder weapons, a gun, in Benedict Canyon.

*   *   *

For Polanski, it was all over. The media pressure would become as intense as that which surrounded the murder itself, even more so when the full story of the Manson 'family', with its overtones of Satanic malevolence, emerged, followed by a mass of investigations, analysis, comment, speculation and, finally, the court hearings, which followed during the next two years.

From a personal point of view, Polanski had become a kind of a walking freak show. He flew to London to find peace and quiet, but the media were in place to welcome him. He went back to New York and met Beatty at Delmonico's where he had a suite, but could not settle. He returned to California and stayed with Richard Sylbert at his Malibu beach house, but was affected by intermittent bouts of weeping. 'He was quite distraught,' said Sylbert, 'and was still affected by what he perceived as guilt for not being there when it happened.' To one friend, Polanski even talked of suicide.

By then, the movie project *The Day of the Dolphin* had collapsed.* Polanski had turned in his completed script, and the producers had posted a budget of around $5 million. But United Artists pulled out. It remained an unalterable truth that in the eyes of many people in power, and certainly of the chattering classes, Polanski was persona non grata.

Once the one remaining obsession about the identity of the killers was resolved – in Polanski's mind at least, if prematurely – he set off for Paris to join Gerard Brach. As soon as he arrived, the Paris media camped on his doorstep in even greater numbers than in London. With headlines about Manson appearing daily by mid-December, Polanski remained the unavoidable focus of a thousand camera lenses.

Before leaving this most dramatic and tragic era of Polanski's life, it is worth recalling Polanski's own view of Manson and his selection of 10050 Cielo Drive for those most gruesome killings. He said publicly that he believed Manson was a spurned performer who sent his 'family' on its raiding party in the belief that Terry Melcher lived there. But he was either putting forward a false premise to cover his own inner feelings of having contributed in some way to the events, or simply refusing to believe that Manson might actually have targeted the house because he

* The option on *The Day of the Dolphin* was picked up by producer Robert E. Relyea, who hired Polanski's friend Buck Henry to write a new screenplay, Mike Nichols to direct, Richard Sylbert as production designer, and George C. Scott for the starring role. Perhaps Polanski was well out of it; the movie, released in 1973, ended up costing Avco-Embassy $8.5 million and was described by the critic Judith Crist as 'a Saturday afternoon special for sheltered nine year olds'.

knew it was the home of the Polanskis. Only years later did pieces of the jigsaw which confirmed this fact fall into place.

Back in Los Angeles in December 1969, Vincent Bugliosi was beginning to pull together all the strands of the Manson story, and much of what he discovered would never be made public. For one thing, he did not want to complicate the issue before the Federal Grand Jury with the complexities of occult and satanic cults. Bugliosi had decided to play down this aspect and go for straightforward first-degree murder, organized by a deranged lunatic and carried out by drug-addled followers.

Privately, however, Bugliosi knew that these undercurrents could not be ignored. As he began to piece together the background of Charles Manson, Bugliosi discovered that far from being a down-and-out hippie, he was an intelligent man who, like Robert DeGrimston Moore, founder of The Process, had been a member of the Church of Scientology.

Bugliosi's combined team of detectives was faced with the difficulty of proving Manson's involvement in the Hinman killing, and with convincing a jury that he had the power to control the minds of a group of people to the point where he could order them to go on their killing spree to Cielo Drive. In order to achieve this, Bugliosi had to upturn all the stones where clues might lie, deep in Manson's past. He very soon discovered the Satanic links – Susan Atkins' involvement with Anton LaVey's Church of Satan, Bobby Beausoleil's starring role as Lucifer in Kenneth Anger's movie, and Manson's own confrontation with the satanic sect of Robert DeGrimston Moore's Process Church when it moved to San Francisco.

The popular theory being offered to the public – even by Polanski himself – was that Manson's killers turned up by accident at 10050 Cielo Drive with the directive to murder whoever was inside. This was a naïve proposition. Sandra Good, Manson's girlfriend and mother of his child, reckoned Manson had been to the house four or five times before the murders, looking for Terry Melcher and/or the owner of the property, Rudi Altobelli. Tex Watson, the leader of the death gang, had been to the house when it was rented briefly to another person before the Polanskis moved in.

After the murders, Altobelli went into hiding. He was scared. It was a fact that he had met Manson previously at the home of Dennis Wilson of the Beach Boys in 1968. He knew, too, that Manson had called at the house on 23 March.

In December 1969 Manson was under arrest, though this did not necessarily render him incapable of ordering the murder of anyone he pleased by those of his 'family' still on the outside; he had already threatened to have Bugliosi killed. Altobelli was a reluctant witness to the time when Manson came face to face with four of the five people his 'family' would murder at Cielo Drive. He did not simply come forward and volunteer the information; Bugliosi had to persuade him to make a statement about what he knew. Altobelli was so scared that he and Terry Melcher, by then back with Candice Bergen, had gone into hiding at Doris Day's beach house at Malibu and would not come out. Terry Melcher hired a full-time bodyguard for months afterwards.

When Altobelli was finally located by the murder investigation team, he pleaded, 'I don't have to testify, do I?' This was the opening gambit of dozens of scared witnesses. Melcher asked if he could give his evidence in a private room and have it broadcast through microphones to the court. His request was refused.

While not wishing to linger too long on the Manson story, which has been told in its fullest detail by Vincent Bugliosi in his book, *Helter Skelter*, it is worth linking up the connections which readers may recall had begun two years earlier when Robert DeGrimston Moore's branch of The Process left London and set up shop in San Francisco just two blocks away from where Manson was living.

Soon after Manson was charged with eight murders, two members of The Process turned up at police headquarters and asked to see the detective in charge. They said they wished to make it clear that Manson was not a member of The Process. However, the following day, the same two people were booked in as prison visitors to see Manson, although it was not until years later, when The Process was being revived back in Britain, that he was finally acknowledged as one of their own.

An article by a Process revivalist in one of Britain's leading occult magazines, *Lamp of Thoth*, recorded in 1989:

Manson went astray where others in The Process have succeeded. He was sucked into the whirlpool of fame and fortune and where he didn't cut it, he decided to cut it up. Despite this, Manson speaks for a generation and is deserving of the cult following his infamy has secured . . . Manson was right when he said he was the scapegoat. In his way, he has a clear right to say he's Christ and also the Devil – Manson's intention was to open up the occult centres of perception by a unique pop-based outlook influenced primarily by The Process: in his terms, 'Getting Fear'. But Manson went astray where others in The Process have succeeded: HE GOT CAUGHT. A pity, really . . .

The article ended on a chilling note, affirming the re-formation of The Process and sending a message to their enemies and detractors: 'As the Family might have agreed . . . you'll get yours, yet. The Process will see to that . . .'

There, twenty years later, were encapsulated some of the underlying – and at the time unknown – beliefs that set Manson and his followers on their killings. He knew Sharon Tate was the wife of Roman Polanski, and that Polanski had made *Rosemary's Baby* in which Anton LaVey, head of the Church of Satan, had the effrontery to appear as the Devil.

Vincent Bugliosi delved deeply into that aspect, but perhaps never wanted this to be made public because theorizing about such matters in such an important case might have damaged the credibility of the evidence. He concentrated on getting a conviction with a hard-hitting presentation of the firmest facts in a case littered with imponderables, blind alleys, bungled investigations and weird occult beliefs. But he was clearly intrigued by the undercurrents. Interviewing Manson in prison one day, he asked him if he knew the Englishman, Robert DeGrimston Moore. Manson replied, 'He and I are one and the same', which the attorney took to mean that they held identical beliefs.

Bugliosi probed further into the occult dimensions, attempting to establish how Manson could control a large group of people. Susan Atkins and others in his 'family' confirmed repeatedly that his whole power over them centred on his claim to be the new Messiah, the Christ and the Devil in one, a duality through which Christ could give orders and the Devil would carry them out. Manson searched for inspiration from sources as diverse as the Bible and Beatles songs. He had memorized virtually all the main Beatles songs of the day, and would quote lines to which he had given his own meaning. At one point during the forthcoming trial, his lawyers were considering calling a number of celebrity witnesses, including John Lennon and John Phillips, to state how they themselves interpreted their songs which, he claimed, had had such an effect on Manson's thinking.

Little of the true underlying forces of Manson's motivation came to public knowledge during this period. But the whole aura which had quickly built up around him was sufficient for some sections of the American counter-culture movement to appoint him their hero.

The media depicted him as the epitome of evil. *Life* had put him on its front cover, a famous photograph with Manson's hypnotic stare which became the focus for the mass media in portraying him as the face of violent, drug-crazed substrata of society: the monster in the heart of every hippie and long-haired supporter of a culture which seemed to encompass an increasing section of youth and counter-culture movement bandwagonners.

Support for Manson was demonstrated at a meeting in Flint, Michigan that winter of 1969, staged by one of the most violent of protest groups, the Weathermen, where the centre-piece was a huge cardboard machine-gun hanging from the ceiling and attached ecumenically to a photograph on a 24-foot poster listing their enemies: Mayor Richard Daley, whose police had attacked peace demonstrators in Chicago; Ronald Reagan, who instructed police to take whatever action necessary to quell campus riots; Lyndon B. Johnson, Richard Nixon – and Sharon Tate.

Her presence in the list was symbolic, to show support for Manson. Never mind that he had murdered so many people. His act was, in their eyes, a guerilla attack. One of the Weathermen's leaders – whose activities so concerned the FBI that they were subject to twenty-four-hour surveillance – went to visit Manson in prison and returned to announce, 'I fell in love with Charlie Manson the first time I saw his cherub face and sparkling eyes. His words and courage inspired me . . . I felt great the rest of the day.'

Manson himself was allowed to write a column while in jail for the underground newspaper the *Los Angeles Free Press*, which also ran free adverts for tapes of his songs. Another magazine, *Tuesday's Child*, depicted him on a cross. When he decided he wanted his life story told on film, he sent for three other great heroes of the counter-culture, direct from their starring roles in *Easy Rider* – Dennis Hopper, Peter Fonda and Jack Nicholson, whose film had become the rage of 1969 at a time when the whole counter-culture movement had taken on an explosive, manic air.

Manson's lawyers fixed up a meeting between Hopper and their client and they had a two-hour session in a room on the eighth floor of the Los Angeles Hall of Justice. Meanwhile, Nicholson himself began attending the daily trial proceedings, taking copious notes. He said he was personally interested in observing the machinations of a non-sequestered jury. 'I just wanted to see for myself,' he said, though leaving unmentioned the effect this connection with and observation of one of the most macabre murders of the last half-century might have had on his friend Roman Polanski.

171

In the event, the film never got made. Not even the fringes of Hollywood from which Hopper and Fonda had secured finance for *Easy Rider* were interested in exploiting the Tate murders for which Manson and his cronies were sentenced to death, the penalty subsequently being commuted to life.

Twenty-one years later, this author made contact with Manson at Corcoran Prison, San Joaquin, California where he is an inmate for life along with the killer of Robert Kennedy, Sirhan Sirhan. Manson was ready to talk to me about the beliefs and contacts he had at the time, and the prison authorities gave their approval for the interview.

At the last minute, however, Sandra Good, who had herself just completed a prison sentence in connection with other matters, telephoned. Manson had sent a message about the proposed visit. 'Charlie is having problems,' she said. 'He wants to talk to you, but they insist on shackling him in irons, hand and foot, for the meeting. He thinks this is degrading and will only meet you if you can get them to take off his irons.'

There was no point in such a request. The prison authorities had already told me of their concern for the security of visitors during interviews and so Manson remained unmet.

What remained with Polanski at the end of 1969, as Manson and the 'family' provided month upon month of murder trial headlines, was guilt that had he arrived in California earlier and not lingered in London, he might have been able to have prevented the murders. In darker moods, he would go over the scene with friends, always suggesting that had he been in the house he and Frykowski might have beaten the attackers off. The 'guilt' in this respect masks several other ifs and buts. If he had been home, Frykowski and Gibby Folger would by then have returned to their own place . . . if he had been home, Jay Sebring would not have been sitting on Sharon's bed or even in the house. If he had been home, he would surely have been murdered with Sharon . . .

Chapter Sixteen

*P*olanski described his rediscovery of sex a few months after the murders as therapeutic, although Kenneth Tynan appeared unimpressed by the explanation. Roman was also telling friends that he doubted whether he could ever again have a permanent relationship, and Tynan was prepared to consider that loneliness drove him towards an obsessive sexual quest which he observed at first hand when they began working together in England in the summer of 1970. After the day's work, Polanski would 'fling himself exhausted into the back seat of his Rolls with its smoked-glass windows and murmuring, "Who shall I gratify tonight?" would thumb through a constantly amended list of candidates'.

It only took a little time for him to reach that position. Having disposed of all his possessions which remained at Cielo Drive, settled the bills from Rudi Altobelli for the damage to the carpets and curtains caused by bloodstains, given away the white Rolls Royce he bought Sharon after their wedding and handed the keys of their Ferrari to her father, Paul, he returned to Paris.

He moved on to Gstaad to join Victor Lownes for Christmas, followed unremittingly by a pack of press cameramen whose own voyeurism showed no signs of a let-up. Polanski remained quiet and moody and given to fits of grief. He was in no mood for the party Victor Lownes had arranged at his rented chalet, attended by his personal staff, a collection of exuberant friends and girls including eighteen-year-old Maltese twins whose beauty was sufficient to command a later centrefold in *Playboy* and whose presence was sufficient for the gossips to talk about their relationship with Polanski. The very setting for his winter sojourn provided a colourful background for continued suitably embellished stories about his 'amorous activities'.

The social scene was lively, with an array of famous names around, including Taylor and Burton, David Niven and Curt Jurgens, but Polanski discovered that the taint of the murders had followed him to Switzerland, and he was not always made welcome. The Eagle Club, at the top of Gstaad's favourite mountain, tolerated his presence when he was a guest of people like industrialist Peter Notz but refused his application for membership. Notz became a close friend in Gstaad and recalled Polanski's variable moods. 'I remember one especially difficult moment,' he said, 'at a dinner party on 24 January 1970. Roman had been quiet all evening, and then suddenly burst into tears. He apologized profusely, saying, "Sorry about that, Peter, but you see it's Sharon's birthday today. She would have been twenty-seven." He left the party and tore away at high speed in his Volkswagen.'

Polanski found solace on the ski slopes, where he demonstrated his spectacular prowess with a bravado which verged upon the suicidal, racing down the most dangerous of the slopes, going where others feared to ski, seemingly intent on driving away the nightmares by physical exhaustion. He moved out of Lownes's chalet and rented one for himself and Andy Braunsberg who had joined the party. It was located away from the social scene, 4 miles outside the resort, a large place with nine rooms. 'I know it seems crazy,' he told writer Reinke Kramer, 'but I am going back to work, and I need the space for inspiration.'

He had begun reading *Papillon*, Henri Charrière's bestselling autobiography of life on Devil's Island and his eventual escape. He located Charrière in Caracas and said he wanted to turn the book into a film starring Warren Beatty. The rights were owned by a publishing company in France, and Polanski began negotiations to get a film deal moving.

In the meantime, there were relaxing, therapeutic interludes with girls from a local finishing school who had befriended him. He met two or three from a school at Montesano at Notz's chalet, and girls of various nationalities, aged between sixteen and nineteen, the daughters of wealthy parents around the world, began calling upon Polanski at his own chalet. He became something of a secret attraction amongst the finishing school population, and for the girls the visits became a frequent and exciting adventure. He gave them the run of the house, and they turned up to listen to music and hear his stories of Hollywood.

It was Polanski's notoriety that in part attracted them. A half-dozen or more girls became his regular companions, sometimes together, sometimes in ones and twos. Occasionally he would drive up to the school in his Volkswagen to meet whoever was to accompany him to the chalet that night. The girls would wait until the lights went out and they were presumed to be tucked up safely in their dormitories. Then, whichever was his date that night would clamber over the wooden balcony, drop into the snow and dash across the grounds to the entrance where his car would be parked, engine running, ready to drive to his chalet. The liaison would often end in the bedroom before he returned the visitor(s) to the school before dawn. It was a routine interrupted only by occasional other visitors to the Polanski chalet, although one – Bruce Lee – provided an extra flurry of excitement among the girls. The 'lure of forbidden fruit' was as appealing to Polanski as it was to his daring young visitors, and he remained in Gstaad for four months, long after the sojourning celebrities around him had left.

Negotiations for *Papillon* were not progressing well. Charrière was impressed by Polanski and visited Gstaad with his wife, staying at the chalet while they discussed arrangements. Financial backers were enthralled by the story, but less sure that Polanski was the man to deliver. He tried to salvage the foundering project by flying to Paris to get Warren Beatty's signature on a contract to star in the film, as Charrière. They had four days of wild parties, and Beatty did not read the book until the fifth day. He said he thought it was terrific but was undecided about making the movie.

The budget remained a problem, too. Polanski, with Andy Braunsberg alongside working out the figures, reckoned it would need $5 million. At that point the deal collapsed and local backers pulled out. Polanski returned to Gstaad still no nearer getting a new film off the ground. (*Papillon* was filmed two years later by an amalgam of independent producers, with Franklin Schaffner directing and Steve McQueen and Dustin Hoffman starring, though it fared badly at the hands of reviewers.)

Polanski lingered for a couple of weeks longer in Gstaad, then returned to his mews house in London to toy with another scheme he had dreamed up and which Andy Braunsberg had said would be 'terrific'. They would 'do' *Macbeth*. Again, it was something pulled from Polanski's past that inspired it – the vision of Laurence Olivier's 1948 version of *Hamlet* was still a vivid memory.

There was also a belief among those close to Polanski that he had chosen *Macbeth* as a kind of spectacular response to media pressure and to show everyone he had not lost control. Orson Welles, a man of similar expansive ambitions which often went wrong, had famously – or, as *Halliwell's Film Guide* says, infamously – tried a similarly extrovert production of *Macbeth* back in 1948, with himself starring.

Although Polanski was no stranger to Shakespeare, he had never seen *Macbeth* performed on stage. He required a collaborator for the project to guide him through what was basically unknown territory. He called Kenneth Tynan as soon as he returned to London. Tynan, fresh from the critical notoriety which followed in the wake of *Oh! Calcutta!* in New York, would have to be wooed. His was a world of intellectuals, of the National Theatre and of strident review. Polanski, as Tynan noted, generally moved in less rarefied circles which he personally regarded with a certain contempt. Even so, Tynan himself was currently in the eye of a hurricane. He was under contract to write for *Playboy* – hardly an organ for the literary man – having been hired by Hugh Hefner as a contributing author, for which he was being handsomely remunerated. Tynan took their money, paid on a regular basis even though *Playboy* had rejected several of his articles, including one in defence of hard-core pornography because Hefner objected to an over-preponderance of masturbation. Thus at the end of 1968, he was in debt to *Playboy* to the tune of more than $10,000 for his unfulfilled commitments.

This involvement with *Playboy* led to some derision back in London, where *Private Eye* published an odd ode about Tynan:

> Now am I grown to Capitalist estate!
> First did I swear upon the Public Box.
> Then *Oh! Calcutta!* Now I swim in gold.
> O Hefner, tremble, exploiter of bare flesh,
> A greater comes.

The establishment press had begun an angry tirade against Tynan ahead of the arrival of *Oh! Calcutta!* in Britain. *The Times* led the attack with an article by Ronald Butt branding him as the purveyor of 'sexual voyeurism that used to be available to the frustrated and mentally warped in the side-turnings of a certain kind of sea-port'. London theatres refused *en masse* to take the show, and it ended up being premiered at the Roundhouse, which was a converted disused railway shed at the end of the red-light mile in North London.

So for different reasons, Polanski and Tynan were a confounding match. Tynan was in the middle of the *Calcutta* mêlée when Polanski called. He was curious enough to agree to a meeting, and in late April 1970 found himself at Polanski's mews house, listening to his elaborate plans for *Macbeth*. His first notion was especially intriguing to Tynan. He said that the play was not often staged successfully because it was invariably played by middle-aged actors, simply because they were the people who normally played Shakespeare. He wanted the Macbeths to be young, in their twenties, and the whole screenplay to be filled with vibrant action. 'I see Macbeth,' said Polanski, 'as an open-faced young warrior who is gradually sucked into a whirlpool of events because of his ambition . . . a gambler for high stakes.'

Further on in the discussion, Tynan would become concerned that Polanski was turning *Macbeth* – Shakespeare's most violent play – into a macabre re-run of the recent events in Polanski's life. He admitted to being uncomfortable about the project but agreed that day to join in. There were a few ground-rules: that the murders would not be discussed, nor would politics, since Polanski was moving towards becoming a right-wing reactionary, which clashed directly with Tynan's own views. In this initial monitoring Tynan discovered that his collaborator held a great mistrust of trade unions, especially those affecting the British film industry, which he believed was a conspiracy to suppress talent. He refused absolutely to identify with the proletariat, which Tynan assessed to be a rebellion against the hard-line Communism he had been exposed to in his youth, in the same way as his unbridled objection to religion, especially Catholicism, had its roots in his childhood when he spent time with the poor Catholic family in Wysoka during the war.

Yet Tynan came to the conclusion that although Polanski abhorred religion, he believed that evil was a quite definite force, and was reminded of his own review of *Rosemary's Baby*, in which he said that it was one of the few films 'that makes one consider the possibility that there is such a thing as absolute evil'.

Polanski's attitude to women also intrigued Tynan. He described it as 'tribal . . . he beguiles them into submission with his urchin charm but if they presume to engage him in argument, he soon grows bored and petulant. Women's lib arouses him to a high pitch of bewildered fury. While we were writing *Macbeth*, there would often be a brace of girls draped around his living room. One evening when we had finished work, a recumbent darling rose to her feet and said she was going out to the kitchen to make some coffee. Polanski rounded upon her as if stung. "What are you, some kind of militant? If you want coffee, ask my housekeeper." I realized then that for him there were only two acceptable female positions: sitting down and lying down.'

This attitude was implicit in the first object which came into view as one entered Polanski's house. It was a piece of sculpted furniture designed by the artist Allen Jones: a coffee table consisting of a sheet of glass supported by a life-size girl on all fours wearing nothing but long gloves, leather boots and a corset. The figure's back was arched and her face contemplated itself in a mirror on the floor.

His overall message could be embarrassingly stark in its delivery, as recalled by Tynan: 'We are driving along in his Rolls and stop at a red light and there is a pretty girl standing on the corner. Without hesitation, Polanski rolls down the window and leans out: "Hey, miss, excuse me, you have a beaudiful arse. Where are you going?" and the girl ends up in the car.'

In spite of the diversions, the screenplay was completed in six weeks. Polanski and Braunsberg formed a production company called Caliban Films (after the offspring from the Devil's copulation with a witch in *The Tempest*) and enlisted the aid of Bill Tennant, Polanski's agent, to attract some financial backing.

This proved to be far more difficult than they had envisaged, although Tennant, being close to the market-place, warned that the mention of Shakespeare to conventional film-backers would immediately invoke a blast of air forced through the lips, accompanied by a shaking of the head on the part of any potential producer. The play itself was in any case always bound up in theatrical superstitions, but the Polanski treatment undoubtedly caused additional apprehension. Because he had made it a young play, full of action, it appeared to contain even more violence and bloody scenes. There was also nudity – virtually unknown on the screen at that time – which Polanski and Tynan claimed was an accurate translation of Lady Macbeth's sleepwalking scene.

Then there was the aura of Polanski's personal problems which could be linked without difficulty to certain lines in the screenplay: the grotesque killing of Macduff's wife and children, the desolate grief: 'Your wife and babes, savagely slaughtered'. The connotations were clear, and recognized by Tynan when they came to write the scene. 'I had not been looking forward to it,' he wrote later. 'And a difficult moment arrived when I queried the amount of blood that would be shed by a small boy stabbed in the back. Polanski replied bleakly, "You didn't see my house last summer. I know about bleeding."'

This was the only reference Polanski made to Tynan about the killings during the whole time they were working together on the script. But no one could disconnect the two, and Polanski in his heart of heart surely knew it. This was certainly the view of his old backer, Michael Klinger, who said, 'Without a doubt, this work has got to be a reflection of Sharon's death.'

The completed package was touted around the usual quarters for weeks, and attracted not a single offer for production money. Then, just as Polanski had used Compton Films as a last resort to launch his career in Britain seven years earlier, he fell back upon a similar organization – though a far more wealthy and prestigious one – to get *Macbeth* moving. Devoid of alternatives and ready to throw in the towel, Polanski decided to lay the screenplay before Victor Lownes to discover if Playboy would be interested in backing him.

Kenneth Tynan expressed great misgivings about this prospect and said that if they went ahead he did not think he would want his name on the credits. Polanski had no qualms at all about accepting Playboy money. It was true to form. As Basia Kwiatkowska has said, he would not mind who he used.

He laid it on the line to Tynan: 'Nobody else is biting.' At the time, Playboy was polishing its image. Though the magazine and the Bunnies were still central to the success of the international group, its London base was earning massive profits from the casinos which it had opened in Park Lane, and others were opening or imminent in major cities throughout the UK. Britain's gaming laws had turned the country into what the American and Middle Eastern high-rolling gamblers called a floating casino, and Playboy was at the zenith of its earning power, awash with money.

A mere 2 million lousy bucks, Polanski told Lownes, was all that would be required. Lownes was building an image too, steering himself away from the sensational tabloid accounts of his champagne life-style, oozing sex and Bunnies, which had become a staple part of the Sunday tabloid diet. He was so famous that even ex-girlfriends could earn money by selling their kiss-and-tells.

Jackie Collins, then a less famous writer than now, went to see Lownes to get some background one day in those early seventies: 'I was supposed to meet him in his office, that cosy warren of Bunny ladies, but at the last minute the rendezvous changed to a more intimate venue – his house. An Italian butler greeted me in fractured English and showed me into the sitting room, adorned with paintings by trendy new artists and with reading matter ranging from Victorian sexuality to the history of world sculpture . . . but he was in his reorientation period, going up-market with an estate in the country and riding with the hounds.'

Polanski caught Victor Lownes at exactly the right moment. He read the screenplay and reported back within thirty-six hours that he was sending it to Playboy's projects department with a personal recommendation to Hugh Hefner that they should back it. In fact the film projects people threw it back, saying, 'Shakespeare? Polanski? Tynan? Forget it . . .' Lownes, more because of his regard for Polanski than anything else, persevered. Hugh Hefner agreed to meet Polanski to hammer out a deal and flew his brand-new black DC-9, decked out in the style of the ultimate bachelor pad, to Marbella, where the whole project was laid out.

Polanski was nailed down to a maximum $2.5-million budget. Playboy was putting in $1.5 million and Columbia, after some arm-twisting, agreed to put up the remaining million dollars for the distribution rights. Polanski and Andy Braunsberg would take an equity share as co-producers, and Polanski would be credited as director and co-writer of the screen adaptation with Tynan. He and Braunsberg registered their Caliban name at Companies House, installed themselves in the former offices of Cadre Films, the disbanded company Polanski had run with Gene Gutowski – and bought a large second hand Rolls Royce to look the part.

Polanski was on the move again. Actor Martin Shaw takes up the story: 'I must prefix my remarks with the admission that I am a Polanski fan. Frankly, I'm a jobbing actor and while his personal life was fascinating, intriguing and tragic, it didn't matter a fuck to me. I was just interested in working with him.' Shaw was appearing in a play at the Royal Court, not far from Polanski's house. One night in the mid-summer of 1970, Polanski went to see the play and went backstage afterwards to ask Shaw to have breakfast with him. Breakfast meetings were a novel experience then, an Americanism virtually unheard of in the UK, especially for a theatrical actor like Shaw who had yet to make his first film:

'We got on extremely well. What impressed me was his energy and complete lack of bullshit. When you meet people as an actor, there is always another agenda going on, and given that very few people in the world – especially in the film world – can tell the truth straight off, you're used to a million messages other than what is happening at the time. What was refreshing about him was that he was just upfront, the straightforward truth. So he said he had seen the play, thought I was a

180

very good actor and was I interested in some action, because he was going to film *Macbeth* and the production was going to revolve around young people who were very fit. He said it was a very violent time, and the film would reflect that; he asked me if I was up to it. I said I was and he arranged a screen test for the role of Macbeth. I was pretty hopped up about that – I was twenty-four and had never appeared in a film before – and suddenly here I am being considered for one of the great roles of all time. He was honest enough to say he was testing a lot of people, including Anthony Hopkins. Afterwards, he phoned me at home to tell me I hadn't got Macbeth but he wanted me to play Banquo which was going to be a more important role in the film than in the play, because he wanted Banquo to be more of a rival to Macbeth to add some puissance.'

Shaw was intrigued by the descriptions of the 'action' and it struck him that it was a surprising choice of film considering Polanski's recent history. 'How do you assess that kind of grief?' said Shaw. 'How do you get inside the mind of someone who has had that happen? Everybody has their own way of expressing or expiating something awful that has happened, and I suppose that was his.'

In between testing Shaw and seeing a couple of dozen other potential Macbeths, all of whom (including Albert Finney) either turned the part down or were not suitable, Polanski and Tynan were returning from Paris in the first week of September. On the plane, Polanski saw a face he recognized but could not place. It turned out to be that of another young actor, Jon Finch, whom he had been looking at in a casting directory. Finch was just returning from completing some television work in France. Polanski asked him if he would come to his house, where he was put through his paces for several hours, doing scenes with Polanski and Tynan playing Banquo's murderers in front of a video camera. Finch left at dawn as Macbeth.

Polanski left the role of Lady Macbeth until the male lead had been cast, and now furiously began testing actresses who responded with varying degrees of seriousness from 'Get lost . . . whatever the money' to 'I'll do it – but no funny business'. One who took the latter line was a former star of the dire Compton Group films, Francesca Annis, now an established actress of respectable accommodation. She was twenty-five years old and very young, in conventional terms, for Lady Macbeth, but that was what was required for this film. Tynan remarked when they heard her read for the part that she spoke her lines like a young girl, childlike. Polanski replied that that was exactly what he wanted, a woman who would be 'manipulated by her husband'. Like Mia Farrow in *Rosemary's Baby*, she was the nymphetic creature of fantasy that Polanski sought in most of his leading women.

The preliminaries got under way at Shepperton Studios in October and the following month the entire unit of 200 actors, extras and technicians moved on location to a remote corner of Wales amid howling gales and driving torrential rain which froze before it hit the ground. A difficult shoot, full of excitement, temperament and vile weather, was in prospect. Martin Shaw again: 'I was inexperienced and in awe of everything, especially Polanski who was providing me with a priceless experience, and something that was priceless in screen credit.

'Working with Polanski was an experience in itself. I know some actors and actresses have described him as a brutal autocratic shit but it depends on your point of view and your resilience. You have to realize that making a film is not just for people who want to swan around in winniebagos and come out when everything's ready, say a few lines and then go back into the jacuzzi. Polanski's approach could sustain none of that kind of prima donna attitude; as far as he was concerned, acting was a job for a jobbing actor who was very serious about it. As with his conversation and the rest of his personality, there was no room for bullshit. It's just, "Get it done". This attitude was very evident while making the film. There was a memorable conference between Roman and Kenneth Tynan where we were just reading through some lines. Ken said, "I suggest that line scans like this . . ." and described the way he thought it should be spoken. Roman just said, "You must be fucking kidding. These guys are going to be sitting on horses in a raging storm with wind-machines blowing all around them and they are going to say it however they can." To me that was very refreshing. You know, he cut out the crap. He had the ability to demystify everything. He expected 101 per cent of everybody and his own enthusiasm was very infectious.'

However they regarded Polanski as a person and a director of actors, few failed to marvel at his all-round skill as a film-maker, in that he really did not need anyone else on the unit. He surrounded himself with some of the best technicians in the world. 'Time after time,' said Shaw, 'when it was a hand-held camera shot for instance, he would take the camera out of the hands of his operator and do the shot himself, he just could not contain himself. He would even involve himself in the make-up. He would come into the make-up room and ask questions. But Tom Smith, his make-up director, who was one of the finest, would say, "I can manage on my own, thank you, Roman." He was one of the few people who could and would stand up to him. Others were less inclined to do so, and would let him have his head.'

Polanski's relationship with Francesca Annis was best described, said Shaw, as a 'very spirited one', full of artistic tension. There was a good deal of aggravation between them because she herself had a lively temperament and fought back: 'I think once Roman realized he wasn't going to pull her, they got on extremely well and she was turning in one of the best Lady Macbeths I have ever seen.'

There was no doubt that Polanski's view of actors was often little short of derisory. To Tynan, he described them as 'comics' and 'monkeys' and had little time for their analytic conversations about characterization or how a scene should be played. His view was that they should just go and do it, and he would tell them if it was right or wrong – as was often shown in the number of takes it took to get the scene right. He resorted to all kinds of cajoling. Once, after several takes in a scene with Francesca Annis in which she had failed to muster the required degree of emotion, he whispered to the cameraman to keep rolling, walked over to her and cracked a popper – a phial of anamyl-nitrate – under her nose and achieved exactly the kind of reaction he wanted.

Macbeth was filled with incident, and occasional amusing interludes. Midway through filming, the witty raconteur and writer Clement Freud wrote a tongue-in-jowel article on Polanski, the extrovert Pole who has never worked in the English theatre, directing a collection of wild young English actors in *Macbeth* with Playboy money on the hillsides of Wales – in broken English. To make his point, Freud used the phonetic disturbances as his theme – a popular method of reporting Polanski. His crew could certainly mimic his oft-heard refrain: 'Thad's mudge bedder, beaudiful, fandastic . . . once again, please.' But thereafter it became difficult to reproduce his accent, especially in print as Freud had tried to do. When the article appeared, Polanski fired off a letter to Freud's editor: 'Zis piece about me feelming *Macbet* vas vonderful, very funny. But being a Pole I deedn't know zet I speak viz accent of an Austrian psychiatrist . . . Loook, ven Hefner reads zis article he vill say, "How can zis alien parrot direct our mooovie!" Zo, I am in beeg trouble . . .'

Like Freud, Tynan was fascinated by Polanski at work and kept a record of events. Though a taskmaster, Polanski played hard, too. In London, he would usually end up in one of the fashionable discos or at the Playboy Club, and if friends like Beatty or Mike Nichols were in London, they would all be out until the early hours. But at 6.45 the next morning, Polanski would be ready to go to work. Tynan penned an amusing portrait of a typical morning as Polanski would climb into the Rolls taking them to the studio: no good morning or formalities – just straight into it:

'You had garlic for dinner last night, my friend. Open the window. How you like my new tape? Elton John. Fantastic, huh? Listen, I screwed a Chinese lawyer last night. She's a barrister from Hong Kong. Beaudiful! . . . You see that guy driving a Jensen, he's wearing a wig . . . Peter Sellers and I and some chicks had dinner at Parkes with this Persian guy who writes poetry the one I told you about who's always stoned out of his mind. When we sat down, he said, "I am estoned" – Persians are like Spanish, they put an "e" before "s" at the beginning of words. We all ordered *blanquette de veau* and the Persian just sat there, not moving, with his head bowed like he was praying . . . That's a 747 over there going through that cloud . . . After we waited for some time, the Persian suddenly said quite loudly, "I want to change my wheel" over and over. Then I finally remembered what we had ordered. All he wanted was something else to eat instead of veal . . . Listen, I'm going to Gstaad this weekend with those two chicks I pulled at the party that Victor gave for Warren . . . You remember there was one in drastic hot pants? Sure you know the type, sort of between a starlet and a secretary . . . Or is it *which* Victor gave? What's the exact difference between that and which? . . . Hey look at that over there . . . what a great arse she's got . . .'

On location, the accent did occasionally cause trouble, though. In the appalling weather, when directorial instructions were barely audible, he had set up a complicated sequence in which rain, the actors, animals, chickens and a farm cart all had to be cued for the scene. He shouted through the bullhorn: 'Okay, cue rain . . . people move . . . okay . . . chickens; get those fucking chickens moving . . . right, rain, cue the rain [from a hose pipe] and now . . . cut!'

Everything halted. Polanski screamed, 'Why have you stopped . . . that was exactly right.' Braunsberg pointed out that he had called 'Cut!'

'No, I didn't,' yelled Polanski. 'I said "Cut!" I meant "Cut". Cut. Bring on the Cut.'

'You mean cart,' said Braunsberg.

'Yes . . . cut,' said Polanski.

It was one of many such stoppages. Polanski's search for perfection would mean going over a scene time and again to get it exactly right. The people, the settings, the detail . . . all had to be correct.

Stunt-men were never used as stand-ins for Jon Finch and Martin Shaw, even during dangerous sequences, and during one of these, Finch's hand was cut by a sword and had to have fifteen stitches. 'To me,' said Shaw, 'it always seemed as if he was daring us to do it. There was one shot where Jon Finch and myself had to ride along a very narrow ridge on horseback and we had to gallop across at a fast rate of knots. He came over to both of us and had this sort of grin on his face, an impish boyish look which said, "I'm going to dare you to do something which I know and you know I could do. Now are you as brave as me?" That was the subtext that went unsaid. So he comes over and says, "I gotta fantastic idea for a shot. You gallop along this ridge but I warn you, I am going to put fire hoses, wind-machines and everything on you. But I don't think you can do it. I'd better have stunt-men, hadn't I?" And he grinned. So of course we said, "No, fuck off, we'll do it." And we did it. It was dangerous but it was fun and we felt that much better for having done it. But let's not beat around the bush – it was all macho bullshit. We were very young and wanted to do it. It was wild and dangerous. There was never any question of "Do it or you're fired". It was all done with a grin – "Go on, I dare you!"

'At the same time, there is another aspect to his direction which is very unusual. We had to set up one shot which was the arrival of the entire court at the Castle of Glamis; it was a huge procession. So the logistics of having about a hundred actors and horses coming into the castle was immense. The scene required it to be raining, so rain had to be cued, the drainage had to be cued, the actors had to be cued, there was lightning on the backcloth; there was a phenomenal amount to be done and it was going to take three hours to set up the shot. In the middle of all the furore that was going on, I said to him, "I've got a question for you about my attitude here." He said, "Not now, Martin, not now." Three hours later, when the shot had been set up, he turned to me and said, "Okay, wadda you want? What was your query?" I thought that was great that he had remembered during all that was going on. Basically, I just wanted to know how I felt about Lady Macbeth at that time. He asked me how I thought I should play it, and I told him, and he said, "Fandastic, fandastic, do it." That's what I admired about him; he had control over the technical aspects, but he also knows about the internal stuff that actors want to do as well.'

There was another memorable moment in the last fight scene between Macduff and Macbeth which was entirely orchestrated by Polanski. As Shaw remembered it, they had a fight arranger, but it was Polanski's invention and he wanted the sword to enter the body at an unusual angle. He said that on film, the blade either went in through the belly or through the chest, straight. He said that in reality it was rarely like that. 'So what is going to happen,' said Polanski, 'is that Macduff is going to insert the sword down by his waist and push and it is going to come out the other side of his body diagonally through his neck.'

He sent the special effects people away to construct a flexible sword and a channel within the armour so that it could be done. He was always setting these challenges for his people, and they would frown and say 'It can't be done' and come back three hours later and show him how they had managed it.

'He is the master of the subliminal detail,' said Shaw. 'He could spot things none of us would recognize. I once saw him rage and almost tear apart a costume someone was wearing because it was machine-stitched. He said, "What the fuck is the madder with you people? This is fucking 1067. How many sewing machines you seen around here?" Another time, when we were filming on a hillside, he looked out and he said, "Can anyone tell me what's wrong with this view?" Whenever he said something like that, everyone looked at their shoes, or up at the sky, and thought, "Oh, please God don't let it be me that's fucked up." Nobody could tell him what was wrong. "So this is 1067 – I'm looking down there and I can see fences and hedgerows." So the assistant director said, "What can we do, Roman, it's the countryside of 1971 – it's like that wherever you look. Perhaps we could blur the shot." So he comes back and says that was no answer, and they should do something about it. And so they went driving around with wadges of fivers and tenners and asked the farmers to lay down their fences and then replace them at the end of the shot. This was one shot we were talking about – but he insisted. It must have cost a fortune, but it had authenticity.

'The chainmail was another example. It was made of chain mail, and not knitted string, and it was heavy and went rusty and it was uncomfortable and we were soaking wet. But it was extraordinarily realistic. This may sound to some like overguilding the lily, but let me say, I would go a long way and make many sacrifices to work with him again.'

Polanski may have gratified some of his actors with his quest for realism, but by January 1971 he had run into severe problems with the money-men – to such a degree that they wanted him fired from the movie. He was over budget by at least 20 per cent and well behind schedule. A company called Film Finances, which was like an insurance company, guaranteeing completion of the shooting against incompetence, acts of God, bad weather or broken legs, had been keeping a watchful eye on the production as it was about to move to the North of England. The schedule became even more demanding, with 1000 extras required for crowd and battle scenes, which was going to cost £4000 a day. Appalled at what they considered Polanski's unnecessary excesses in his quest for realistic settings, Film Finances called a halt and demanded that Playboy remove him from the production altogether. They had another director and one of its own executives on standby to take over as producer. They wanted the production trimmed back, they wanted filming speeded up and they wanted the movie completed within four weeks. There was no doubt it could have been done – but Polanski wasn't budging from his stance.

That night, as they drove home from their day's filming, Polanski confided to Kenneth Tynan and Andy Braunsberg: 'I am not going to cut a single shot out of the script; I am not going to cut a single adjective, not a single semi-colon.' He reassured them he intended to film at his own speed. An hour later, having mapped out his arguments on a sheet of paper in advance, he telephoned Hugh Hefner direct at the Playboy headquarters in Chicago, and proceeded to tell him why it would be a disaster if he was pulled off the picture. Hefner accepted that without Polanski and Tynan on the credits the whole project might collapse into the muddy mire of the Northumberland countryside where they were now filming.

With Film Finances still breathing fire, Hefner flew to London, took the penthouse suite at the London Hilton and called a meeting of all concerned, including Victor Lownes and Polanski. Polanski presented a detailed accounting of money spent so far and gave his projections for completion. The money-men would not be easily placated. Was it true, one of them asked, that he had spent three hours filming a candle because it wouldn't flicker in the way he wanted it to flicker? Polanski said he did not remember.

Film Finances were still in favour of replacing, but that solution remained unappealing to Playboy. At the end of the day, Polanski agreed to forgo a third of his fee, and Hefner stumped up an extra half-million dollars, though there were conditions. Film Finances insisted that Polanski and Braunsberg should be removed as producers and replaced by their own man, who turned up the following day in a chauffeur-driven car and proceeded to keep tabs on the movie, every pound note and paper clip, every delay and retake, until its completion in April – ten weeks late and $600,000 over budget.

Chapter Seventeen

T he summer months of 1971 passed in the hot atmosphere of editing suites making ready a new masterpiece that would be the result of a twenty-five-week nightmare of appalling weather, constant bickering over money, cast injuries and abject tension. There was much to be done, and a good deal of sound-dubbing of inaudible lines attempted over the sound of howling winds and driving rain. Victor Lownes had managed to arrange a Royal Command performance for December which meant that the final work had to be completed on time. Martin Shaw said everyone was pretty hopeful of the outcome. 'I think we were all agreed that though it had been an absolutely nerve-racking, muscle-aching job with all kinds of pressures, it had the makings of being a very good film. As it turned out, I think it was recognized, and still is even today in 1993, as one of the best films of a Shakespeare play. And even the piss-taking over the label "A Playboy Production" could not take that away from us or him.'

Such a conclusion could only be seen with the benefit of hindsight. At the time, a farcical aftermath to the making of *Macbeth* was developing. Columbia sent a team to view Polanski's completed rough-cut at the end of the summer and they declared that the film needed careful marketing and suggested that it was perhaps a touch too long for the average audience. What they were really saying was that it needed to be much shorter, and only an expensive marketing operation might salvage some of the production costs.

The London premiere was postponed until the New Year to give Polanski more time and *Macbeth* was booked into New York theatres for a January 1972 opening. There he would be at the mercy of critics who can kill a film stone-dead, and this occasion would be no exception. With Columbia half-heartedly releasing it in a graveyard of a month, *Macbeth* was received with a mixture of pretentious mirth and disgust

– but most evidently, it was not Polanski's movie that was to be reviewed, but his life.

First, the *New York Daily Mirror* recorded that the only noticeable audience reaction was the laughter that greeted the line 'A Playboy Production'. Then Pauline Kael, reviewer for the *New Yorker*, who was not Polanski's favourite person – and vice versa – weighed in with an analysis which was as powerful and articulate as anyone might have feared:

> In the Manson murders, there was an eerie element that the public responded to. Even though we knew that Roman Polanski had nothing whatever to do with causing the murder of his wife and unborn child and friends, the massacre seemed a vision realized from his nightmare movies. And there was an element of guilt and embarrassment that this connection was inevitable . . . [but] one sees the Manson murders in this *Macbeth* because the director has put them there.

Other reviewers kept up the barrage. Paul Zimmerman of *Newsweek* wrote:

> The parallels between the Manson murders and the mad, bloody acts of these beautiful, lost Macbeths keep pressing themselves upon the viewer. All that is good here seems but a pretext for close-ups of knives drawing geysers of blood from the flesh of men, women and children. No chance to revel in gore is passed up . . .

Roger Ebert, syndicated critic of the *Chicago Sun-Times*, said:

> It is impossible to watch a film directed by Roman Polanski and not react on more than one level to such images as a baby being 'untimely ripped from his mother's womb'. Polanski's characters all resemble Manson . . . they are anti-intellectual, witless and driven by deep, shameful wells of lust and violence.

There were better reviews, however, and the National Film Board of America voted *Macbeth* the best film of the year. Martin Shaw said he heard from friends in the American Academy that he and other members of the cast eventually appeared on nomination lists for Best Actor and Best Supporting Actors but none made it through to the final stages. By and large, Polanski and his movie had been massacred by the American critics and sank quickly into the depths of nowhere.

The British critics were much kinder, far more objective and less concerned with recent events. Anxious to try to quell some of the implications of his wife's murder being re-enacted in the film, Polanski gave an interview to Sydney Edwards of the London *Evening Standard* in which he tried to divert attention to earlier events in his life. 'If anything,' he said, 'the scenes were prompted by something I went through a long time ago in Poland . . . when two young Nazi officers walked into our apartment . . . and I saw them drag a woman down the stairs by her hair from the fifth floor. The attitude of the murderers [in *Macbeth*] is the attitude of those two Nazis.'

It was a sentence from Polanski's interview with Sydney Edwards that caused a furore in London – and ended his ten-year friendship with Victor Lownes. Asked by Edwards why he had taken the investment of Playboy to fund the film, Polanski replied, '*Pecunia non olet*,' adding, 'You know what that means in Latin . . . money doesn't smell.' Victor Lownes was furious and took Polanski's remark as an insult against Playboy, and indirectly himself. At the Royal premiere in London on 2 February, Lownes had to introduce Polanski to Princess Anne – to whom the director joked, 'I'll never make another film with horses in it' – but he never spoke to Polanski again. He wrote a long letter to Hefner lamenting that their association with Polanski had turned so sour: 'It is distressing to me that for years I did everything to help this son-of-a-bitch and only recently come to realize that I was being exploited by him . . . it bugs me that I dragged everybody else into this mess.'

Lownes took a parting swipe at Polanski, returning a gift he had received from him and Sharon some years earlier, which was a statue cast in pure gold in the shape of an erect penis, commonly known by them as The Golden Prick Award. Lownes attached a note stating that he could no longer bear to have this 'life-sized portrait' of Polanski around the house and he was sure that he would have no difficulty in finding another 'friend' to shove it up. Polanski donated the statue to Release, the drug rehabilitation charity, who auctioned it off amidst some embarrassing publicity suggesting it was actually a cast of Polanski's own organ. Lownes reached for his pen again, saying he had not seen a retraction and could only assume that Polanski relished this totally erroneous implication!

*　　*　　*

Polanski did not hang around for the inquest on *Macbeth*. He cleared off to France to rejoin the surreal world of his collaborator Gerard Brach. He was virtually broke, his production office was shut down, and he was in a gloomy state of mind, wondering what he was going to do next to claw himself back from the oblivion which now seemed his certain fate. London life had dried up, one of his best friends had become an enemy, and Hollywood seemed to have crossed him off its list. There were two or three projects which never went beyond an exploratory discussion, one for an erotic film which Kenneth Tynan had been writing at Polanski's suggestion after he'd visited Bangkok but which hit the decks in the wake of the flare-up of media attacks in the wake of *Oh! Calcutta!* and *Macbeth*.

Polanski and Brach moved on to Gstaad with Andy Braunsberg to catch the last of the winter skiing and, reverting to type, began tossing ideas at each other based on a low-budget, small-cast movie in the mould of *Knife in the Water*. They settled on a plot outline about a movie producer and an actress and were writing away furiously when Jack Nicholson arrived in Gstaad to join Polanski on the ski slopes. Polanski explained that he had been 'kicking a few ideas around' and was writing a part especially for Jack in a film provisionally entitled *The Magic Finger*. The title had rather risqué connotations considering Nicholson's own current reputation after the release of Mike Nichols' erotic, sex-filled *Carnal Knowledge* in which Nicholson had co-starred with Candice Bergen, Art Garfunkel, Ann-Margret and Rita Moreno. The film had caused uproar for its explicit sex. Nicholson chuckled and said kindly that *The Magic Finger* wasn't quite him but he would look out for something else for them to work on when he returned to the States.

A change of scene was forced upon Polanski. London and Hollywood were out, and France had never really warmed to him. Now, he struck out for Rome to find Carlo Ponti, and talked him into parting with $1 million to put his new project into production. The title was changed to *What?* and the script totally rewritten so that its central character was based on an oil magnate. There was no real plot or story as such but a mélange of scenes with varying degrees of soft-porn sexuality.

The scenario contained elements Polanski had explored previously in *Two Men and a Wardrobe*, *Knife in the Water* and *The Fat and the Lean* – notably one character's power over another. He chose the young actress Sydne Rome for his female lead. She had arrived in Italy a couple of years before, to test for a not dissimilar role in Christian Marquand's sex satire, *Candy*. She had stayed on in Rome and now found herself being wooed for Polanski's own sex romp which was basically a series of interlinked scenes in which she appears with another of Roman's pals, Marcello Mastroianni, losing an item of clothing in each scene and participating in sado-masochism. The woman, as usual in the Polanski–Brach scripts, is shown as the victim, the one who must submit to the demands and manipulations of the male. *What?* was not a good film; it achieved little attention anywhere other than Italy where soft porn was good business and the name of Ponti counted.

Polanski, Brach and Braunsberg, along with a couple of others, lived and stayed together in Italy for almost two years in a villa they rented at high cost from an Italian contessa. Their intention was to set up a kind of creative commune, a new approach to art movies which could also make money, and in this he was encouraged by a new group of friends. Andy Warhol and entourage had also temporarily decamped to Italy, and they struck up an accord.

Warhol was himself exploring film-making possibilities and borrowed Andy Braunsberg from the Polanski commune for assistance with two ideas, one on Frankenstein, the other on Dracula. Their artistic minds seemed drawn to such gothic blood-letting, and their creative powers were also supposedly being enhanced by various substances which were freely available, but at the end of a long and sterile period in which the only production was *What?*, Polanski's commune experiment foundered on the rocks of pecuniary disharmony. They had not earned a penny between them and the rent on the villa alone was $3000 a month. Polanski was already beginning to look around for a return to civilization when Jack Nicholson called . . .

Chinatown was the quintessential 1970s movie, embodying some of the major themes of that decade such as corruption and conspiracy, and commenting metaphorically on Watergate. There were also some secret ingredients to the film's other theme of tangled sexual relationships and incest that helped make it the success it became and finally launched Nicholson into the superleague of Hollywood stars. *Chinatown* was the coming together at last of Nicholson and Roman Polanski in a professional capacity, and there is a belief that the mercurial little director brought to the film a moodiness that turned it from something confusingly average to a work of classic proportions and put Polanski himself back into a glowing spotlight.

Scene of the murders, in August 1969: the house Polanski rented in Bel Air, where Sharon Tate and four others were shot and stabbed to death. One of the bodies still lies on the lawn, covered by a blanket. (*Associated Press*)

The haunted face of Charles Manson whose 'family', known as Satan's Slaves, were sent to carry out the murders. The swastika sign, emblem of a satanic order formed in Britain, is visible on his forehead. (*Yardley Collection*)

Police patrol the house where, the day before, Sharon had been discussing the decoration of the nursery for the baby she was carrying. (*UPI*)

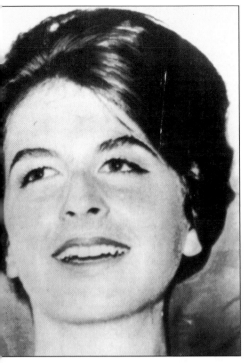

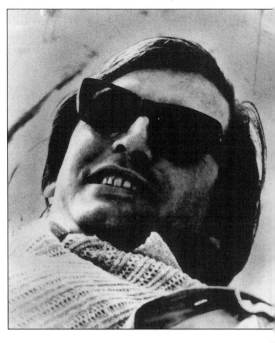

Other victims *(clockwise from bottom left)*:
Sharon's former lover and 'hairdresser to the
stars' Jay Sebring; heiress Abigail Folger and
Polanski's friend from Poland, Wojtek
Frykowksi. (*Yardley Collection*)

Polanski arrives in Los Angeles from
London after the murders, accompanied by
Victor Lownes. (*Yardley Collection*)

The man who helped Polanski re-establish his film career after the killings: the British critic and writer Kenneth Tynan, collaborator on *Macbeth*. (*Courtesy British Film Institute*)

On the set of *Macbeth*. Polanski, with his stars Francesca Annis and Jon Finch, gives Finch a piggy-back for the camera on a windswept location. (*Courtesy Columbia Pictures*)

Jack Nicholson discussing a scene on the set of *Chinatown*, Polanski's most acclaimed movie of the seventies. Polanski himself took a cameo role as the thug who slit Nicholson's nose. (*Yardley Collection*)

Polanski co-wrote, directed and starred in *The Tenant* with Shelley Winters in 1976. (*Yardley Collection*)

In drag, as the disturbed leading character in *The Tenant*. (*Courtesy British Film Institute*)

Polanski is arrested for the alleged rape of a thirteen-year-old girl whom he took to Jack Nicholson's house. He pleaded guilty to a lesser charge, and then fled the United States. (*Rex Features*)

Nastassia Kinski was fifteen when she and Polanski first met. He brought her to America to star in his next movie. Events, however, took a dramatic turn; he was fired from the movie, though he would eventually cast her as his lover and the star of *Tess*. (*Yardley Collection*)

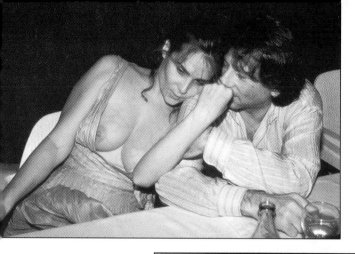

The paparazzi captured a revealing night-club encounter with the new love in his life, Emmanuelle Seigner, who would be billed as the girl who tamed him.

Polanski cast Seigner in his next movie, *Frantic*, in which she co-starred with Harrison Ford. (*Warner Bros*)

By now married to Polanski, Emmanuelle Seigner took the lead in the controversial *Bitter Moon*, described as a cross between a black comedy and a blue movie. (*Yardley Collection*)

Still smiling – Polanski faces the nineties, married and a father.

Nicholson, from the beginning of his involvement with the film, wanted Polanski to direct, though there was some opposition from both Paramount boss Robert Evans and writer Robert Towne. And it was Nicholson who called Polanski and suggested he should get his 'ass over to Los Angeles pronto' to get involved. The new movie, he said, was his for the asking.

It already had a history. Robert Towne had just come through a harrowing time during the production of *The Last Detail* which he had written and which starred Nicholson. It was his first major screenplay, though he and Nicholson had long been friends and collaborators in the Roger Corman film factory. *The Last Detail* is the story of a final night of freedom for a young naval recruit about to go to jail for thieving. The movie contained a good deal of explicit language, including forty-seven 'motherfuckers', and for a time it seemed that Columbia might scrap the whole thing because the censors were balking at the swearing.

Towne, wearying of these problems, dreamed of writing and directing his own movie and had conceived a detective story. The idea was inspired by his casually reading in a west coast magazine called *Chandler's LA* an article recalling the troubles between farmers and land speculators earlier in the century. Out of it came an intriguing private-eye tale, with sufficient detail for Towne to approach his old friend Robert Evans, still the boss at Paramount.

They went to lunch because it so happened that Evans was looking for a writer to sort out some problems on *The Great Gatsby* which was proving to be rather difficult to get on to film. Having dealt with his own troubles, he listened to Towne's idea for a new screenplay, liked it instantly and gave him some money to proceed with an outline. Evans, incidentally, was also seeking a vehicle for his new deal with Paramount which allowed him to produce independently, and he wanted to provide a starring role to amuse his new wife, Ali McGraw, who had been languishing since the runaway success of *Love Story* which his studio had also produced. He believed that Towne's screenplay might be the ideal vehicle on both counts. They both agreed that the leading role, that of the detective Jake Gittes, should go to Jack Nicholson, who was brought in almost from the beginning and was able to offer his thoughts as the project progressed.

Another year passed. *The Last Detail*, meanwhile, was a major hit in 1973, and so was *The Godfather*, which Evans had produced and for which Marlon Brando was up for an Oscar. Evans, Towne and Nicholson were flushed with pride for different reasons, and great expectations now rode on the bulky script Towne had produced for *Chinatown*, whose title was as enigmatic as the film itself because it was largely devoid of any oriental characters or setting.

Polanski entered the scenario after Nicholson's telephone call which was followed up by a firm proposal from Robert Evans who, it will be recalled, had also been the instigator of *Rosemary's Baby*. Evans knew that Polanski's recent work had reaped neither success nor financial reward, but believed he, as producer, could steer him back to both. However there was one slight altercation at the beginning. Evans had just seen a personal screening of *What?* when Polanski arrived, and said it was one of the worst films he had seen in years. Polanski, in need of an urgent revival in his bank balance, shrugged and signed on the dotted line.

His return to Hollywood received a mixed reception, ranging from welcoming handshakes to sidelong glances which said, 'What in hell's name is *he* doing back in town?' The Sharon Tate murderers' death sentences had just been commuted to life, and headlines continued about Manson. Nicholson was still of the view that the 'moral majority was out to punish him because his wife was murdered'.

That apart, Polanski now hated the Hollywood syndrome and was paranoid about the attacks he had suffered across the board by the media, and having been branded a megalomaniac by some he had previously worked with. Robert Towne disliked him and his 'I-know-better-than-you' attitude, not so much personally as for the abruptness of Polanski's decision to make substantial changes to the script Towne had been working on for almost two years and which he felt was the best work he had ever done. Polanski conceded patronizingly that it was a masterful play, brimming with ideas and packed with some sensational dialogue; hidden away in the 200 pages was, he said, a powerful movie. 'But it's too long and complicated. There are too many people in it. It wants stripping down to more manageable levels,' Polanski told Towne over lunch at Nate 'n' Als, the Beverly Hills eatery. 'It cannot be filmed as it stands. I am going to take it over and rewrite it from start to finish,' he pronounced.

'No, you're not,' said Towne.

'Yes, he is,' said Evans.

'It should be trimmed,' agreed Nicholson.

Towne insisted on making the changes himself and Polanski went back to Rome while the cuts were made. He returned to discover that the script was still almost as long. He offered to spend two months with Towne on a rewriting effort and they worked long hours for eight weeks

194

until a new draft was finally complete. For moments of relaxation, and to get away from Towne's procrastinations and infuriating habit of finding things to do other than write, like taking his sheepdog for a stroll, Roman began taking flying lessons at Santa Monica airport.

Polanski altered the thematic base of the story so that it had a very definite Chandleresque quality, with shades of *The Maltese Falcon* and *The Big Sleep*. J. J. Gittes was a cool and cynical former police detective who had once worked the Chinatown district and was now out on his own as a private eye, largely in divorce actions. He was hired ostensibly by a woman client who produced evidence to show that her husband was involved with another woman. But then the story fragmented along several different and eventually converging paths as Gittes realized he had stumbled into something big, with sub-plots and undercurrents by the score: corruption reaching into high places, violence, sex, incest and death.

By early 1973 they began casting the actors who were to join Nicholson in the venture. These were the subject of almost as much pre-production discussion as the script itself. Ali McGraw, whom Robert Evans had wanted for the lead, had since decamped with Steve McQueen, her co-star in *The Getaway*. Then Evans wanted Jane Fonda but she turned it down without discussion. She was not keen on Polanski and 'I was fed up with people telling me how good Jack Nicholson is.' Polanski suggested Faye Dunaway. Evans was uncertain because he thought she could be difficult. Polanski knew she was, from conversations with Beatty after *Bonnie and Clyde*. But she was a powerful actress, and she got the part. It was also Polanski's idea to go for John Huston, gruff and great, as Dunaway's father. All in all, the sparks were ready to fly once again.

One example was later recounted by Polanski himself. It concerned a scene involving Faye Dunaway in which loose strands of her hair kept catching the light. The hairdresser made several attempts to flatten it, until finally Polanski went over to her and distracted her in conversation while he grasped the offending strands between his fingers and pulled the hair out, hoping she wouldn't notice. Dunaway, not unknown for her ample adjectival vocabulary, burst out, 'I just don't believe it. He's just pulled my fucking hair out.' She stormed off the set, with Evans running behind trying to persuade her to return.

Polanski complained that she was hesitant and nervous in her delivery which, he claimed, was the result of her insecurities, and she would explode in hysterical, expletive anger every time he altered or cut one of her lines because she was convinced that he was attempting to massacre her role.

But there are two sides to every story. Dunaway complained, 'That little shit wouldn't talk to me about the part. He just kept telling me, "Just do it the way you feel . . ." He would explain nothing and give me no clue as to the motivation of the character. What was I supposed to do . . . read his mind?' When she repeated her question to him about the motivation for the part, he screamed, 'Motivation! I'll tell you motivation! All the money you're being paid to do it. That's motivation.'

Freddie Fields, Faye's agent, demanded an apology from Polanski, who gave one half-heartedly and then ruined it by adding, 'She's nuts anyway.' Faye was not pleased and 'the little bastard', as Polanski was called on the *Chinatown* set, was lambasted with some more familiar phrases and sayings before work resumed. He also had one more surprise for Dunaway. During the shooting of the final scenes, Polanski began to reconsider the ending. The Dunaway character survives in the Towne version, but at the last minute, Polanski argued that she should die, and he won the day. So Dunaway was killed off and made the ultimate victim, a fact which annoyed several critics.

Nicholson remained cool throughout. He agreed to do something he hadn't done since he was a boy actor – line-reading with Polanski. Others objected and considered it an insult. Nicholson just raised his eyebrows and fell in line.

He and Roman were good friends. At night after filming, they often went on the prowl together and would appear next morning fragile and hiding behind black shades. Nicholson's eyes were bloodshot but by and large he generally refused attention. Life's like that, he would say. People have late nights even in the movies; sometimes their eyes get bloodshot and sometimes they get baggy. So what?

He never cared much how he looked and in *Chinatown* must have become the first male lead to spend half the picture with half his face covered by plaster and bandages to the slit in his nose, affected by Polanski himself who was doing a Hitchcock and playing a bit-part as the knife-wielding punk. It looked so effective that audiences actually thought it was a real wound.

Relations between leading male and director remained peaceful until the very last day, when there was a basketball game on television that Nicholson particularly wanted to see; his favourite team, Lakers, were playing the New York Knicks. Polanski was retaking a shot and could not get it right, because of some complex lighting; between takes

196

Nicholson kept running back and forth to his dressing room to find out the Lakers' score until finally 'the little bastard' screamed for him to return.

'I told you we wouldn't finish this scene,' Nicholson shouted.

Polanski came back, 'Okay, if that's your attitude . . .' and then he called, 'It's a wrap,' hoping that Jack, realizing the scene had not been shot correctly, would stay until it had been. On this occasion, however, he did not. The Lakers game had gone into overtime and he shuffled off back to watch it. Polanski stormed after him, barged into Jack's dressing room and smashed the television which exploded with glass shattering everywhere. 'You are an asshole,' he fumed at Nicholson, grabbing what was left of the television set and hurling it forward out of the door, and Nicholson also delivered a few choice lines.

Later, as they were driving home, they pulled up together at some lights. Jack was in his old VW. They turned and looked at each other. Nicholson mouthed the words, 'Fucking Pollack'; Polanski grinned. Nicholson grinned back and the fight was over.

Chinatown would be ready for 1974 release and Nicholson instinctively knew he had done a good job. This was confirmed when Robert Evans called him to view a rough cut.

'Mogul,' said Nicholson, 'we've got a hot one. Get those cheques ready.'

Polanski's interpretation of Towne's script took the film on to a plane that even Towne did not envisage. It presented a metaphorical view of an America where nothing was ever what it seemed, of a country being laid low by corporate greed, political corruption and betrayal. Watergate had spread like an infected wound across the body of America; Vietnam had torpedoed the nation's credibility abroad and its self-esteem at home. *Chinatown* conveyed the message through a social history with metaphorical eloquence, just as *Blow-Up* had done in another way in its sardonic view of Swinging London. Though occasionally lumbering and slow, *Chinatown* is a magnificently composed film, filled with potent images defining the often complex undercurrents of American society.

Nicholson was perfect, and could not have been bettered. Faye Dunaway, in spite of the tension which Polanski contrived between himself and his female lead, gave probably the best performance of her life.

The critics generally raved about Nicholson but *Chinatown* received a patchwork of reviews, with the sub-text obviously causing some confusion. Notably, however, Polanski's old media adversary Rex Reed commented that 'He proves, with the right material and the right producer to ride hard on his excesses and tendency towards pretentiousness, he is capable of brilliant work.'

Gradually, the film took off. It was a box office success and there was much hype for the Academy Award nominations towards the end of the year. The Oscar night celebrations in April 1975 turned out to be a rout for Robert Evans and Paramount studios. The two major films of the evening were *Chinatown* and *The Godfather, Part II* – when the lists were tallied, each had eleven nominations. Nicholson and Dunaway were up for Best Actor, Polanski for Best Director, Robert Evans for Producer of the Best Picture and Robert Towne for Best Original Screenplay. In the end, *The Godfather* collected the lion's share of the honours – six in all – and on *Chinatown* only Robert Towne converted his nomination into an Oscar for his outstanding script.

Nicholson was by then already making *One Flew Over the Cuckoo's Nest*, which would secure his first Oscar. He was also very happy about his life because Anjelica Huston had just walked into it. They had met at a party at Nicholson's house during filming of *Chinatown*. It was an opportune moment for Polanski and Towne to insert a mischievous but meaningful line – an in-joke – into the script when John Huston's character had to ask J. J. Gittes (Nicholson), 'Are you sleeping with her yet?' Nicholson was, and continued to do so for the next seventeen years of a chequered relationship. Before the year was out, Nicholson's house in Mulholland Drive – located in a compound he shared with Marlon Brando – had become the focal point of Anjelica's life in every respect. And it was here that she was to become unwittingly embroiled in part two of Polanski's own Hollywood scandals.

Chapter Eighteen

*I*n Hollywood parlance – packaging was the 'in' word – the Polanski–Nicholson partnership ought to have been a valuable package on the strength of *Chinatown*. A hot director is put together with a hot property and a hot actor or two and in theory they should have a hot picture. Warren Beatty had already shown how with his own package which he had put together as producer, co-writer and star of *Shampoo*, with Julie Christie and Goldie Hawn, which had its premiere in February 1975, and gave Beatty a multi-million-dollar payday in fees and share of the equity, while the rest of his crowd in Hollywood looked on in amazement and envy at this latest financial coup.

Polanski believed that if he and Nicholson could make another picture as a follow-up to *Chinatown* they would all be in the money, and just as Beatty had garnered a large equity share as originator and producer of *Shampoo*, Polanski was going to attempt to emulate his success. He returned to Rome and the rented villa where he had left Gerard Brach and Andy Braunsberg, intent on reactivating their plans for independent productions. He had left Hollywood under a slight cloud. In the publicity hype which surrounded *Chinatown* Robert Evans had let slip in a newspaper interview some unflattering comments which stung Polanski, just as Polanski had stung Victor Lownes with his remarks about money not smelling at the time of the release of *Macbeth*. Evans said Polanski was a good director as long as he was kept on a very tight rein, and properly managed. But he had a problem of surrounding himself with sycophants who flattered his ego, 'and then his films turn out badly'. Evans, making it clear that the success of *Chinatown* had not been achieved without considerable effort on his part, added that 'It takes guts to be a producer and eventually Roman realized I was right all along.' He was referring specifically to the musical score for *Chinatown* which had been written by a new friend of Polanski's, a

199

young composer named Philip Lambro, who, said Evans, virtually walked in off the street. The music was felt to be quite wrong for numerous scenes, and Evans held up the picture's release until Jerry Goldsmith had composed a new musical score in double-quick time.

By then, Polanski had high-tailed it back to Italy, where he took a brief interlude from the movie business to direct Alban Berg's unfinished opera *Lulu* at the Spoleto Festival before returning to join Brach and Braunsberg. They were to begin work on a rapid screenplay designed especially for Jack Nicholson in the leading role. It would be an independent production set-up in which Polanski's own company, Caliban Films, would be the lead organization. He and Braunsberg would co-produce as they had done on *Macbeth*, he and Brach would write, Polanski would direct and Polanski would co-star with Nicholson, more or less following what Warren Beatty had done with both *Bonnie and Clyde* and *Shampoo*. The whole project was commercially oriented to make them all a lot of money.

That, at least, was the plan. But Polanski did not have Beatty's contacts. Leslie Caron summed up the difference which made Warren the star of this triumvirate of friends (Beatty–Polanski–Nicholson) around that time: 'Warren had all the attributes of star quality and, of course, very good looks. He had a great deal of dynamism, always on the move . . . with talents and disciplines far above acting, which was demonstrated when he became a producer. He was obsessive about his work and his career, a very passionate man in every respect. He never made any secret of the fact that he wanted the world. He loved power and went for it . . .'

Polanski did not possess those motivations, but the underlying intent was the same – to make an assault on the big league. For this Polanski set aside all his previous explorations in the macabre, and went for comedy. *Pirates* was to be a period piece, whose slender storyline concerned a British buccaneer cast adrift on a raft and taken aboard a Spanish galleon where he causes a string of allegedly comical situations to occur. It was not something that had been dreamed up on the spur of the moment, either. Polanski's desire to make a period adventure dated back to his seeing Errol Flynn as Robin Hood. 'It was a childhood dream of his to make this film,' said Basia Kwiatkowska. 'I remember vividly in Kalatowki [a famous Polish resort in the Tatra Mountains where artists gather] in 1959 he was already trying out various scenes for it. He was carrying this idea around in his head and handling it as if it was something very precious.'

With years of plotting the movie in his mind behind him, Polanski completed the screenplay with remarkable speed and Braunsberg was assigned to put the package on the market. There was one difficulty which they had overlooked. Nicholson had not actually signed a contract and did not appear especially keen to do so. Every time Braunsberg contacted him, his fee went up, starting at somewhere around $750,000 which was his current asking price for a picture after *Chinatown*, and rising to double that. The truth was, he did not want to do the picture.

They touted the package around Europe and Hollywood. Polanski arranged to meet the new head of production at Paramount, Barry Diller, who had just taken over from Robert Evans. Paramount read the screenplay and expressed a strong interest, but backed off when their own production department forecast that the movie would cost far more to make than had been projected by Polanski's team – probably as much as $15 million. Four months passed without an offer and Polanski began to look elsewhere. United Artists also took an interest but negotiations were prickly and dragged on until UA production executives said they would only contemplate making an offer if Polanski himself set up a completion guarantee to insure them against delays and excessive costs. Polanski did not have the funds to make such a commitment and the deal collapsed. He had wasted a year in talks which came to nothing. He was desperate again. Caliban Films had exhausted its funds and they had to put *Pirates* on hold and go back to square one to find a new offering.

The speed with which Polanski and Brach proceeded to prepare and cajole a new project, a screenplay entitled *The Tenant*, into motion belied the need for a cash injection: from the moment they began to write the screenplay to its actual showing as a film took less than a year. It was a rapid and a well-researched scheme. Polanski had been tipped off that Paramount already owned the rights to the novel by Roland Topor on which the screenplay would be based. The book had been lying on the Paramount pile for years, and no one had ever done anything about it. Polanski and Brach wrote their screenplay in six weeks and sent it to Los Angeles. Paramount liked it so much that they actually increased the budget to allow Polanski to hire major Hollywood names to join himself in the cast list.

Once again, Polanski had rummaged around in his past for inspiration. *The Tenant* took him and Brach back into familiar territory, exploring human emotions and paranoiac terrors. One reviewer described it as a male version of *Repulsion*.

It concerned a young Polish clerk named Trelkovsky with transvestite tendencies – to be played by Polanski himself – who takes over a faintly sinister and dreary apartment in Paris, previously occupied by a woman who flung herself from the apartment window. The woman does not die immediately and must do so before Trelkovsky can take possession of the apartment. He visits her in hospital where she lies heavily bandaged, mummy-like and grotesque. There he also encounters the woman's lesbian lover, with whom he becomes involved. He moves into the apartment and gradually comes to believe that other tenants in the building are trying to drive him to suicide. We see him gradually disintegrating, like Catherine Deneuve in *Repulsion*. He tries to escape but is gradually drawn back to the apartment.

Polanski had read the novel ten years earlier. Topor, a surrealist painter who made the animated film *Fantastic Planet* a few years before, was part of the crowd Polanski used to hang around with in his meagre years in Paris. Like *Pirates*, the character of Trelkovsky had been rolling around at the back of his mind for years, and he was familiar from personal experience with the atmosphere of a Parisian apartment building, where the story unfolds. In the story, Trelkovsky was a naturalized French citizen, which fell neatly in line with Polanski's own real-life position. He had just applied for and been granted French citizenship to avoid the constant need for visas on his Polish passport. He also had a physical similarity to the character he was playing, and knew the kind of troubles he might have been through as a Pole living in a city steeped in bourgeois tradition, which he believed was the cause of its harshness towards foreigners.

With the bonus of an increased budget, Polanski was able to recruit three Oscar-winning Hollywood stars to his cast – Shelley Winters, Jo Van Fleet and Melvyn Douglas. For his co-star, as the suicide's lesbian lover, he selected Isabelle Adjani, the current golden girl of the French movie scene after her appearance in Truffaut's *The Story of Adèle H*, for which she had just won that year's New York Critics' Award for Best Actress and an Oscar nomination.

The cast list and the very fact that Polanski himself was both starring and directing his own picture attracted a good deal of media attention during filming at the Epinay Studios by the Seine, 20 kilometres from Paris. A colleague who visited the set reported, 'I had watched Polanski working once before, years earlier at Shepperton Studios, and frankly he hadn't changed much at all. He still spoke in that clipped sort of accent, though it wasn't so pronounced, but he possessed that air of determined authority, the autocrat. He enjoyed working with French technicians far more than with the British whom he spoke of with derision for their restrictive practices. But the pursuit of perfection to the point of driving his actors to dementia was apparent. I frankly did not know what to expect. A lot of people were saying he had lost it, but then *Chinatown* was so good that you had to wonder. During my brief visit to the studio, he was doing a scene with Isabelle Adjani which took twenty-five or more shots to get right. It still wasn't, and they did it again another twelve or fifteen times the following day. He was having difficulty with Adjani's own accent, which was far more pronounced than his own, and since they were both supposed to be drunk on tequila in the scene it became even more difficult. He tried using real tequila instead of water, but it didn't improve matters at all.'

Shelley Winters, she of the speak-your-lines-loud-and-clear brigade, played the concierge of the apartment building and was both intrigued and complimentary. 'He's a very fascinating man. The camera is him – and it can drive you crazy. One minute, he's acting with you and then he has his back to the camera and he's the director. He tries to make every situation real – with God knows how many takes. I've never known anyone else quite like him.'

Very few actors have made a success of simultaneously taking the role of director or vice versa. The most quoted exceptions, of course, are Laurence Olivier with *Hamlet* and Orson Welles with *Citizen Kane*, two of Polanski's own favourite films. *The Tenant* could not begin to be discussed in the same breath as either of these, but the point is always whether a director is able to make and maintain the transition from behind the camera to in front of it without causing a kink in the flow.

The Tenant was badly flawed in other ways, and far from bringing Polanski the critical acclaim he had hoped for after all the media attention the movie had received prior to its release, it returned him to the arena of controversy and derision, especially in France where it was shown at Cannes in May 1976. He was strongly reprimanded for the way he had presented Isabelle Adjani in unattractive mode, and the film was panned for its changes of mood, from tragic to comic. His own big scene drew especially hostile comment: it comes at the end, where he re-enacts the suicide of the woman who has become his obsession, and the camera pans down on him in his brunette wig, suspenders, green panties and high-heeled shoes, covered in blood after jumping through the apartment window. One reviewer complained, 'Polanski has taken over the role played by Catherine Deneuve in *Repulsion* – and one misses Miss

Deneuve.' Leslie Halliwell summed up the feeling of many critics: 'This wearisome case history shows the total dissipation of whatever talent [Polanski] once had.'

Such stinging criticism brought a now familiar response from Polanski, that he and not the film was under review, though in this case it could hardly be true. Viewers had to be Polanski buffs to see any real artistic merit in the production. Too many previously well-explored areas of the human psyche were being regurgitated: Polanski had failed to offer anything new or innovative. It would take years for *The Tenant* to be given that dubious rating of 'cult' movie, but in the meantime it flopped everywhere.

It was also true that the darker side of Polanski himself remained the object of lurid fascination, yet his own behaviour did nothing at all to divert the kind of public voyeurism that he had complained of so bitterly ever since the events at Cielo Drive. He realized this at Cannes when the media mob surrounded him and Brach, but it was not the star treatment savoured by the great and the good or the beautiful.

Polanski was the star of his own life, and he remained good copy. The press hounds who surrounded him did so not out of their quest to photograph or interview an attractive, awe-inspiring film person or to discuss the artistic merits of a great director. They grouped around his hotel entrance or outside the theatre or restaurant where he happened to be with a crowding hostility which sought to show a different kind of 'star' – not one who was simply famous, but one who was famously notorious.

Polanski knew this, and though he continually proclaimed his total distrust of and disgust at the popular media all over the world, he none the less played up to them when the moment was necessary, such as for publicity purposes for his film. He also knew that the press were always on his tail. 'In many ways,' said Basia, 'he was creating his own problems. He liked, for example, to surround himself with people from the demi-monde. It is hard to tell why these curious people became such good friends of his. Perhaps it was because he liked to dominate them.'

Polanski certainly continued to take risks of further unsavoury headlines – and that risk was undoubtedly present when he turned up in Germany and embarked upon a three-in-a-bed situation with two teenage girls, one of them aged fifteen.

Chapter Nineteen

*T*here ought, by 1976, to have been a pattern to Polanski's work, the kind of progression that is evident in the endeavours of even the most undisciplined artists, but his career was becoming almost unplottable. He was forty-three years old and had been making films professionally for fifteen years, yet his was the oddest curriculum vitae. The only recognition of continuity lay in the elements he built in to any of his films, which could be readily identified as Polanskian: quirky sex, nudity, madness, varying degrees of violence and an obsession with the central theme of domination of women both from his personal point of view and as an ingredient in his work.

This lack of any sense of direction was reflected in his unstable, nomadic life and equally spasmodic approach to work. From time to time, he vaguely referred to the Sharon Tate murders as having thrown him right off course, but since these did not appear to have inhibited his personal life in any way whatsoever – other than his occasional bouts of melancholia – it is difficult to see a connection. Jack Nicholson once tried to analyse his friend's attitude by saying he just wanted to make good pictures which need not necessarily be mainstream events. But art movies could never finance his life-style of Ferraris, Rolls Royces and expensive villas in Italy and Gstaad, a home in London and an apartment in Paris, and so there had to be commercial impetus too. Another of his erstwhile cronies, Richard Sylbert, reckoned Roman only came to Hollywood when he wanted money, because he hated the American press and the Hollywood system, largely because he could not stand the hidden undertones in negotiations and discussions. However, Hollywood was the only place where he could obtain major money.

Even that explanation does not bear close scrutiny, because after the early low-budget movies on which he cut his teeth and earned the tag of 'genius', the only films in recent years which had been remotely successful were those which were the glossiest of Hollywood products, *Rosemary's Baby* and *Chinatown*. *Macbeth* had outstanding merit as a Shakespearian film but suffered through the American system of critique. *What?* and *The Tenant* brought neither critical approbation nor monetary reward.

Polanski had reached a point of stagnation, it seemed, because the exploration of those darkest corners of human behaviour had already been well covered. Basia identified his problem as being linked to a theme which was central to many of his successful plots – the victimization and domination of women. 'When I look at his films,' she said, 'I think this stands out – women are usually the victims who have no one to turn to for help. It was apparent in various ways in *Repulsion*, *Cul-de-Sac*, *Rosemary's Baby*, *Chinatown* and *Macbeth* (and, in a more perverse way, in *The Tenant*). He portrayed women as if they deserved to be humiliated. Why? As I have said, I think it dates back to our own relationship – because I left him and he wanted revenge on me. He took it in his films. In the film we made together, *When Angels Fall*, in spite of some terrible crude and cruel things in it, there was a tenderness, just plain tenderness – a thread of pure love. Even in *Knife in the Water*, written when we were still together, the woman has some dignity, some freedom of choice. Afterwards, his women are only used, crushed. I escaped his humiliation. I ran away from Romek.'

In a way, life had overtaken the kind of portrayals Polanski and Brach dreamed up for the screen, and in the wake of the furore in France over *The Tenant*, Roman found himself in a creative void. His plans for *Pirates* had gone no further and the production commune formed with such high hopes had run out of steam. He had no work ahead of him, except for another opera. The Bavarian State Opera company had booked him to direct their production of *Rigoletto* at the 1976 Oktoberfest in Munich. His arrival was well signposted. Opera buffs in Germany are almost as passionate as their counterparts in Italy, and the hiring of a film director for such an important event aroused some bitter protests in the newspapers.

The engagement entailed a three-month stay in Munich which Polanski planned to intersperse with return visits to Paris. However, his attentions were rapidly diverted by the arrival in his life of Nastassia Kinski, a girl of classic Teutonic beauty. Looking for some action in Munich's lively night-life, Polanski had teamed up with a recent acquaintance and ended up sharing a double date with Kinski and her seventeen-year-old girlfriend in a late-night disco.

It was the beginning of a long relationship which would culminate in Nastassia starring in a later movie, *Tess*. When asked at that time by an interviewer for *American Film* magazine what had attracted him to her, he admitted she was still only fifteen when they first met 'but was a woman . . . woman and child at the same time. Her looks were quite unique and I knew almost instantly that she had star quality.' In Munich, in 1976, though, his future ambitions for Nastassia were not a principal concern. What he omitted to mention for the benefit of the interviewer was that on their very first meeting, Polanski ended up in bed with her – and her friend. After a night of disco dancing and drinking, they had all ended up in Polanski's luxurious hotel suite, paid for by the Bavarians. They sat around drinking and Polanski eventually retired to his bedroom with the seventeen-year-old. Some time later, he discovered that his own acquaintance had wandered off in a half-drunken stupor, leaving Nastassia alone slumbering on a couch. The foursome became a threesome as Polanski gently woke the girl and led her to his bed to join himself and the seventeen-year-old.

For the next two or three weeks, he spent much of his spare time in the company of the two girls, though gradually it was Nastassia who transfixed him. The daughter of the eminent German actor Klaus Kinski, she had made her movie debut at thirteen playing a deaf and dumb girl in Wim Wenders' *The Wrong Move* and then appeared in the 1975 Anglo-German adaptation of Dennis Wheatley's novel, *To the Devil a Daughter*, which starred Richard Widmark, Christopher Lee and Honor Blackman.

Whatever thoughts were developing in Polanski's mind about his relationship with Nastassia, they ran parallel to the ambitions of the girl's mother, who felt that with the right guidance, her daughter could become a big star. Polanski provided a bridge to those hopes. At some point, he suggested that Nastassia might like to move into his London house, to improve her English and prepare for the future. Her mother agreed, with the proviso that she went along too.

The arrangements were put temporarily on hold towards the end of October when Polanski was invited by French *Vogue* to be guest editor of its Christmas issue, following in the footsteps of such luminaries as Alfred Hitchcock, Marlene Dietrich and Federico Fellini. It was an eminently appealing opportunity for various reasons, but mainly because it would be a major feature about himself and his work over which, for once, he had control.

He also immediately devised a plan to promote his dormant film script, *Pirates*, by using it as a theme for the lay-out of photographs he had been asked to select. He told the *Vogue* editors that he also planned to feature an exciting new young actress who would become an international star with his next movie. Her name . . . Nastassia Kinski.

The selection of material for the magazine would include a clutch of personal photographs from his childhood and on through his developing years, coming right up to date with him at play, captioned dining on champagne and caviare at Maxim's and smoking an expensive Havana cigar. The major part of the feature would centre upon the women who had appeared in his movies, including Sharon Tate but with the notable exception of Basia Kwiatkowska who had helped him on the road to such fame as he now enjoyed. And then, for the present, he wanted to feature Nastassia. *Vogue* agreed to fund a photographic session in the Seychelles.

They arrived there in the first week of November, Nastassia surrounded by an entourage of make-up artists, dressers and hair stylists, and Polanski with a couple of photographers. It was an elaborate casting-couch scenario that was obvious to all present as an opportunity for them to be together in an idyllic setting. The photographs were glossy and extravagant and provided an unreal, rose-tinted portrayal of Polanski's life and the women he had worked with, passing quickly over the heartache and tragedy that several had suffered through their encounter with him. For Kinski, it was a miraculous and almost unbelievable entry into the realms of international focus, with shots of her in restrained sexual poses, apparently acting out scenes from Polanski's 'next major movie', *Pirates*.

There was also a photograph of Polanski himself taken on the white beaches of the Seychelles, buried vertically in the sand with only his head showing and with the waves lapping around his ears – a kind of 'up-to-his-neck-in-it' idea which, in a very short while, would be proved to be uncannily prophetic.

And so the Christmas issue of *Vogue* presented Polanski in a new light – and one which he relished. For once, he was being featured without the usual attributes of sinister innuendo and darkness. This was Polanski the famous director and star, positively dazzling-white. He was called for interviews by various magazines, and to one Polish journalist he announced that he would like to go back to his homeland for the first time in fifteen years. The fact that he had recently acquired French citizenship, which freed him of any complications, may well have had some bearing on his decision to return home for a visit, although later, when he faced questions in Warsaw from the newspapers about why he had come back after such a long lapse, he denied this. The Polish journalists seemed to treat this with some scepticism, however.

There was an emotional reunion with his father and Wanda who were living in an apartment building in the centre of Krakow, where their most valuable possession was a blue Mercedes car which Polanski had bought for them a couple of years earlier. The following day, he borrowed the car and began driving around the city, looking up old friends and revisiting old memories.

Krakow itself had not changed a great deal physically, but was a blacker, darker place, grim and grimy and severely affected by smoke and chemicals from the steelworks and aluminium plants. Roman moved on to Warsaw and to the old film community and former colleagues from Lodz. Though some of his former friends were wary of him, he was in great demand at the festive parties where he regaled his enthusiastic listeners with stories of Hollywood. 'I could not understand why he had stayed away for so long,' said cinematographer Witold Sobocinski, his former close friend who in 1993 had become a professor at the Lodz National Film School, 'because I know Poland was very close to his heart. He had not changed much. He still wanted to be the centre of attention. He was a leader, not in an ideological sense but as one who always had to be on top of what was going on. If there is a banquet, all remain standing until Polanski tells them where to be seated. I came to meet him on that first visit, and do you know, he did not even remember me at first. As far as we were concerned, he was recognized as the only Pole from our circle who had made it really big abroad, although his career was reported mostly from the scandalous and not the artistic angle – and would continue to be so. For the younger generation of Polish film-makers Polanski's art became traditional, if not classical. But I don't think he was a particular source of inspiration to them, nor of envy either.'

But there were serious questions to be asked, and with film people pressing him for details of the Western world, Polanski agreed to give a question and answer session at the Warsaw Film Club on 3 January 1977 at which over 400 film-makers, actors, writers, journalists and photographers crowded in to listen.

Among them was another old friend, Jerzy Skolimowski, with whom he had written *Knife in the Water*. Jerzy arrived late, causing speculation as to whether he would come at all. Since joining Polanski in London and having a couple of failures directing pictures for Gene Gutowski, he had returned to Warsaw where he lived with his wife and two sons in reduced circumstances. Though he would soon make a come-back with *The Shout*, with Alan Bates and Susannah York, at that time he had not made a film for six years, and the villa he was building had been abandoned for the time being through lack of funds.

The differing circumstances of the two men who had started out on the same road together were well known to the audience. Skolimowski was cheered on his arrival. Polanski had always denied that material considerations and money were major motivations for him in his career, but this was another aspect of his life and times which his fellow Poles quite obviously distrusted. One of Polanski's questioners asked if it was easy to make money as a film-maker in the West. Polanski replied that it was 'very difficult'.

'Why hasn't Skolimowski worked for so long?' asked another questioner.

'Ask him not me,' came the reply.

As the meeting progressed, Polanski noticed a growing hostility toward him, especially from some of the more intense film-makers among the audience, to whom he appeared conceited. He seemed deliberately and unnecessarily provocative to a group of people who had gathered with genuine interest to listen to him.

'Aren't you worried,' one asked, 'that you have made no kind of statement in your films, and now it is too late to do so?'

'I know you are making fun of me,' Polanski replied, 'but I can only say I'm interested in life as much as you and perhaps more because I have had more occasion to experience life.'

The reply provoked another questioner who referred to the title of a film made by Andrzej Wajda, pointedly described by the speaker as Poland's greatest director – *Everything For Sale*. 'Do you think everything is for sale . . . are there any limits for you personally?' he asked, and then paused before inquiring, 'Are there any tragedies in your life that you would not use to sell a film?'

Polanski brushed the question aside with a flippant remark about experiences in life itself being a necessary ingredient in the work of any artist, whether painter, writer or film-maker. Later, after the meeting, he gave an interview for Poland's leading weekly, *Kultura*, in which his attitudes to films, money and life were further explored. There was one question which was posed with such surprising abruptness by the interviewer, Janusz Glowacki, that it drew an answer which would have a surprising relevance to the next major episode in Polanski's life.

'Did you ever really love anyone?' Glowacki asked.

'A few women.'

'Normal love does not feature in your films . . .'

'Normal love is not interesting. I assure you', said Polanski, drawing upon his personal experiences again, 'that it is incredibly boring. And, as I said, I love spectacles . . .'

Polanski returned to Paris a few days later and telephoned Nastassia Kinski regularly. Hollywood was beckoning again, which was just as well because he was virtually broke. He had recently changed agents, by necessity since Bill Tennant had had some emotional trauma and given up his agency business. Polanski had been taken on by Sue Mengers, known for her association with the artistically inclined though a powerful negotiator in monetary matters. She knew everyone and was a particular friend of Andy Warhol.

Mengers was pressing Polanski to return to Los Angeles on a more permanent basis. It was the only place, she said, where he could obtain a real showcase for his talent. The Americanization of Polanski might well have been in the bud, had it not been nipped by what followed.

Mengers had fixed up a deal with Columbia Pictures for Polanski to write and direct an adaptation of Lawrence Sanders' novel, *The First Deadly Sin*, and at the end of January he took off for Los Angeles as she had suggested and began to get himself back into the swing of Hollywood life. He checked into the Beverly Wilshire Hotel where Warren Beatty had a penthouse apartment, and discovered that Andy Warhol was there too. Their paths crossed a couple of times as Polanski rejoined the incestuous social scene, at the same time discovering that many of his old friends had disappeared from view.

He seemed to be ready to adopt Sue Mengers' suggestion of a long stay in Los Angeles and began sounding out the authorities for the necessary visa and immigration papers. He also made arrangements for Nastassia Kinski to join him. After her appearance in *Vogue*, he had discussed her future with an agent he knew, Ibrahim Moussa, who also thought she had great potential although obviously her lack of acting experience and her European accent posed a problem. Polanski did some horse-trading at the Lee Strasberg School of Drama and enrolled his protégée as a pupil in exchange for lectures which he would give to the school. He called Nastassia immediately. She shrieked with delight when she heard the news, as did her mother, who said she would come too.

In the meantime, another curious development began to unfold. It was a complicated and dramatic sequence of events which brought the world's media back to Polanski's doorstep, and there were differing accounts of how it all began. Roman claimed that in the wake of his guest editorship of French *Vogue*, he had revived his interest in still photography and had been given a commission from the men's magazine, *Vogue Homme*, to prepare a photographic feature on 'young girls of the world' in a target age range of around thirteen. According to him, the magazine wanted a selection of photographs taken by himself in various countries which would show the provocative, sexy style of young girls of the day. It was a dubious idea which an executive of *Vogue Homme* would later dismiss as 'an unlikely prospect – we are not into paedophilia'.

So the route to Polanski's involvement with a thirteen-year-old whom we shall call Mary (a pseudonym) was steeped in some mystery. Dark rumours suggested that she had been introduced to him by John Huston, while others said that Polanski met her mother in a Hollywood bar a year earlier and came looking for her – and found the daughter instead. Polanski's own story was that a friend had talked about a fabulous-looking teenager who was the sister of a girl he was dating, and Polanski proceeded to get in touch.

The girl's mother, he said, had been warned to expect his call, and when he rang, she invited him over to her house. It was she, said Polanski, who reminded him that they had met at a club some months earlier. Mary's mother, an actress who lived with a journalist on the staff of a magazine called *Marijuana Monthly*, was keen for the contact with Polanski to develop because she was seeking work and thought he might open a few doors.

Her resident lover also sought to use the contact with Polanski to promote the idea of Jack Nicholson giving him an interview for his magazine. And so, with benefits available all round, it was agreed that Polanski should take Mary out on location for his photographic sessions.

After a preliminary visit to the girl's house to take some 'test shots' he made a date for a complete photographic session with her on 10 March. Later, the girl's mother would tell the police that she made a point of telling Polanski her daughter's age and that on no account was she to be alone with anyone.

Jack Nicholson, as Polanski may well have known, was not in Los

Angeles at the time. He had gone to his home in the ski resort of Aspen and was spending some time in the company of, among others, Polanski's old friend Jill St John. Nicholson's love life was well documented in the papers. He had recently had a very public split with Anjelica Huston, followed by a pre-Christmas reunion. During the New Year festivities, their relationship had struck another bad patch over Jack's wandering eye, which was why Nicholson went off to do some skiing on a separate vacation while Anjelica prepared to move out. Nicholson did not expect her to be there by the time of his planned return in the third week of March.

Polanski entered stage left with the thirteen-year-old whose mind was filled with dreams of becoming a star. Unbeknown to Nicholson himself, his house was to become the scene of what followed . . .

The girl was to have been accompanied by a friend who, in the event, did not go. However, her mother insisted that Polanski leave telephone numbers of the locations and call in if there were any changes. He drove to Mulholland Drive where Jack Nicholson lived but went first to the home of another friend, the British actress Jacqueline Bisset, who lived across the road with Victor Drai.

On the way, according to Mary's version of events to Los Angeles police, Polanski talked about sex. He asked her if she was still a virgin and if she knew anything about masturbation. Would she like him to show her what masturbation was? Her story was at variance with that of Polanski, who claimed she told him how she slept with her boyfriend and that she had first experienced sex at the age of eight.

They arrived at Jacqueline Bisset's house around 4 p.m. Bisset had been shopping and arrived home laden with parcels. Victor Drai and two other friends stayed indoors while Polanski and Mary went outside to begin the photographic session by the pool. By now a cold wind had blown up and the sun was going down behind the trees.

While they were there, Mary's mother called to check on her daughter and was told by a woman who answered the telephone not to worry. Mary and Polanski were out by the pool and there were other people in the house. Soon afterwards, Polanski decided he had chosen the wrong location for his photographs and suggested to Mary that they should go across the road to Jack Nicholson's house, which they did. He parked his rented Mercedes outside the security gates to the compound which contained Nicholson's two houses and Marlon Brando's mansion. Polanski called Nicholson's housekeeper, Helena Kallianiotes, who lived in the smaller of Nicholson's two properties, and said he was sure Jack would not mind if he used the house for his photographic sessions. Helena let them in.

'Is there anything to drink?' Polanski asked.

'Champagne in the fridge,' said Helena. 'You know where it is . . . and now, if you'll excuse me, I have to get on with my work.'

She waited to take a glass of champagne from the bottle of Cristal which Polanski popped and then left him alone with the girl. They sat drinking for a few minutes. The young model was apprehensive. She said that the last time she drank champagne she was ill. Polanski reassured her; this was good champagne and would do her no harm. She claimed he told her that Nicholson would be arriving soon, knowing full well that he would not, but, it was said later, playing on the fact that Mary desperately wanted to meet him and even have her picture taken with him, so that she could boast to her friends.

'I don't know how much I drank,' she was to tell the police. 'I just kept drinking it for the pictures he was taking.' The photographs were posed in various parts of the house. In the kitchen, for example, he had her sitting on the table licking an ice-cube, and in Nicholson's main living room, he photographed her in the bay window overlooking Franklin Canyon.

They moved to the jacuzzi area; the girl was intrigued by the clouds of steam and Polanski suggested she should go topless. He produced some pills, Quaaludes, took one himself and persuaded the girl to take half. The scenes that followed, ostensibly for photographic purposes, had the girl topless in Nicholson's elaborate jacuzzi in which she was joined by Polanski.

In the middle of this misadventure, the girl's mother telephoned and was assured that all was well, though soon after, feeling the effects of the champagne, the hot jacuzzi and the pill, Mary wanted to lie down. Polanski took her to what used to be the spare room where he once slept. Now it housed Nicholson's huge television screen and his stereo, and was furnished with deep sofas.

'I can barely remember anything that happened with any clarity,' the girl said in her police statement. Polanski followed her into the room and began making love to her almost as soon as she lay down on the sofa, first orally, then with vaginal intercourse, and finally, anally, when he climaxed. As he did so, there was a knock on the door.

Anjelica had returned home. He called out to her, and Anjelica shouted back, 'Roman?'

He opened the door slightly and Anjelica could see he was naked.

She had never cared much for Polanski and now she was angry that he should be using Nicholson's house for what appeared to be sexual purposes.

'What are you doing here?' she asked sternly.

'I'm doing a picture session for *Vogue*,' Polanski replied. Anjelica was not convinced and complained to Helena about allowing him into the house.

Undaunted, Polanski returned to the sofa and attempted to make love again. The girl froze; she wanted to go home. Twenty minutes later, they both emerged from the room, dressed and ready to go. Polanski made some half-hearted attempt to introduce the girl to Anjelica but neither was especially interested. He took Mary home and she ran straight upstairs to her bedroom, too ashamed, she said, to face her mother.

Polanski talked to the mother and said they had done well; he would call back again when the pictures had been developed and printed. Later that night, however, the girl broke down in tears to her boyfriend and elder sister, describing what had happened in the Nicholson house, and unsuccessfully pleaded with them not to tell her mother. The mother called the police, and at midnight, the girl was taken to the Parkland Hospital for medical tests for sexual contact. That night and the following morning she was interviewed by detectives in the presence of deputy District Attorney James Grodin. By the end of the interviews, the DA's office was sufficiently convinced by her story to issue a warrant for Polanski's arrest, charging him with suspicion of rape against a minor, a charge which if proven carried a statutory penalty of between ten and fifty years in prison.

Later that day, Polanski was walking across the lobby of the Beverly Wilshire Hotel with some friends, on his way to the theatre, unaware of what had been going on the previous night and earlier that day.

'Mr Polanski,' said a quiet voice as he strode towards the exit doors, 'I am from the LAPD. I have a warrant for your arrest.' The police had arrived mob-handed, and Polanski asked where they wanted to talk. The senior officer suggested his hotel room, for which they had a search warrant. He agreed, but asked if the police would split up, to avoid speculation from the passing hotel guests to whom he was instantly recognizable. In his room, Polanski denied everything, and said that nothing untoward had happened with the girl. The police took away undeveloped rolls of film, slides and photographs and a phial of Quaaludes found in the bathroom. Grodin now asked him if he would accompany them to the Nicholson house in Mulholland Drive. Polanski agreed.

Two other officers carrying a search warrant arrived in advance at Mulholland Drive and the rest arrived soon afterwards. Anjelica was preparing to move out of the house. 'I'm sorry,' she said, 'but I can't stay . . . and anyway I answered questions to a detective earlier when he called about Roman Polanski being here yesterday. It isn't my business, anyway.'

'I'm sorry. It is your business. You live here, don't you?'

'It isn't my house. I have been staying here.'

'Is Mr Nicholson still in Colorado?'

'Yes, I spoke with him on the telephone a few minutes ago. He doesn't know anything about this.'

'Well,' the officer said, taking Anjelica's arm, 'we have court-authorized papers for a search and we have to ask you to step back inside.'

'Where do you want to start?' she asked, resigned now to cooperating with them.

'Your handbag. We'll start there.'

A half-hour later, Anjelica was charged with possession of cocaine. Detectives also took various items from the house, including a small brick of hashish; the police had already made it known they would like to have the opportunity of taking Jack Nicholson's fingerprints so that they could be checked against those on the hash container. Nicholson remained in Aspen, rejecting all approaches from the near-frantic journalistic activity that had blown up around him. His lawyers and advisers told him to stay away from Mulholland Drive at all costs so that he did not become even remotely involved in a public manner.

One who did reach Nicholson, by coincidence, was Jerzy Skolimowski who, after talking with Polanski when he visited Poland at Christmas, had obtained Nicholson's telephone numbers. Polanski had told him that Nicholson was a big shot in Hollywood, and that if anyone could get him work, it was he. Skolimowski, deciding to make one major effort to re-establish himself in the West, telephoned Nicholson who invited him to Aspen to talk things over. Skolimowski managed to rustle up some funds and caught a plane to New York where he landed on the very day the newspapers were blaring out the headlines of Polanski's arrest.

Horrified and confused by what he read, Skolimowski believed that his own chances were now finally blown. Nicholson, he was sure, would not wish even to talk to any contact of Polanski. None the less he telephoned from New York, and Nicholson told him to continue his journey to Aspen anyway. There was nothing either of them could do about or for Polanski for the time being, and he told Skolimowski that he was remaining in Aspen.

When Nicholson had not returned to Los Angeles by 1 April, police requested a warrant from Santa Monica municipal judge Robert Thomas authorizing detectives to obtain his fingerprints. Nicholson cooperated and had his prints taken by Aspen police. They did not match those found on the hashish container and on 19 April the police announced that he was cleared of any suspicion in the case, though Anjelica still faced possible prosecution over her alleged possession of a small quantity of cocaine.

The weeks and months of headlines were only just beginning as the story developed through its various stages, and Columbia executives, shocked by the mess, did not wait to allow the court to decide upon Polanski's guilt or innocence and arbitrarily announced that it was cancelling his contract to make *The First Deadly Sin*.

Anjelica Huston's lawyers negotiated the non-performance of the action against her if she agreed to testify in the case against Polanski, and a twenty-one-member Federal Grand Jury was convened to hear the evidence in secret. The jury then indicted Polanski on six counts:

1) Furnishing a controlled substance to a minor
2) Committing a lewd and lascivious act on a minor
3) Committing unlawful sexual intercourse with a minor
4) Act of rape by use of drugs
5) An act of perversion, oral copulation with the sexual organ of a child
6) Sodomy

Even Roman's best friends were at a loss to see how he could recover from these devastating accusations, and a *Vogue* executive in Paris joined those who were distancing themselves from him by denying to Polanski's defence lawyers that he was on any official assignment for them when these events occurred. So the scenario was in place for a mass of media attention between the Grand Jury indictment and the eventual trial, set for August 1977.

Chapter Twenty

Nastassia Kinski and her mother arrived in the midst of his troubles, but Polanski was as good as his word and contributed towards a course at the Lee Strasberg Institute for Nastassia. Her arrival did not go unnoticed by the prosecution in the drugs, sex and jacuzzi case. Meanwhile, Polanski had moved out of the Beverly Wilshire, now that the expense-account for making *The First Deadly Sin* had been withdrawn, and into the less salubrious and far cheaper Château Marmont.

Top-class lawyers do not come cheap in Los Angeles, and with counter-investigations, defence submissions and character witnesses to be marshalled, the bills were enormous. Whatever the outcome, Polanski needed some money fast, and Sue Mengers came to the rescue, negotiating a new picture deal with the producer Dino De Laurentiis to direct a remake of the John Ford 1937 classic, *Hurricane*. Polanski was reported to be getting a million-dollar fee to direct the picture – the largest he had ever been offered.

He ploughed into it as if there was nothing on the horizon which might deter him – even to the point of telling De Laurentiis that he wanted Nastassia Kinski, currently ensconced in acting classes, to be his female lead. He was overtly confident about the future and, after a couple of months in seclusion, was venturing out into Los Angeles night-life, telling anyone who would listen that what had happened was not his fault. His story was that it was Mary's actions as much as his own that led to the situation he now found himself in. She had introduced sex into the conversation, she had taken off her blouse, she had been a willing participant in the sex, he had never given her drugs and only a couple of glasses of champagne. How could he be blamed for that?

There were a number of other incidentals that could only occur in Hollywood. Polanski's first appearance before a judge was at Santa Monica, known as the 'celebrity' court, and he arrived to discover that the case was attracting almost as much attention as his wife's murder had done. Dozens of reporters and cameramen from around the world were joined by the local population, including a large number of school-kids and students who variously jeered and cheered, yelled and whooped as Polanski arrived. It was reminiscent of one of Hollywood's famous celebrity sex trials from the past – Fatty Arbuckle, Charlie Chaplin and Errol Flynn came to the minds of writers looking for comparisons.

Observing this explosion of local interest, an enterprising theatre manager began running an extended season of Polanski films, which provided an admirable opportunity for Roger Gunson, the District Attorney assigned to lead the prosecution's case, to back-track through Polanski's work and attempt to discover if there was any pattern in his films which might be applied to the case. Gunson decided that there was, and he believed it could be used, if necessary, as evidence to demonstrate a consistent tendency in Polanski's artistic output over the previous decade.

Meanwhile, the lawyers on both sides began negotiations for a plea-bargaining deal whereby Polanski would admit to lesser charges to save the need for a trial, which had been set for 9 August, coincidentally the anniversary of Sharon's murder. Polanski's lawyer, Douglas Dalton, had offered to have him plead guilty to 'contributing to the delinquency of a minor'. The DA would accept nothing less than a plea of guilty to one of the six charges. Gunson knew by then that his evidence would not support some of the more serious charges. The girl was not a virgin and had admitted experimenting with drugs. A medical report had shown there were no signs of 'anal or vaginal damage', and the girl's family were concerned about the intensity of media coverage. Already a photograph of her and her mother taken with a telephoto lens had been published with her name by a German magazine, and the build-up to the trial had brought the media circus to Santa Monica on a scale not seen in years. European newspapers and magazines were already installing telephone lines for their reporters and photographers to use during the trial. The family lawyer, Lawrence Silver, said the case was going to provide the world with a daily diet of sex and scandal for weeks, and the girl herself would become the central focus of it.

A day before the trial was due to begin, Gunson agreed to a deal with Polanski's lawyers. He would enter a plea of guilty to one felony count of 'unlawful sexual intercourse' with a thirteen-year-old girl. Even that carried a jail term potential of one to ten years, and the possibility of Polanski's deportation. And so, when the media from around the world crowded into Rittenband's courtroom on 9 August, they were to be disappointed. There would be no trial; the whole business had been wrapped up and the lawyers had rehearsed their speeches.

Prosecutor Gunson announced that Polanski was ready to plead guilty to unlawful sexual intercourse and asked Judge Laurence J. Rittenband to dismiss all other charges. He read a statement from the District Attorney which said that this 'would achieve substantial justice with respect to society's interests through the felony conviction of the defendant yet provide the victim with the opportunity to grow up in a world where she will not be known as the young girl with whom Roman Polanski had intercourse'.

This point was picked up by Lawrence Silver for the family. He said they supported this resolution to the case because if the trial proceeded 'she would have to testify within the glare of world-wide publicity and a stigma would attach itself for a lifetime. Justice is not made of such stuff: whatever harm has come to her as a victim of this case would be exacerbated in the extreme . . . reliving the sorry events with their delicate contents would be a challenge to the well-being of any person.' He said the family did not seek Polanski's incarceration, merely an acknowledgement of his wrongdoing and undertaking to seek counselling. There was 'no money involved' in this decision, though it went unsaid that a conviction might have led to a civil action being brought against Polanski by the girl for psychological damage.

At that moment, the case seemed to be swinging in Polanski's favour. Observers would have put money on him being freed on probation. But they reckoned without the reasoning of Judge Rittenband who asked if Polanski knew that the girl was only thirteen. He replied that he knew that before they set out on the photographic mission. Standing before the court in a smart, doublebreasted, pin-striped suit, he was asked to summarize the crime he had committed: 'I had sexual intercourse with a person not my wife, under the age of eighteen.'

Judge Rittenband sat back in his chair, reviewing the evidence, and finally announced he would adjourn the case until 19 September to allow Polanski to undergo examination by two court-appointed psychiatrists who would report back on whether he was 'a mentally disordered sex offender'. Later that day, the District Attorney said the judge could not recommend Polanski's deportation, but it would become inevitable for an alien convicted and imprisoned for a crime involving 'moral turpitude' to be barred from the USA. That prospect hung over Polanski like a black cloud.

In the six weeks before the next hearing Polanski's work with Dino De Laurentiis on *Hurricane* had reached the point where they were ready to cast the film. His passport had not been confiscated and he was even given permission to travel abroad to survey sites for location filming. He had several discussions with his probation officer, Irwin Gold, who produced a long report which became a focus of much mirth later when pirated copies surfaced and were mysteriously circulated around the social watering-holes of Los Angeles, New York and London.

The report made fascinating reading. The descriptions of the sex scenes were sensitive and erotic, and added a note about the interest in the case and the number of supporters who had come forward to support Polanski: 'Not since Renaissance Italy has there been such a gathering of creative minds in one locale.'

The report also listed unsolicited letters written to the probation officer in praise of Polanski's character from such names as Robert Evans, Mia Farrow and Dino De Laurentiis. Farrow wrote: '. . . he is a loyal friend and a distinguished director, important to the motion picture industry and a brave and brilliant man important to all people.' Evans was similarly gushing: 'I know the suffering [he has endured] and I feel the press has maligned him terribly. He may make for provocative headlines, but with rare exception, the press never captured the beauty of Roman's soul. If ever a person is deserving of compassion . . . it is Roman.' His former partner Gene Gutowski similarly went over the top when he described Polanski as 'virtually a teetotaller who never imbibed much more than a couple of aspirin'.

Polanski, whose mentor Andrzej Wadja once described him as a better actor than a director, managed to draw some sympathy from Irwin Gold, who also made a point of delving into his past. All the horror stories had poured out: life in the ghetto, losing his mother, the harsh post-war period, even the attack by a man who would be convicted of murder, the flight from Communism, the Manson murders and so on. Gold noted: 'Although the defendant has been under abnormal periods of stress throughout his life, he has never sought psychiatric help or other professional assistance . . . implying that any psychiatric care could conceivably interfere with the creative process.'

Polanski's version of events at Mulholland Drive that day in March were diligently recorded by Gold: the girl mentioned she liked champagne . . . she got drunk at her father's house . . . she talked about sex . . . she first had sex when she was eight . . . she was not inexperienced. He denied offering the girl drugs. They went to the bedroom because he thought he heard a car coming; there were 'some maniacs who used to come to the compound', which was a thinly veiled allusion to the Sharon Tate murders . . . the fear. She was a willing partner in all that they did . . . it was all very spontaneous . . . he withdrew before climax, etc., etc.

By now, Gold had clear sympathy with Polanski, as was apparent from one of the closing paragraphs of his report: '. . . he expressed great remorse . . . he expressed great pity and compassion for the victim . . . he stated that because of the many tragedies that he himself has known in his own life he feels greatly for the young person in distress . . .' Polanski went on to say how he had often been kicked in his life. Gold asked whether it was possible that he too had kicked someone. Polanski broke down and cried, and word had it that Gold almost wept with him. But in his report the officer did suggest certain restrictions as a condition of probation: 'that he not associate with children under the age of eighteen, except in the presence of responsible adults', which seemed to undermine everything that went before.

A new hearing had been set for 19 September, but a couple of days before, Judge Rittenband summoned counsel for both sides to his chambers to assess their feelings. His own would soon become apparent. He thought the probation report was an absolute whitewash. He announced he intended to send Polanski to Chino State Prison for a period of ninety days for more extensive assessment.

Dalton objected and at the full hearing on 19 September pleaded that Polanski was a 'criminal by accident' and that there were many 'complex and psychological factors in this situational event which was otherwise a complete departure from his normal mode of conduct'. Gunson angrily rejected the implication that all that had happened was with the girl's consent.

The objection did not wash with Rittenband either. He laid into Polanski: 'Although just short of her fourteenth birthday, the girl was well developed and regrettably not unschooled in sexual matters. However, although she was not inexperienced or unsophisticated, this fact was not licence for the defendant, a man of the world in his forties, to engage in an act of unlawful sexual intercourse, however submissive and uninhibited she might have been. You will go to the prison of Chino for ninety days so that an in-depth diagnostic study may be conducted upon your character and mental state so as to enable me to reach a fair and just decision.'

Dalton immediately rose to ask for a stay of the order because Polanski was involved in making a film involving millions of dollars and the employment of many people would be imperilled by his non-performance. Such matters had to be taken account of in Hollywood, but the judge noted laconically, 'He contracted to make this film after he had been charged on the probable assumption that, at worst, he would get probation.' But he agreed to allow a ninety-day stay before Polanski was required to report to Chino, to give time for the picture to be completed. In the meantime, he was free to travel – and travel he did.

Ten days after the hearing, and unknown to Polanski or the public at large, a newspaper cutting was placed in front of Judge Rittenband. It was from the *Santa Monica Evening Outlook* and showed Polanski pictured in Munich surrounded by several women at a table covered with mugs of beer. The accompanying news item said: 'Movie director Roman Polanski puffs a cigar as he enjoys the companionship of young ladies during his visit [on 28 September] to the Munich Oktoberfest, the world's largest beer festival. Sources say Polanski came to Bavaria's capital as a tourist and just wants to relax. A Santa Monica court ordered Polanski to undergo a ninety-day diagnostic study at a state prison but permitted him to finish a film first.'

The judge was furious and the situation was not helped when he discovered that Nastassia Kinski, who he knew had come to Los Angeles at Polanski's bidding, was also with him in Munich. Rittenband banged on the table and said Polanski had shown utter contempt for his court. He immediately summoned the District Attorney and Douglas Dalton to his chambers. 'It's nothing short of contempt,' he raged. 'This son-of-a-bitch speaks of remorse and here he is playing around Europe with a sixteen-year-old.' He ordered that Polanski should return forthwith, and set a hearing for 21 October for him to explain himself.

By now Polanski and Nastassia had moved on to London, where Kinski was due to do some screen tests at Pinewood Studios. They stayed at Polanski's mews house and it was there that he learned of the rumpus back in LA. He had resumed work on the film script for *Hurricane* and had arranged to fly to Tahiti to scout the locations. An airline strike prevented him from getting back to Judge Rittenband's court for the due date, and the hearing was postponed for three days. Then, the judge demanded to know what he was up to, and why he appeared to be travelling the world with Miss Kinski, also apparently under the age of eighteen. Polanski explained that his interest in Kinski was purely professional and that she had been chaperoned throughout by her mother. He also pointed out that the photograph in the Santa Monica newspaper had been cropped – there were other men in the original picture and the 'lovely young ladies' were with them. His journey had been necessary for work on the picture, he said, and the defence put Dino De Laurentiis on the stand to confirm that he had 'sent Mr Polanski to Munich on business, to meet a German distributor because I was personally unable to go'.

Later, in chambers, the judge said he did not believe Laurentiis, and the whole thing smelled of a cover-up. However, he agreed to allow Polanski to remain free until the date originally set, so that he could continue work on the film, but warned him that there would be no further extension. He should report to Chino, as arranged, on 19 December; the judge showed no mercy. Polanski would have to spend Christmas in prison, and fellow director Tony Richardson arranged a last supper with himself, Jack Nicholson, Kenneth Tynan and others in Hollywood on the eve of his surrender.

He arrived at the gates of Chino in a silver Cadillac owned by Douglas Dalton. A huge press pack was waiting to catch a last glimpse of the current 'most notorious man in tinsel town' before the gates slammed shut and he began his ordeal inside a prison where his fellow inmates were perpetrators of a fair cross-section of crimes against society, ranging from cop killers to fraudsters. Polanski was placed in protective custody, meaning virtual isolation, because, as one of his jailers had frighteningly observed, he was a 'sitting duck for a rear-end funnelling' himself.

Between visits to the psychiatrists he worked as a cleaner, and spent the rest of the time reading letters of sympathy from various friends. In the second week of January he heard from De Laurentiis who had reached an absolutely critical stage with the production of *Hurricane*. He needed to hire actors and book the locations and studio time. In view of the uncertainty, he had no alternative but to replace Polanski as director. Furthermore, he could not take the risk of having a totally unknown actress in the leading role – Nastassia Kinski was therefore no longer required either. Instead, De Laurentiis signed Mia Farrow.

Polanski was shell-shocked now by the succession of events, but the last bombshell was yet to fall. The first stage of the diagnostic tests took forty-two days, and Polanski was released from Chino on 29 January 1978, with both defence and prosecuting counsel convinced that he would not have to return. Judge Rittenband, however, had other ideas. On 1 February, he informed both the defence and the District Attorney that he planned to send Polanski back to Chino to complete the ninety-day diagnostic sentence and added a devastating rider. Unless Polanski was prepared to give his undertaking to leave the country voluntarily upon his release, he would consider an additional prison sentence which would result in involuntary deportation upon his release. Either way, the judge was effectively saying, Polanski would be required to leave the country.

Although the District Attorney had pressed for a custodial punishment, even he was bemused by Rittenband's handling of the case. Some claimed that he was conducting a vendetta against Polanski on behalf of the Hollywood establishment who wanted to get rid of this 'evil little bastard troublemaker' once and for all. Shelley Winters and others went so far as to suggest that Polanski had been set up from the very beginning.

Faced with a no-win situation – deportation either way – Polanski decided there was no point hanging around for the finale. He borrowed $1000 from Dino De Laurentiis and bought the last available seat on British Airways flight L589 to London which left at 5.57 that afternoon, arriving in London at 11.40 the following morning. As he peered out of the aircraft window at Los Angeles growing ever distant beneath him, Polanski was in tears resulting from a mixture of emotions.

Who was to blame? Not Polanski, in his view. It was the lousy, rotten judge, of course, and that silly little girl and her scheming mother, and it was . . . everyone. Everyone but himself.

Chapter Twenty-One

*S*urrounded on all sides by pressures that might drive any man to despair, Polanski's resilience to adversity was being tested to a greater degree than at any time in his life. Yet despair does not come easily to him. Anger was a more appropriate word to describe his mood at the time. According to one of his friends, he was 'devastated, personally and morally, yet bursting to call a press conference as he arrived in London on 2 February 1978 to put his side of the story. He had now convinced himself totally and without reservation that he was the one who had been wronged – and he could see it no other way. Rittenband was his enemy and the cause of his troubles; that's as he saw it and he could not be shifted.' Michael Klinger, whom he telephoned soon after arriving in London, advised him against speaking to the newspapers: he would be overwhelmed by a deluge of questions over which he would have no control.

Disgraced and out of work, harassed at every turn by the press pack, and with some so-called friends deserting him as if he had the plague, Roman was like an escaped convict on the run, except that he had avoided the formality of climbing over the prison wall. On the flight across the Atlantic, his brain had been teeming with possibilities, that there might be a squad of police waiting to arrest him at the other end, that somehow the American law enforcement agencies would track him down and bring him back to face the music. His financial plight added to the trauma but was the lesser of his considerations.

He went straight to his mews house, which was cold and unwelcoming in the grey and damp London winter. He telephoned a few friends, explaining that he had been imprisoned with the scum of the earth, a collection of morons, and had no intention of allowing 'that bastard Rittenband' to return him to Chino. He had no idea how he stood in England if the Americans issued a warrant for his arrest, as seemed likely, but quickly established from a lawyer that under the British extradition treaty with the USA, it was quite possible, indeed very likely, that Scotland Yard would cooperate and take him into custody if so requested.

This prospect was very soon confirmed by the District Attorney's office in Los Angeles later that day, when they discovered that Polanski had flown the coop. 'We've got the dogs out,' assistant DA Stephen Trott said in a press statement, 'we shall pursue him and extradite Polanski from anywhere, provided we have a treaty.'

Roman did not hang around long enough to test England's mood. There was still no warrant for his arrest; and later that day, he caught a plane to Paris and went quickly to his apartment in the Avenue Montaigne. He called his lawyer, Douglas Dalton, in Los Angeles and told him he would not be coming back. This news was reported officially to Rittenband at the hearing set for 1 February, when it had been intended to send Polanski back to prison. Rittenband postponed the case for fourteen days to allow Polanski to return voluntarily and Dalton gave his undertaking to attempt to persuade his client to return. However, when the newspapers reported Polanski's movements the following morning, Rittenband issued a bench warrant for his immediate arrest, which in effect meant that the police could begin extradition moves right away.

Dalton arrived in Paris forty-eight hours later, and met Polanski to discuss the options. He talked in gloomy terms of Polanski's future as a fugitive from American justice, a convicted felon who could be arrested in any country where the Americans had a treaty for extradition for such an offence. 'Would it not be advisable to return?' said Dalton. 'We'll fight Rittenband. He's done some remarkably stupid things. He cannot deport you himself – that's up to the Federal authorities. But at the end of the day, you have got to get this cleared up otherwise it will hang around your neck like a millstone for the rest of your natural. Serve your sentence and get a clean sheet – then we can fight any moves to have you deported.' John Lennon, he cited, had fought a similar battle with J. Edgar Hoover and the United States Immigration Service, and won.

Polanski listened but would not budge. There was no way he was going back to prison. What was the point? If Rittenband or the US Immigration Service still tried to get him deported, he had achieved nothing. If he served his sentence and then had his multiple-entry visa revoked, there would be no point. 'But think of the future,' Dalton said with realistic reasoning. 'Do your time and there is a possibility of having the ruling set aside. As a fugitive you can never go back. Period.'

Polanski said he was exhausted. 'They can all go fuck themselves,' he said after an hour or more of discussions. 'I'm not coming back.'

In Paris, he was safe. As a French citizen, the charge with which he had been convicted was not one which the French authorities recognized as worthy of invoking an extradition order. One respectable French daily even likened his plight to that of Oscar Wilde, and the French had no time for the hypocrisy of American moral standards.

Dalton returned to Los Angeles to report to Judge Rittenband. The judge, who was himself giving his version to the press, angered by leaks from the probation officer Irwin Gold who had stated that the psychiatrist's report on Polanski while in prison was favourable, recommended a non-custodial sentence. Rittenband was virtually saying 'Good riddance'. Polanski, he stated, did not belong in America, he was not welcome.

Dalton was still fighting. He launched a judicial attack on Rittenband and filed a complaint with the Superior Court of Los Angeles, claiming bias, prejudice and violation of ethics. The judge, who was threatening to sentence Polanski *in absentia*, strenuously denied all of Dalton's claims, but soon afterwards he announced that for the sake of expediency he was relinquishing the case. It was assigned to Judge Paul Breckinridge who made it clear that he had no intention of pursuing it until, and if, Polanski returned to Los Angeles. The case was removed from the active list – but for Polanski it would remain a hovering threat.

Outside the apartment in the Avenue Montaigne, the press pack was camped mob-handed on the doorstep. Photographers with long tom lenses were trying every trick to get a snap of Polanski. His apartment had itself become a prison. The doors of the building, in one of the most fashionable parts of Paris, just off the Champs-Élysées, were electronically controlled and watched over by a concierge who repelled all unauthorized would-be entrants.

After two weeks of virtual isolation Polanski decided he had to do something to try to get rid of the press watch. He telephoned his old friend Sveva Vigeveno, a Swedish photographer living in Paris, and suggested a meeting. Polanski slipped unnoticed through a rear entrance of the building and met Sveva in a boulevard café. She was shocked by his appearance: he was almost unrecognizable. The beard he had grown in Chino was black and bushy, his eyes were puffed and his face drawn and lined, and for once he looked his age. The clothes he wore were dated; his overcoat was buttoned tightly and looked too small; he looked like a refugee. 'He asked me if I liked the beard,' said Sveva, 'but I think if I had said no, he would have shaved it off. Otherwise, he seemed in relatively good spirits, though his face was a mask, really. Not the Polanski I had known.'

Sveva was to take photographs of him in the café and out on the street at a news-stand, and sell them around the world. Then, he said, once they had been published, perhaps the photographers would leave him alone. He was right about one thing; the photographs were picked up by newspapers and magazines around the world; the *Daily Mail* in London, for example, billed them as 'Exclusive: first on-the-run pictures of the man who fled Hollywood'.

Less responsible organs were writing some pretty dastardly things about Polanski, and he had good cause to be swamped by a renewed complex of media persecution. But the image portrayed in the gossip columns of a lonely and embittered Polanski holed up in his apartment was only partly true. He was certainly not uncomfortable. The apartment was modern and spacious, an indication of better times. But after the initial shock-waves of each day's developments began to subside, Polanski realized that he had to do something urgently to draw himself back from the brink of bankruptcy. The options were remarkably few and could be summed up with a corny old cliché: sink or swim. He swam.

He needed money and he needed it fast and the only way he knew how to get money was to make a film, immerse himself in work. What? Where? Who? How? The ponderables were almost imponderable. Who in the world was going to back him now? Again, the number of people he could approach could be counted on the fingers of one hand and there would probably still be a couple of digits to spare.

The man he targeted was a friend from years back, a former actor named Claude Berri whom Roman had first met in the early sixties and who had since become head of Renn Productions in Paris and a partner in France's leading independent film distributors. They had talked in the past of making a film together and Polanski had once broached the possibility of making a screen adaptation of the Thomas Hardy novel, *Tess of the d'Urbervilles*. He called Berri and suggested a meeting. Berri was apprehensive, if not surprised.

The subject matter alone was near the bone, considering all that had passed in the previous twelve months: the story of Tess involved the

229

rape of a young girl, and the young girl would be played by Polanski's lover, Nastassia Kinski. As the *Hollywood Reporter* wryly commented on news of his intention, 'You'd have thought he would have had the decency to do a war film or something.' It could all have been part of the plan. The publicity value would be terrific. For Polanski and an unidentified girl in Jack Nicholson's jacuzzi, read Alec d'Urberville and Tess.

Polanski was giving Berri the hard sell; it was going to be the best movie he had ever made. He picked up a paperback copy of the novel and began flicking the pages, saying, 'Tess is above all a great love story. What happens to Tess is the epitome of Victorian melodrama. She is seduced when young, bears a child who dies, is deserted by the man she later marries, and finally is sent to the gallows for the murder of her seducer. The detail Hardy supplies is astonishing.'

Berri nodded, but he was worried. The cost of a major period costume piece set in the nineteenth century would be enormous, and how in the world would they be able to film it in the realistic setting of rural England if the director could not go there? Polanski said he could overcome that problem by shooting in northern France.

Berri was still not convinced – until he saw Nastassia Kinski. 'One night,' he recalled, 'Polanski turned up at my house with Kinski in her blouse and little skirt . . . I knew then I was going to accept. I felt the whole film rested so heavily on the right actress for the lead and she was that person. I was convinced.' The one major flaw in the equation had not occurred to Berri at that point – Kinski had a severe language difficulty in that her English was limited, and strongly accented.

Polanski was talking and thinking big. With this movie, he would show them all that it was a two-fingers-to-the-world situation. Claude Berri had the feeling that he was being carried along by Polanski's own enthusiasm and determination to fight back. He would later discover, to his great personal cost, that he had been chosen to fund an extravaganza whose aim and intent was largely motivated by one thing: the self-preservation and aggrandizement of Roman Polanski.

Berri mortgaged future income from his French distribution rights of various films to start the ball rolling and began scouring the European film world for backers to join him in financing the project. Polanski had talked in terms of a $7-million budget, which turned out to be a gross underestimation, but at that time they had no script and no schedule. It was pure guesswork and, as always, Roman was a great talker.

No one seriously considered the possibility that any major US studio or distributor might wish to be associated with anything to do with Polanski while he was a fugitive from American justice. In truth, as Kenneth Tynan sardonically observed, no one would touch him with a 5-foot pole.

The first major expense was to obtain the rights. It would be the first time that Hardy's novel had been made into a talking film – a silent movie version was made in 1924. David O. Selznick bought the 'talkie' rights in 1946 and later planned the movie to star his new wife Jennifer Jones. He always said his two greatest dreams had been to film *Gone With the Wind* and *Tess of the D'Urbervilles*. The second still eluded him when he died in 1965, and the rights remained with his estate. Berri explained: 'We discovered that the copyright for Hardy's novel ran out at the end of 1978 but Roman was anxious to secure it before anyone else and was also keen to go ahead right away. By then, we were all high on the idea of Tess, so we paid $50,000 for the rights for the remaining six months. I suppose you could say that at that time our enthusiasm was at its peak.'

They made contact with Selznick's son Danny who was so pleased to receive such an unexpected windfall that he dispatched a package to Paris containing the yellowing pages of his father's production notes. Polanski pored over them with unrestrained glee. They contained a complete list and description of characters prepared by Selznick's researcher, Muriel Elwood, who had written of Tess: 'Sixteen years old, oldest of the D'Urberville chain, fine-featured, roundly built, deep red lips, deep dark eyes that are neither black nor blue nor grey nor violet, a mass of dark hair . . .' With a couple of minor differences, they described Nastassia Kinski to a tee. 'Fantastic!' said Polanski. 'Fantastic!'

With the rights secured by the beginning of April, Berri agreed to put the movie into pre-production mode, even though he had not secured any major backing. Kinski was dispatched to England for four months to become more proficient in the language and to study the Dorset dialect and local ways. Polanski hired Kate Fleming, a dialogue coach with the National Theatre, for an intensive period of speech training, going through exercises and readings day in and day out to the point of complete frustration for both women. At the end of it, Kate Fleming had produced from Kinski an English accent that was both historically and dialectically correct and in which her Teutonic tones were only recognizable in moments of high drama.

By May, they were well advanced. Polanski and Gerard Brach, recruited once again for a joint writing collaboration, had been working day and night to produce a screenplay. A number of well-known technicians had already been booked, led by Geoffrey Unsworth, the renowned cinematographer of such movies as *2001: A Space Odyssey*, *Cabaret* and *Superman* which he had just finished. Oscar-winning costume designer Anthony Powell had agreed to design the all-important wardrobe, which would be one of the most costly fixed items in Berri's budget.

Between writing and planning, Polanski drove frequently to northern France to scout for locations. Unable to go to England, he needed scenery and buildings that would pass for the Dorset countryside. The work needed authentic nineteenth-century transport and even a full-size replica of Stonehenge, which would cost Berri a small fortune. At the end of that month, he had still not found a partner to join the venture. Two or three had taken a look at the project, but backed away when they saw the figures.

In the hope of generating some interest, Berri took a major advertisement in the issue of *Variety* published to coincide with the Cannes Film Festival, announcing the forthcoming movie. 'Tess, by Roman Polanski', and for a time the telephone did not stop ringing. The inquiries, however, gradually faded with no new investor on the hook, and by the time filming was scheduled to begin in July, Berri was heavily mortgaged – and worried. There was a point at which he might have cut his losses and run, but it was almost too late for that now. Only a deal with Société Française de Production, who took a 33 per cent equity in the film in return for use of its production facilities, enabled the lumbering project to continue.

By then, the cast, crew and support staff had grown to a massive 200 people who moved *en bloc* to Normandy where filming was scheduled for completion by the end of the year and first showing at Cannes, 1979. Claude Berri nervously watched the costs mounting: the transport, the costumes, the sets, the people. Four million. Six million. Eight million. He could have wallpapered an entire office block with the bills. The money became of lesser importance than getting the film completed at all.

Polanski's own well-known battle for perfection and his now familiar insistence on complete accuracy in every shot, down to the minutiae, would provide heartaches enough. Polanski's insistence on finding scenic accuracy as near as possible to the countryside of southern England called for filming in eighty separate locations, and carting several busloads of personnel, four tons of costumes and other paraphernalia through the countryside of France also had its very obvious and expensive drawbacks. Then there was the unaccountable – a succession of debilitating setbacks which no one could have foreseen and which affected everyone in ways other than the physical.

Two months of freak weather put the schedules in disarray, and then, during the summer, the production service company went into dispute with the craft unions and there were strikes at the Joinville studios. For four weeks, the sets for *Tess* were locked up and could not be touched. The delays kept coming. The intensity of Polanski's focus on his protégée Nastassia Kinski amazed those around him. Some scenes were reshot time and again. Claude Berri was at his wits' end. Like producers before him, he began imploring Polanski to speed things up. He was still without a financial partner, and had put just about everything he owned in hock to keep the film going. He had no other choice, except perhaps bankruptcy.

There was tragedy too. First, Kate Fleming, who had become Kinski's mentor, died from cancer. Then, with more than half the film completed, Geoffrey Unsworth, upon whose camera skills Polanski had relied heavily, suffered a heart attack in October after a day's filming at Morlaix. He collapsed at his hotel that night, and died soon afterwards.

In spite of the tragedy, Polanski decided he would carry on filming. He called everyone to work the following day, using an assistant cameraman until a replacement for Unsworth, the Frenchman Ghislain Cloquet, was brought in to replace him. 'I thought it was necessary to continue,' Polanski later recalled for an interviewer. 'It was a bizarre atmosphere, an emptiness, but I knew that if we stopped we might never recover.'

In November, with the elasticity of his schedules already stretched to breaking point, it began to snow in northern France. Winter had set in early, and so the creation of *Tess* which began in the early spring of 1978 had now stretched throughout the year: it must be one of the few films in history where the passage of time in the story was marked in actuality by real-life changing seasons – except that the changes often came at an inappropriate moment in the script.

Claude Berri's fingernails were now bitten down to the quick. When filming finally ended in the early weeks of 1979, he instructed Polanski to get a rough-cut version ready for the Cannes Film Festival in May, so that he could provide a private preview for potential distributors. Polanski doubted whether that would be possible, so when the time came, Berri insisted that Polanski and Kinski should appear at a press conference to stir up some interest. Polanski, by then in the middle of editing his thousands of feet of film down to a manageable length, was exhausted. Sam O'Steen, the Hollywood editor who had worked with him on earlier movies, was summoned to add his expertise. Polanski went off to recuperate on a walking holiday in the Himalayas. When he came back, he rejected Sam's work as ruining the rhythm of his film.

The final bills for making *Tess* would exceed $12 million; it was the most expensive film ever made in France. With the rights being touted around the world, the talk in the trade was that Polanski's excesses had doubled the cost. As always, he would deny this, pointing to all the problems encountered along the way. 'It's not my fault,' was the familiar cry. 'How could I account for everything that happened during the making of this movie? How could I?'

He did not want to go to Cannes in May either, but Berri, by now a desperate man, insisted. The media had been warned in advance: 'Polanski's coming . . . and he's bringing Kinski.' They had booked a suite for him at the Carlton Hotel – the prime spot to be in at Cannes – and hanging down from the front of the building when he arrived was a gigantic poster promoting the film. In the middle of a powder-blue background was the huge face of Kinski, framed in a white bonnet, and below it, the word 'Tess', with a red heart dripping specks of blood underneath.

True enough, Polanski was back, and the press conference Berri had arranged at the Carlton was bulging with journalists and photographers from around the world, baying like wolves as Polanski and Kinski took their places upon a dais in front of them. The questions came thick and fast, but no one there that day was interested in *Tess*.

Polanski agreed to answer questions about his legal status in connection with the American case and about Miss Kinski. Then he was hit with a barrage of questions:

'Will you ever go back to the United States?'

'Yes, if my lawyers can negotiate . . .'

'What kind of sentence do you expect?'

'I cannot say, but . . .'

'How old are you, Miss Kinski?'

'Are you his lover?'

'Are you going to marry?'

And so on. With a cool mixture of candour and diplomacy, Polanski tried to steer himself through the minefield of questions which became progressively more pointed. In French, he answered a reporter from *Paris Match* who pressed him about his private life: 'I have never hidden the fact that I love girls and I will say once again for all, I love very young girls.' He planted a kiss on Kinski's cheek and deftly tried to switch the questions to *Tess*: 'I'm here to talk about my picture – ask me about my picture.'

There was no let-up: 'Why did you make a film about sex and rape – a girl's loss of innocence?'

'Ugliness', replied Polanski, 'is in the eye of the beholder.'

He had lost control, and the questioners persisted, 'Tell us about the film and its parallels to your own life – the violated young woman?'

Polanski looked up at the ceiling and whistled . . .

Chapter Twenty-Two

*I*f the filming of *Tess* had been a nightmare, the post-production stage was a fiasco. All through the summer, Polanski and his editing team were frantically trying to cut the film into a manageable screening length in time for a promised German premiere, set for the end of October 1979, and a similar launch in Paris on 1 November. Apart from the rush to have the final print ready on time, sound-dubbing for the foreign-language versions also had to be completed, along with the musical score.

Although the film was made in English, Claude Berri had been unable to sell any English-language distribution rights and he had demanded that Polanski supply him with a rough-cut version, without the music score, so that he could attempt to drum up some interest and try to salvage something from what appeared at that moment in time to be a major catastrophe. Responses from abroad continued to be negative and it looked as if American and British distributors were staging a boycott. When Berri was finally given a private screening of the completed film, with music, a month before it was due to open in Germany, he exploded with rage. 'Too long!' he yelled. 'Too long! Nobody is going to buy it.'

Berri was resting his hopes now on a successful opening in Germany – and once again he was to be sorely disappointed. The reviews damned the film and were highly critical of Polanski. Nastassia Kinski, in her home country, was so shocked by the hostility of the German critics that she telephoned Polanski in tears. *Tess* fared better in Paris where the critics were far kinder, but the audiences were not flocking to the cinemas to rescue Berri from what seemed certain financial ruin. The $12-million movie, which one German critic had described as a documentary on nineteenth-century farming, seemed destined to abject failure. The movie did not deserve such a fate, nor warrant such

236

devastating criticism. It was a film that showed a different Polanski, at least in the artistry of the work as opposed to how he achieved it. He had been quite meticulous in his portrayal of Hardy's novel, and the quest for accuracy, given his inability to leave France, had created some enormous logistical problems. One could question what had drawn Polanski to the subject matter which, as with *Macbeth*, was rather close to home in view of his recent troubles. But for all its incredible production problems, *Tess* was a very watchable film and Kinski was groomed to low-key perfection.

However, far from attracting interest as Berri had hoped, *Tess* remained unsold in the crucial international market-place. No major British distributor was interested in making an offer, not even a derisory one, although the attitude of Rank executives seemed to have more to do with a dislike for Polanski personally than with the film itself. In America, Columbia said it was not sexy enough, and United Artists offered a minuscule $200,000. The word was that in the current vogue for Hollywood blockbusters, they were concerned both with Polanski's fugitive status and the box-office potential of a literary classic. If it had been something like Roman Polanski's *Blood Alley*, there might have been an auction.

Berri, who had been dealing with Francis Ford Coppola's company on *Apocalypse Now*, contacted Coppola, who brought two executives of his own production company to Paris for discussions. They looked at the film, but they were not enthusiastic either. If they took it on, Coppola said, they would want to perform major surgery, taking the rough print and re-editing the movie completely. Polanski drew on a few choice Anglo-Saxonisms to express his views on this suggestion, and Coppola and Co. exited stage left without making a bid.

Gradually, however, *Tess* began to take on a life of its own – without the help of the Americans or the British. In February 1980, the French Academy awarded *Tess* three Césars – their equivalent of the American Oscars – for Best Picture, Best Director (Polanski) and Best Cinematography, in the joint names of the late Geoffrey Unsworth and Ghislain Cloquet. A number of film festivals began calling for prints, and Polanski was suddenly in demand, including a trip to a festival in Argentina which he and Kinski attended together, although by now their own romance was over. Kinski was making a life of her own too. She had received numerous offers from European and American directors and looked set to blossom.

Then, at last, the Americans came back for a second look. Columbia, among the first to turn the movie down, made an offer for limited showing in America, and almost a year after its disastrous premiere in Germany, it finally opened in New York – at just two cinemas.

Tess attracted a clutch of decent reviews – and eventually Academy nominations. Roger Ebert, whose syndicated reviews appear in 200 newspapers, including the *Chicago Sun-Times* and the *New York Daily News*, wrote:

> Roman Polanski's *Tess* is a love song with a tragic ending . . . he tells a story of a beautiful young girl, innocent but not without intelligence, and the way she is gradually destroyed by the exercise of the male ego. This is a wonderful film – full of exploration of doomed young sexuality that makes us agree that lovers should never grow old.

A good deal of newsprint would be used to debate the Polanski technique of story-telling, and on the strength of critical acclaim and audience, Columbia extended the run in America. *Tess* finally reached London in the early spring of 1981 and was welcomed by George Perry of the *Sunday Times*, who wrote: '. . . it validates Polanski's claim to artistic respectability in the face of the notoriety of his private life.' *Tess* played in London's West End for more than a year.

By then it was known that *Tess* was collecting the most coveted accolades, and Jack Nicholson called Polanski from Hollywood to say, 'So the little bastard's done it again.' There were two Golden Globe awards for Best Foreign Film and Best New Female Star of the Year (Kinski). It won the Los Angeles Film Critics' Best Director award – and six nominations for American Academy awards for Best Film, Director, Musical Score, Cinematography, Art Direction and Costume Design. The last three of these nominations were converted into Oscars at the ceremony in April 1981 – for Geoffrey Unsworth (posthumously) and Ghislain Cloquet, designers Pierre Guffroy and Jack Stevens, and costumier Anthony Powell. The official record of the Oscars includes a note which in part explained American reticence to take the film in the first place, with studios concerned as to whether they might face prosecution for making payments, albeit indirectly, to a man who was a fugitive from American justice. It merely states: '*Tess*, embroiled in some controversy because of the complicated legal/illegal status of its director Roman Polanski who'd earlier fled Los Angeles on the eve of being sentenced in a case involving his relationship with a minor, won three of the evening's awards.' However, the Academy did choose to demonstrate its sympathy towards Nastassia Kinski whose own status during her three-year relationship with Polanski had been dragged through the very pits of tabloid journalism. Though not nominated for an award herself, she was invited to take part in the Oscars night along with Lillian Hellman, Lily Tomlin, Steve Martin, King Vidor and Diana Ross.

Tess eventually fared well at the box office but it would be a long time before Claude Berri would claw back his momentous investment in the work of Roman Polanski. It had been a shattering and knife-edge experience in which Berri had become submerged almost from the outset of agreeing to fund the production, and, just as had happened in the past with the likes of Compton, Ransohoff, Victor Lownes, and, to a degree, Paramount, over the making of *Chinatown*, the whole business ended on a sour note. As one of Berri's aides said, 'No amount of threatening memos or cajoling could deter Polanski from the belief that he knew best, that he had to have the best, and that what he directed would be the best. Sometimes it was painful to watch his attempts at artistic perfection; he seemed completely oblivious to everything that was going on around him. I just do not know how Kinski kept her cool. If it had turned out well, then fine. But it did not. Sure, Polanski had his problems and sure, *Tess* was a very good movie in the end, but the making of it and the selling of it was a shambles, a living nightmare, and was only partially rescued at the thirteenth hour by the turn-around that was experienced in the States.'

Polanski was floored by the experience and would not make another movie for almost five years. The lay-off began as a self-imposition but lasted far longer than he would have liked. He said he was exhausted and worn out and wanted some time to himself to recharge his energy. At the same time, however, he was already floating the prospect of resurrecting *Pirates*, the screenplay he wrote with Gerard Brach back in 1973, with Jack Nicholson in mind. But for the time being *Pirates* remained 'my next film'.

Almost eighteen months had passed since the Germans fired their broadsides at *Tess* and the American critics rescued it from oblivion. In the meantime, Polanski had kept a positively low profile. It was a reflective period in which his continued eagerness to prove himself again was temporarily set aside. The American Department of Justice had made no move at all to get him back. Conversely, he had made no attempt to smooth things over. It was not an opportune time for such an attempt, he told George Perry in February 1981 – the media were still gunning for him. Perry was among the few who got to talk to him: others were Michael Glazer for *Rolling Stone* and Harlan Kennedy for *American Film*. In each interview, he bemoaned his fate at the hands of the media. 'The press want you to conform to their fantasies,' he said. 'The nature of my notoriety is such that almost whatever is printed about me hurts. The most well-intentioned journalists have to ask certain questions and it doesn't matter what the answer is, it's the question that makes the headlines.' He said life had become so surreal that it was necessary to turn back to the essential, simple, sometimes even simplistic things. That was why, he said, he wanted to make the *Pirates* film, because it was a comedy adventure in the vein of *Treasure Island*.

It was also noticeable that he was reflecting upon the past again, remembering his upbringing, talking about the ghetto, the Nazis, his dead mother and his lost childhood, which might explain a lot of things, and especially his predilection for youth, in other words, because he experienced none of the normal childhood explorations. Was he looking for sympathy? Or suggesting psychological excuses for what had happened? Or just responding to the interviewer to help publicize the movie?

The latter option seemed to be the least likely. The publicity was necessary, but Polanski was a reluctant participant. When asked if he would attempt to go back to America some day, he replied that he might – but not yet. 'Any move now would be seen as a promotional stunt. I do not wish to mix my private and personal affairs, or legal matters, with my professional career. I will choose the moment, when there is less noise.'

Financially, his position had improved. The staged payments from Berri for his $300,000 director's fee for *Tess*, which had stopped for a while as Berri ran into difficulties, had been paid over in full. He had equipped himself with a silver Mercedes and a young English model named Sabina. The London mews house was to be disposed of as he could no longer use it.

In March 1981, he continued the theme of looking back into his past, remembering what was once a simple life when he was invited to Poland for the opening of *Tess* in Warsaw. He was treated like a visiting VIP by some, like a long-lost relative by others, while others still circled him with a curious mixture of disgust and curiosity.

Polanski's arrival in Warsaw coincided with attempts by the proletariat to bring a thaw in the rigid controls imposed on Polish society. Lech Walesa and the Solidarity movement were on the march. The previous month, as the Polish government collapsed in the face of social and economic strife, General Jaruzelski came to power. Two days after Polanski arrived in Warsaw, the Polish workers defied their Communist masters and began a strike which paralysed the nation for four hours. It was touch and go whether or not Russia would send in the troops. While Walesa was demanding recognition of concessions promised to Solidarity the previous year, the hard-liners were demanding martial law – which they got before the year was out.

On this visit he was drawn back to some old haunts that he had not visited since he had left Poland at the beginning of the sixties. He returned to Wysoka and the old houses where he had stayed. Some had been demolished long ago. The Wysoka family with whom he had lodged had split up after the parents died. He found precious few traces of his past, but the return to his roots may well have provided him with the inner peace he was seeking at the time and explained why he suddenly decided to stay in Poland for a while in order to go back into the theatre, in which he had last worked as a boy.

One of his former heroes of the Polish stage, who was now an elder of the theatre, invited him to stage a play of his choice and both to act in and direct it. Polanski agreed, and not for the money, because there was little on offer. He wanted to perform in person for his countrymen, and perhaps his choice of play may have had a subconscious connection to the moment almost thirty-five years earlier when he was attempting to get into drama school and was refused on the grounds that he was too small: 'We do not have many plays which call for people of your build,' he had been told.

He chose Peter Shaffer's *Amadeus*, which was a hit on Broadway, and began commuting between Paris and Warsaw, bringing props and costumes and other incidentals that were not available in Poland, until he was ready to go into rehearsals. Polanski was typecast as Wolfgang Amadeus Mozart, the diminutive, charming, self-mocking genius who was prone to spells of rebellion and occasional explosions of vulgarity and obscenity. To interviewers intrigued by this latest development in the Polanski saga, he said, 'Like Mozart, I was deformed by childhood success. I was forced to succeed early, to become an adult before my age and so everybody thinks you are unbearably arrogant.'

That was certainly true, and it was interesting that he should have admitted it at last after going back to the scene of his own childhood.

He came up with a quite logical excuse for his arrogance, though one which would not wash with a number of his friends, especially Jerzy Kosinski who had heard this explanation before and could virtually quote the next line: 'Because of my experiences, I was always looking for ways to remain a child while others grew older.'

Kosinski marvelled that Polanski could still come up with this kind of reasoning which he honestly saw as an explanation for much of what had happened in his life. They had argued about it after appearing on a television programme a few months earlier, Polanski having agreed to be interviewed on the American *60 Minutes* show to give his version of events at the Nicholson house. There is no point going over that ground again, but the aftermath was interesting. Kosinski was exceedingly put out by Polanski's attitude on television when he said that the girl was not a child, but a young woman. But she was not, said Kosinski. She was thirteen.

'I know that,' said Polanski, 'but she had the mind of a young adult.'

'That really isn't the issue,' Kosinski argued. 'The issue is this: the girl was thirteen. When you were thirteen you were a child – in spite of your experience. If she had been over eighteen, there would have been no story, no offence. She was a child.'

Polanski still could not see it. 'But she was like a young woman,' he kept insisting.

'But she was a child!' screamed Kosinski.

There was a linkage somewhere in all of this to Polanski's thoughts as he returned to Poland, retracing lost youth and following the footsteps to a non-existent childhood. The moment could have been the start of a deep and meaningful plot for one of the Polanski–Brach films, exploring the subconscious of the man to discover what he was thinking as a boy and a youth, because now he was forty-seven and talking about never having grown up. And here he was back on the stage, where it had all begun, as the outrageous little Wolfgang Amadeus, performing to audiences in a city where he had a few enemies who might well have been willing him to fail. But *Amadeus* was tremendously successful – a sell-out for its two-week run in July 1981. After Polanski had given his final performance, the audience gave him a standing ovation. When he returned to Paris, he began negotiations to stage a French version and took a crash course in diction to soothe the Polish lilt from his voice, ready for the opening in February 1982. The reviews were mixed, with some complaining that his command of French was less than fluent. That did not stop the ticket sales, however. The theatre was full night after night. *Amadeus* ran at the Théâtre Marigny for 246 performances, before audiences totalling more than 200,000.

There was one other task gnawing away at Polanski that he wanted to complete: his autobiography. There were two reasons for this. First, he needed money again, and the literary agent Ed Victor said he could get him plenty. Second, a scandal-filled biography of him by Thomas Kiernan had recently been published in America which caused him immense anger. The book, dashed off in the wake of the court case involving the thirteen-year-old girl, had become a bestseller and painted an unsavoury portrait. 'The man has invented my life,' he told George Perry, and for once Polanski's protests were not without cause.

While still appearing in *Amadeus*, Polanski began work on his book, though surprisingly for a man who was capable of writing at speed for his creative work, he found the prospect of setting down 130,000 words of memoirs arduous and daunting. He admitted to Ed Victor that he lacked the discipline to bind himself to the typewriter alone – much of his past writing had been with a collaborator, usually Gerard Brach. Ed Victor suggested he should get help, and he had three professional writers and editors to assist him. One of the few journalists he trusted was Edward Behr, the European contributing editor of *Newsweek*, based in Paris, who was principal ghost writer. Using as a model an earlier biography of Polanski by Barbara Leaming, an associate professor at Hunter College, New York, and with a plentiful supply of press cuttings to jog his memory, Behr began to put together the raw bones of his story to which were added the personal reminiscences Polanski dictated into a tape-recorder. Later, when Polanski had completed his theatrical commitments, he was able to spend more time on the book himself and took over from Behr in the final stages. Ed Victor, based in London, sent an outline of the work to several American publishing houses and then flew to New York for an auction. 'The best bid we received,' he said, 'was a joint offer for hardback and softcover rights with William Morrow the principal publisher. They paid us more than half a million dollars for the American rights. Heinemann in Britain and Laffont in France then came in with another 150,000 dollars, and there were subsidiary sales to other countries.'

Victor had told Polanski from the outset that he had to be frank in his recollections, and the publisher's blurb insisted that 'He never shrinks from revealing himself and the real person behind the brutal headlines and supermarket scribblings.' Polanski himself was more interested in

243

correcting some of the inaccuracies that had been written about him of late. 'Rumour, harnessed to the power of the media,' he said, 'creates an image of public figures that clings to them forever – a sort of caricature that passes for reality.'

However inaccurate and hysterical some of what was written about him may have been, there were elements of truth throughout it all. He always seemed to miss the point, both in his own memoirs and in many interviews past and present, that the underlying reason for bad publicity was Polanski himself. His autobiography really did nothing to alter that, and when serializations were published he was disappointed that the headlines focused not on Polanski the genius and the artist, but on Polanski the central figure in a series of lurid situations. The sentence which he used in the closing stages of his book, 'I am widely regarded as an evil, profligate dwarf . . .', taken out of context, eventually became the prefix to newspaper features on him – which was exactly what he had hoped to avoid. Though the book was frank in certain well-known areas of his life, he would himself later admit that there were many gaps in the coverage of his life. As Martin Amis wrote in his review for the *Observer*: 'This book is a tribute to the searing power of the cliché. It can't have been easy to make a life as violent, melodramatic and profligate as Roman Polanski's sound humdrum . . . alas, the ghosts have made a ghost of Polanski . . . and the result is lifelessness.'

But, as his former wife Basia pointed out in her interview for this book in 1993, Polanski's version of events was always one-sided. 'The last time I heard from him was when he was writing his book. He rang me for some memories and to confirm some facts. It was interesting eventually to read them and see his point of view, which was the only one he offered. Romek often knocks me and I would not do it to him in that way. He seemed to have forgotten some of the basic flaws in our marriage. When I was with him I cried so much that since then nobody has ever seen me cry.'

Polanski's recollections were devoid of insights which showed the reality of his relationships, especially during his pre-fame days when 'the genius' was emerging. He did not mention scenes of physical violence, either. 'Yes, I know his first girlfriend Kika suffered it,' said Basia. 'He tried it with me only twice and I left. It hurt me so much when he wrote in his book I was cruel to leave him poor and hungry on the streets of Paris. In a way it is true, but does he realize how he was crushing me? I was growing up with him, developing, and no doubt we both became wiser in the time we were together. His recollections were selfish. He said to me – and he was absolutely serious – that he did not want a clever wife, that he felt aversion to an intelligent wife. Those were some of the things he would not mention. His vision of life and the cinema, his creativity in music, paintings and action, were a revelation to me. But maybe his writing was not so good.'

For Polanski himself, the book served a purpose. He'd had his say, answered back, gave little quarter to the views and feelings of others – and earned himself a small fortune in the process.

Chapter Twenty-Three

'*I*f the door slammed shut in his face,' said Basia Kwiatkowska, 'he would climb in through the window.' This time, even the windows looked locked, and even some of Roman's friends had already written him off as a spent force. Who, in that competitive business, could go five years without making a film and just walk back into it as if the absence had been a mere blink of the eye? The notoriety had faded. The book put him back in public focus for a while but it had been left to the gossip columnists to record the trivia of his comings and goings in recent months, because there was nothing else to report.

There had been a lot of activity behind the scenes in the last twelve months of his seclusion, and in spring and early summer of 1984, Polanski struck gold. After ten years of trying, he confounded the trade press pundits by marshalling substantial backers for *Pirates*. Endless meetings of poring over scripts, plans, cost projections and production schedules had climaxed with a Yes vote, and Roman was ecstatic. The film that he was convinced would bring him out of the shadows of cinematic oblivion and put his name in lights once again was given the go-ahead by a group of money-men, led by the Arab multi-millionaire financier Tarak Ben Ammar and the independent production company of Dino De Laurentiis. But it went deeper than this. To get *Pirates* sold represented a long dream; it was a movie that had been swirling around in Polanski's brain since the late fifties. As Basia has recalled, he first had the idea back in 1959 and had been building on it ever since to the degree that it became almost an obsession.

This project really meant something to Polanski. When the news broke, there was a good deal of head-scratching and snide, even envious, commentary around Hollywood. What is the little bastard up to now? Pirates? Spanish galleons? Swashbuckling comedy? Why? And how?

246

Twenty-five million dollars . . . how did he pull that off? The audacity of the man in securing a deal of that size – the largest in his career – brought quiet admiration, though for the diehard Polanski fans it was more of a mystery as to why he should be pushing to make a rather juvenile comedy that was nothing like anything he had done before. Polanski's own explanation when he was questioned about this latest turn in his career was typical of him – he used the analogy of sex: 'It's like a playboy who wants to make it with every available type of woman – blondes, blacks, Chinese, whatever.' It also harped back to his desire to get away from the surreal, because the world itself had become surreal.

But in that very world, *Pirates* looked decidedly old-fashioned. The current era of movie-making had spawned another kind of swashbuckling, with modern heroes in successful science fiction movies, hard-hitting socio-dramas, Sylvester Stallone's *Rocky* series, *Superman* and, most recently, Steven Spielberg's rip-roaring adventures of Indiana Jones starring Harrison Ford, which though set in the past was bang up to date in appeal. Polanski even acknowledged himself, when he had completed filming, 'It has come ten years too late.' By then, he surely knew he had given birth to a turkey.

That possibility was never even considered in 1984 – otherwise *Pirates* would never have been made. At the time his enthusiasm was bubbling and the money-men must surely have been carried away by the gargantuan nature of a project which they presumed could not possibly fail. Wrapped up in a complicated Hollywood-style contract was a $1-million potential for Polanski if he delivered on time and inside budget.

It would be a 'spectacular extravaganza' in every respect. Dino De Laurentiis said as much. He would produce the movie himself and, once the ink had dried on the contracts for finance, they were giving immediate approval for the commissioning of a 14,000-ton, purpose-built, full-size replica of a Spanish galleon called *Neptune*, 220 feet long and 98 feet wide, which alone would cost $8 million.

The cast list was of similarly epic proportions, more akin to the Golden Days of Hollywood when they made films like this on the studio back-lots. There were forty-six separate character parts and hundreds of extras.

It was going to be a blockbuster and make them all lots of money. There was also a degree of the Emperor's New Clothes syndrome in the discussions. As one production executive observed later, there seemed to be an air of suspended reality. 'People were talking bullshit, in telephone numbers, ridiculous images were being created in people's minds – and no one said STOP: This is fucking ludicrous.'

This was to be supposedly hilarious escapism, a tale of buried treasure, love and piracy on the Spanish main with an 'adult' measure of sex and violence, the obligatory rape and a fair drop of blood. And so, while De Laurentiis began ordering up the timber, Polanski was looking for his star. Nicholson had priced himself out, perhaps deliberately so: *Pirates* did not match his own list of recent movies, which had included *The Shining*, *Reds*, and *Terms of Endearment* for which he had won an Oscar, and anyway, he was currently working on John Houston's *Prizzi's Honour* and was charging $2 million a film plus a share of the profits.

Michael Caine was wooed but turned the role down, giving rise to speculation that he believed working with Polanski might damage his career. The craggy Walter Matthau had no such qualms and was signed to play the terrifying Captain Red, 'the most treacherous pirate to roam the high seas'. The role of Dolores, a Spanish noblewoman, which Polanski had originally reserved for Kinski – now a distant figure in his life – went to an unknown young British actress, Charlotte Lewis, an eighteen-year-old former model of dramatic looks. She was the only woman in the character part list and her scenes would include the predictably controversial rape. Charlotte's presence also fuelled the equally predictable speculation about whether Polanski seduced his young star – she said not – but for once, the making of the movie itself engaged the interest of the media, through its vast scale which required no exaggeration, just a mere statement of fact.

The building of the galleon was by far the main event. It kept 500 shipyard craftsmen and 2000 labourers fully engaged for almost a year. The ship was to be a sea-worthy vessel that would double as a set and production headquarters. Using the drawings of original seventeenth-century galleons as a guide for the exterior, designer Pierre Guffroy, who won an Oscar for his work on *Tess*, had long conferences with Polanski and the ship's professional architects to perfect their creation. 'The kind of galleon we wanted,' Polanski told a press gathering, 'wasn't to be found anywhere. What we needed was not so much a ship to beat the record crossing for the Atlantic, as a floating set and headquarters.'

When it was delivered a year later, he just stood there open-mouthed, looking at the great and marvellous monstrosity. It was a credit to the ingenuity of the designers and builders and a great monument to the extravagance of the film-makers, but an incredible piece of workmanship in itself. Polanski could only utter the most familiar of his complimentary adjectives: 'Fandastic. I can't believe it. Fandastic!'

There were three decks, the top one reserved for the action in the film. Below, and behind the gun ports, were dressing rooms, wardrobes, showers and make-up studios. Anthony Powell, the designer, was again in charge of the costumes and spent weeks researching for his designs. The third deck housed the mechanical and technical quarters, including two huge diesel engines so that the ship never had to rely on wind-power during filming. A sixteen-man crew was hired from England for the duration to man the yard-arms.

So the ship was the centre of attraction and a huge cost to bear for the financiers, although De Laurentiis reckoned that if *Pirates* was the success they expected, there could be a sequel – *Pirates II* – which, next time round, would not be so expensive to make. That was the theory, anyway.

On land the expenses were equally daunting. With the entire film being shot off-season in Tunisia, a complete new studio facility had to be built because there were none. For this, the holiday town of Port El Kantaoui became a kind of miniature North African Hollywood, teeming with film people and providing employment to no fewer than 10,000 Arab workmen on a 4-acre site close to the marina. The marina itself was dredged to accommodate the galleon and around it were enormous sets built to resemble a Caribbean port. It took three months to build the massive defence walls, typical of many Caribbean islands, on which replica cannon were housed. And the resort area of Hammamet was also partially taken over for the building of more sets.

The logistics were incredibly complicated, and perhaps that is where the trouble began. Filming started on 25 November, and almost from the off, Polanski was hit by problems which were remarkably similar to those he encountered during the making of *Tess*. There were numerous injuries among actors and extras in the fight scenes, filming was stalled completely by heavy gales which tossed the galleon around like a duck in bath-water and at times the difficulties seemed almost insurmountable. 'Even on sunny days, there were complications,' Jean Harbous, the assistant cameraman recalled. 'The whole thing took a great deal of man management, so much detail, so much action that sometimes we shot only a few minutes' usable footage in an entire day's filming.'

Polanski came under severe scrutiny from Dino De Laurentiis who had given him categoric warnings about going over schedule in view of the overtime that would have to be paid. But none of them could account for what Polanski described as 'communication problems' in handling a temperamental local work-force of some 2000 people.

The star, Walter Matthau, is an easy-going type who normally lets his feelings be known in a quiet way, but is always capable of an expletive-filled rage or three to clear the air. In the making of *Pirates*, he became increasingly ill at ease. He did not find the comedy particularly amusing, not in his particular style. He thought some of the lines he had to speak were banal and irrelevant. This, coupled with all the other problems going on around him, caused him considerable discomfort. He did not like Polanski much, either. 'I'll just say he wasn't my kind of director,' said Matthau. 'But in fairness, I think he had too much on his plate. It was a massive production and I believe quite unlike anything he had tackled before. Someone described the making of *Pirates* as *Cleopatra* in miniature and it probably was. Oh God! There were all kinds of mishaps and problems that weren't his fault but frankly he did piss around a lot.'

Two-thirds of the way through filming – a crucial stage for all directors – Polanski knew that it was not a blockbuster. 'Everything that could go wrong went wrong,' he would say in excusing this latest failure to interviewers. 'Literally every shot of that film was like a fish torn out of the mouth of a shark. I don't know any other film-maker who would have finished it.' Thom Mount, a former president of Universal Pictures and now in the lesser role of executive producer of *Pirates*, recalled sitting in Polanski's rented Tunisian apartment as they got towards the end of filming, discussing the problems they had encountered. Polanski was obviously pessimistic about the movie. It had gone badly both from his point of view as director and from the production side of the film's delivery, where costs became, as ever, a non-stop debating area as filming extended into a full ten months and was not completed until the early summer of 1985. The grandiose spending on the galleon, the floating studio, the massive sets in Tunisia eventually gave way to a situation where every paper clip was being counted. Polanski's relationship with De Laurentiis deteriorated in familiar fashion to exchanges of memos. 'Enough of this stuff,' he said to Mount. 'Let's get back to civilization and make a real picture.'

At that moment, the idea for his next picture came into his mind. It would be a thriller set in Paris, he told Mount, and when *Pirates* was done, that is what he would concentrate on.

Pirates was wrapped up. Polanski had been in Tunisia for almost eleven months from start to finish and now faced the marathon editing task and then the musical score. When the final cut was nearing, most of those who saw it began to have their doubts. It was to be made ready for exhibition at the Cannes Film Festival in May 1986, and then world-wide release. By the time post-production costs and publicity had been added, the bill for *Pirates* exceeded $33 million and ended once again on a note of disharmony between the director and the producer.

It always came down to money in the end. 'Dino screwed me,' Polanski complained, 'because I was thirty seconds over the top. He screwed me rotten.' De Laurentiis had a completely different view of the situation, of course, and held Polanski to some contractual penalties. If the film had been good enough, the money would have been recouped and everyone would have been happy. They would not have ended up snarling at each other and saying, 'If only . . .'

But it was not a good movie. As the magnificent galleon sailed into Cannes and moored up along the Croisette to give the film buyers and media a spectacular view of the movie's mechanical star, the reviewers were already priming their cannons to blast it out of the water. There were very few kind words written about it. One critic described it as over-elaborated truculence. Halliwell branded it 'a disaster from a director who should never be allowed to attempt comedy . . . this one is revolting when it is not a crushing bore.'

Some did praise the humour and the way Polanski had cleaned up his act. This, in turn, was a disappointment for those seeking the Polanskian traits of old. There were few of these, except in the tepid humiliation of Matthau's Captain Red and the sex scenes, which were mild in comparison to his usual flamboyant style. 'It was nothing but a collection of visuals,' said Basia, 'and that's what ruined it for him. There was nothing to it underneath – somewhere along the way his original idea had been diluted.'

Pirates sank with all hands, and Polanski headed back to Paris to lick his wounds and wonder whether he would ever work as a director again. There were already too many 'If onlys' in Polanski's life, and this was another.

Supporters of the view that Polanski was a spent force would see *Pirates* as absolute confirmation of it. Throwing money at him had resolved nothing. And he knew, better than anyone, that he had to rescue himself. Even as *Pirates* was sinking and the possibility of a sequel going down with it, a word which appropriately described his life at the time – *frantic*

– was also the title of a new screenplay he had begun plotting with Gerard Brach and his now close friend Thom Mount who had been at his side for most of the previous eighteen months from inception to completion of *Pirates*. In spite of all that had passed during the making of the film, in which Mount as executive producer was at the sharp end, Thom possessed an affection and admiration for Polanski that persuaded him to join the resurrection of his career, before it could be nailed down and laid to rest by the critics abroad and creditors at home. *Pirates* had floored Roman financially as well as professionally. Once more, he needed money fast.

With that well-known Hollywood adage, 'You're only as good as your last picture' reverberating in their minds, the trio began to move quickly to restore faith in Polanski before it was too late. There were very few people now to whom he could turn. There were close friends and socializers in Paris, a dentist, a football player and a few film people who joined him on his excursions into Parisian night-life which he enjoyed because of the freedom that Paris gave him – no hassle, no hounding and no hostility. That all came from abroad. He could go down to his favourite girl-packed night-club, the Élysée-Matignon or the Bains Douches and know he would seldom be molested by the paparazzi. Girls came and went from his life without record. In that respect, he had become a lesser figure in the tabloid pursuit of the salacious and more of a personality to be explored by the magazines servicing the intelligentsia and the film world. So it was to his France, his Paris, that he turned for the setting for his new movie, in which he plotted scenes from clubs and places he frequented himself.

Thom Mount, meanwhile, had pledged his support for the new project and was a good PR man. 'When I watched him on the set of *Pirates*,' said Mount, 'I saw an extraordinary performance by a director. He acted, helped stunt-men, worked on lights and was even his own script girl when he had to be. He knew as much about the craft of film-making as anyone I had ever worked with. And notwithstanding the way *Pirates* turned out, I did not waiver from my view that he was a world-class director.' Fortunately for Polanski, there were others around who were prepared to agree.

By the late summer of 1986, Polanski and Brach had outlined the plot for the new thriller and Thom Mount was to be producer. He took the idea to Warner Brothers in Hollywood with a budget of $20 million – 'Not a high price by Hollywood standards at the time,' said Mount. Though some at the Warner studios were apprehensive about dealing with Polanski at such a distance, the doubts were overcome and, in Hollywood parlance, they agreed to 'come to the party'.

Warner executive Bruce Berman, who was given overall charge of the movie, was also prepared to give Polanski the benefit of the doubt, and consider that he could take his place alongside a number of other directors working in America who had ridden bumpy patches in their careers but earned megabuck salaries for everything they touched, whether or not it was a box office hit. Francis Ford Coppola, Stanley Kubrick, Martin Scorsese, Sidney Lumet . . . they had monopolized the genre of movies for which Polanski had once shown such talent and promise, and whose ranks he might well have joined had his 'situation' been different.

Berman was positively bullish: 'Roman is a great director and the saying "You're only as good as your last movie" just doesn't apply in his case, or with five or six other major directors. It didn't matter to us that his last movie did not do well. We just looked at his overall body of work – and his previous one, *Tess*, was near brilliant.'

So despite all that had passed and everything that Polanski had had to worry about in the previous two decades, there remained a certain enigmatic quality about him which appealed to those who ultimately had to make the decision to back him or not. Also, the image of a man racked by scandal was becoming a less resonant backdrop to his work, though occasionally he still managed to stir the memories of earlier days when he was billed as the master of macabre and mysterious. The mystery had long gone from his public persona, but his own thoughts and aims for the future remained of interest to those who came to talk to him. 'My goal now,' he said to one, 'is to have goals. It is very important. It's very important just to want something. And I want more than I ever did before.' Then he would return to a more esoteric theme that threw all previous quotations into doubt.

When the French daily, *Libération*, published a hefty special edition in which 700 film-makers were asked why they made movies, Polanski's response was a terse 'I wonder.'

Chapter Twenty-Four

*E*mmanuelle Seigner had been in Roman Polanski's life for several months before anyone noticed. Her age gave cause for caution and discretion. She was eighteen when they met; he was fifty-three. It was another 'situation' that could easily be exploited by gossips to show that Roman Polanski had returned to his penchant for the nubile. Seigner was quite aware of the potential dangers although she was more concerned for her own safety when she nervously ventured into his apartment in the autumn of 1985, while he was still involved with the making of *Pirates*.

She had been introduced at a party to a casting director who had made an appointment for her to give Polanski a reading in the privacy of his own home. It was a tactic he had often used in the past when casting his stars, male or female. Polanski's interest was aroused when he heard her name, a notable one in the French theatre: she had also recently worked for Jean-Luc Godard. Conversely, she had never heard of Polanski. Her youthfulness showed immediately she was given his name. 'Roman who?' she inquired of her contact. She had no memory of his fame, or infamy, because when he was scuttling towards Los Angeles airport that afternoon in 1978, she was eleven, and had been a mere babe-in-arms at the time of the murders.

She did her homework on Polanski's history. Such was her astonishment at the discovery of his past that when she went to his apartment she did not drink the champagne and refused to eat anything 'in case he had put drugs in it'. He gave her a cake and she did not touch it. She sat on the edge of the deep sofa so as not to give the impression of giving him the come-on; her sexual attraction was apparent enough and she did not wish to emphasize it at that moment, nor was she in the casting-couch business. 'I don't mind telling you, I was scared shitless,' she said. 'I didn't sleep around and if I went to bed with someone it meant I was involved.'

254

The nervousness did not last long, though Polanski noticed her unease and began to talk about his work. Seigner was otherwise a strong-willed, almost brash young woman, and her everyday clothes gave clues to her own confidence: leather jacket, Mexican boots and lace stockings visible through torn jeans. She had strange, translucent green eyes, beautiful without make-up, and, when she had settled down, was a frank and comfortable talker without a hint of phoney sophistication. Polanski asked her about her life and her own career and ambitions.

She told him that she was keen on acting but lacked the discipline and intellect to go into the theatre, although she had strong theatrical links. Her grandfather, Louis Seigner, a former professor at the Conservatoire National and a renowned Comédie Française actor, was a legendary name in the French theatre in whose backstages Emmanuelle had spent countless hours in her childhood.

Her father had not followed her grandfather into the theatre, as he had hoped to do, but had become a photographer. Her mother was an interior designer and they had lived their lives in relaxed, liberal style which allowed their children freedom. Emmanuelle and her younger sister went to a Catholic boarding school and until recently she had led the 'normal' life of a young girl just out of school. At seventeen, she began some small-time modelling and then Godard gave her a small role in his 1985 movie, *Detective*. 'Godard told me I could make it big in pornography,' she said. 'He reckoned I had a great ass.'

Polanski told friends that he liked her honesty and the fact that she was uncalculating and straightforward. She had no aspirations towards the intellectual, and conformity bored her. That was a definite plus-point in Polanski's view of her. As Basia remembered from long ago, he was never keen on intellectual women, especially any woman with sufficient intelligence or knowledge to outdo him in conversation or argument. In that respect, Emmanuelle surely reminded him of Sharon Tate, and in the half-light she resembled her facially, too. Her beauty was certainly on a par with Sharon's. Polanski talked about his own work and later he gave her private viewings of some of his films, including *Pirates* and *Repulsion* and discussed his plans for a new film which were in the earliest stages of development.

After the first meeting, Polanski began calling Emmanuelle for dates. 'Initially, I did not want to go,' she later recalled, 'because I knew he just wanted to fuck me. Gradually, I was drawn to him by his respectful nature and honesty. He was totally upfront about everything. He knew I knew what he wanted and there was no point going around in circles.

As far as I could see, there was nothing hidden. I liked that. The age thing might have been a problem, but I suppose it's the price you pay for maturity – twenty years being happy instead of sixty bored out of your mind.' The relationship developed to the point of sharing their lives. She reckoned Polanski did not show his age at all, and it did not occur to her that he was actually older than her father. 'Anyway, it's not about age, it's about soul and Polanski's is beautiful. I think my father saw that in him and did not object.' And, of course, she would star in his next film – a line which goes way back through his movies.

By the early months of 1987, Polanski and Thom Mount had secured their deal with Warner Brothers for *Frantic*. Polanski sent Emmanuelle Seigner to London for a three-month crash course in English at the Berlitz School in Oxford Street, which was another interesting aspect of his relationships with his female stars which had remained relevant through the years. To his mind, they never needed qualifications in either speech or acting. In fact, someone was given to recall that well-known Sam Goldwyn line: 'Baby, how would you like to be a movie star?' To which the unknown beauty might reply, 'Oh, yes, honey.'

The Polanski–Kinski relationship and now the Polanski–Seigner togetherness both had echoes of Sam Goldwyn's own affair with the Russian actress Anna Sten, whose real name was Anjuschka Stenski. The little verse Cole Porter wrote about Sten might well have applied to Polanski and Seigner:

> If Sam Goldwyn can with great conviction
> Instruct Anna Sten in diction
> Then Anna shows
> Anything goes.

Goldwyn spent a million dollars to have her anglicized and groomed for stardom, but it didn't work. After three pictures she faded away. Polanski, as director of his girlfriend's work, had visions of a more enduring career.

While Emmanuelle was learning to speak English, the star of the film was found. Polanski had a chance meeting with Harrison Ford in Paris and decided instantly that he wanted him for the leading role as an American professor plunged into a Parisian mystery. The story had echoes of past material spun from the joint force of Brach and Polanski. Polanski explained to Ford that it was based upon an obsession he had

256

with waiting for someone to arrive and who is late. 'You wait half an hour and then an hour . . . there was a limit, a line which is crossed between the past and the future, because the present does not exist, and you begin to worry . . . that is the basis of *Frantic*.'

Ford would play the role of Dr Richard Walker, for which the script called for 'a strong, moral type whose wife had pushed him to where he is today', who is visiting Paris with his wife Sondra for a medical convention and unwittingly becomes involved in international terrorism. There is confusion at the airport and their luggage gets mixed up. At their hotel, Dr Walker is in the shower . . . the water is running and he can't hear what is going on. By the time he comes out, Sondra, played by Betty Buckley, has disappeared. He waits, thinking that she has stepped out for a moment . . .

The movie develops into a cat-and-mouse game, with dark scenes in smoky Parisian night-clubs and gun battles resounding in underground parking garages. He meets Michelle, played by Seigner, a mercenary courier whose suitcase Sondra Walker had inadvertently picked up. As a thriller, *Frantic* began promisingly with an opening sequence which reminded audiences of Polanski's talent and on through some chilling early scenes which meticulously set up the plot.

Filming took four months entirely on location in Paris and was marked by a definite maturing of Polanski's view of his actors and actresses. He paid great attention to Seigner. 'I wasn't very good,' she admitted, 'but he made me look good. He never pushed me – in fact, he under-directed me if anything and left me too often to my own devices, although he was strict inasmuch that my work had to conform to his own thoughts.'

Witold Sobocinski, whose work on *Pirates* had been praised by Polanski, and it was indeed one of the better elements of the film, was brought out of Poland again as cameraman for *Frantic*. He agreed with Seigner's assessment. 'Every director has a different temperament,' he said. 'Some need more help from the cameraman, some less. With Polanski, there is no improvisation in his work and although he does not discuss things in advance, he himself is fully prepared when filming begins. For example, Andrzej Wadja, who I have worked with in Poland, surrounds himself with people who bring a lot into his creation. Method is not important; what counts is the result. Polanski differs from others in the way he does not allow people to hide under his wings. He prepares everything himself, rehearses scenes . . . down to the composition of the frame, the visual shape of the film.'

Surprisingly, Harrison Ford, who is known for his own firmness of opinion on the way he should tackle a particular character or scene, found Polanski an easy director to work with. He saw the role of Dr Walker from a somewhat different perspective to Polanski, and explained why and how he intended to play it. He was going to do it his way, and Polanski accepted this without argument, readily admitting that Ford's alternative was better than his own original idea. It was a relatively new experience for Polanski, finding himself having to adapt to an actor, and ending up admiring him. Long gone were the days when actors were just 'monkeys'.

Ford joined in the mutual admiration club. 'What I liked about him,' he said, 'was his attitude and activity. When I was doing a stunt, say on a rooftop, he would be up there with me, right alongside, even on the dangerous stunts. He is a very fit man; he could do anything he asked me to do.' Some of the old Polanski tricks of manipulating, sometimes daring his actors – as Martin Shaw described in the making of *Macbeth* – were still evident. Sam O'Steen, his veteran editor, brought over from Hollywood for the duration of the film, was watching the filming from a safe distance on one occasion and was so concerned that Ford and Polanski were in danger of falling from a steep roof, that he cried out, 'Be careful!' They were clambering around like a couple of mountain goats. In the end, O'Steen could not watch, and left the set.

Then there was a particular scene where Harrison's kidnapped wife, Betty Buckley, had to kneel down beside a woman who had been shot in a gun battle. Polanski told her to imagine that the woman had a very bad injury, so that she could get the correct facial reaction when she saw the wound. It was a fleeting but important shot. After several takes, Polanski was still not satisfied. He told the actors to take five, and unknown to Betty called over a make-up artist to create a particularly bloody wound which he placed inside the woman's jacket. The actors took their positions again, and when Ford lifted the coat, Buckley saw the wound and was visibly shocked. 'It was so ugly,' she said, 'I wanted to vomit – I totally lost it on camera for a moment, which was not by choice. But the reaction was exactly what Polanski wanted.'

When it was done, Polanski retired to the editing suite with his cutter and splicer, Sam O'Steen. When the rough-cut was ready, Harrison Ford flew into Paris to review it. 'Great,' he told Polanski. 'Don't change a fucking thing.' In fact, Warners did ask him to make changes to the ending, and – another sign of Polanski's maturing temperament – he agreed and said they were right. A few years previously, he would have objected 'as a matter of principle' whether they were right or wrong.

Frantic was one of the smoothest productions Polanski had ever been involved in. There were few tantrums, except from Seigner when she could not get her lines right and cursed in self-deprecation. It was probably more to do with Polanski's own attitude than anything else. He had made friends with his cast and his producers, and everyone was happy. In that respect, there had been few productions like it in his entire career. Friends looking in found Roman far more relaxed than he had been for years, and no longer driven by internal mechanisms that few could fathom. *Pirates* had rid him of one of these – obsession. That film, exactly like Warren Beatty's fifteen-year obsession to make *Reds*, had been with him for over twenty years. He had got it out of his system, and because it had blown up in his face it hurt. Obsession, and deception – because he deceived himself too about *Pirates* and others were caught in the deception. A film was never so good that he should spend so much of his life chasing it.

Frantic was altogether smoother, but although it was perhaps more in the Hitchcock mode than any of his previous works, it was not one of his great movies. The reviewers, when they saw the title and the word 'thriller', were anticipating a return to Polanski's darkest hours. *Frantic* was not like that. The thriller element petered out, so that the audience's imagination could run ahead of the unfolding plot; they could work it out for themselves. There was no blood and gore and none of Polanski's original, authentic weirdness. Those who were familiar with his work would be reminded of his real talent as one of the modern masters of *film noir* and the thriller. *Frantic* could have done with a more severe edit than his good friend Sam O'Steen was permitted, and perhaps Polanski's new-found calmness allowed his edge to slip; it certainly showed in the film. *Frantic* was only moderately successful, but being back with a big-budget thriller was undoubtedly where Polanski belonged, and though the reviews were patchy, the movie generally got a warm reception, especially in France and America.

Although Seigner's performance was competent enough for a first major role, she had not set the world alight, and she was honest enough to admit it. When they had finished filming, Polanski wanted her to appear with him on the stage. He had planned a brief return to the Paris theatre and while in the latter stages of editing *Frantic*, he was directing and starring in Steven Berkoff's adaptation of Kafka's *Metamorphosis*. Polanski was appearing in the difficult role of the clerk who turns into an insect and wanted to cast Emmanuelle alongside him. She went as far as going for a group reading, then dropped out. 'I just could not do it,' she said. 'Listening to those theatre professionals made me realize I wasn't ready for that kind of pressure. Working with Polanski on film was bad enough – but easier by comparison.'

In the play, Polanski's agile performance at the age of fifty-five brought acclaim and standing ovations. Then he was gone, off to promote *Frantic* with a few selected interviews for magazines which would give him the right kind of publicity: no sensations, no stark headlines. He didn't need them, and especially not now, for reasons of which few were aware.

Jack Nicholson had caught up with Polanski in Paris, and during several excursions into Parisian night-life with Harrison Ford, they began talking about what Nicholson had really come to discuss – getting Polanski back to Hollywood. There were rumours at the time that Nicholson was to act as the go-between to attempt to get matters resolved between Polanski and the Los Angeles judiciary. He had been in exile for eleven years, which Nicholson believed was punishment enough. Nicholson, it will be recalled, was among those ardent supporters of Polanski who was prepared to give him the benefit of the doubt about the morals charge, taking into account the possibility offered by Shelley Winters, that Polanski had been set up. Even if he had not, the girl was no angel herself, and considering what has since been learned about the private lives of some of America's most famous politicians and personalities, with the passage of years Polanski's crime looked like no more than an unfortunate indiscretion. That, at any rate, was the thinking of his supporters in Hollywood in 1988, and remains so today, and if there was a chance of getting an amicable solution to the situation, Nicholson was prepared to try to pull a few strings.

His motives were not entirely selfless. He was desperately looking for a director for *The Two Jakes*, a sequel to *Chinatown* in which he had a stake; he had already lost a fortune in one abortive attempt to get it made. The story went back to 1985, when Nicholson, producer Robert Evans and scriptwriter Robert Towne formed a triumvirate to put *The Two Jakes* into production. At the time, Evans had his own troubles. He had gone deeply into debt producing the mega-flop *The Cotton Club*, for which he had obtained backing from dubious sources: he entered into an arrangement with a Puerto Rican banker and an unsavoury New York promoter who, unknown to Evans, was involved in drug rackets. Things turned sour, and the promoter ended up murdered by contract killers in a row over a missing consignment of cocaine. His body was found riddled with bullets in a remote canyon in California, and Evans found himself embroiled in what became known as The Cotton Club Case – a trifle unfairly, because the murder was about drugs, and nothing to do with Evans or the movie.

It took the LAPD five years to unravel the mystery, virtually putting Evans's career in suspension and dragging his reputation through the mire. The District Attorney's office, having first indicated that Evans might be charged with conspiracy to murder, failed to produce any evidence and eventually listed him as a prosecution witness.

Evans faced financial ruin, made worse when *The Cotton Club*, which had cost $40 million, flopped at the box office, and then his partnership with Nicholson and Towne collapsed in acrimony. Towne wanted him sacked as producer, Nicholson refused, and Paramount, hearing of this upset, pulled the plug, leaving a million dollars' worth of sets, already built, standing idle and unwanted. The three partners were sued by creditors, which cost them $3 million and a lot of bad publicity.

Early in 1988, Nicholson was intent on reviving *The Two Jakes*, and as he had starred in several major movies in the meantime – *Heartburn*, *Witches of Eastwick*, *Ironweed* and currently *Batman* – Paramount agreed to back him once again and allotted him a $19-million budget. Evans and Towne had made it up, and the three men were back together. All they needed was a director, and Polanski was on the list, along with Mike Nichols and Bernardo Bertolucci (both of whom turned it down). If Polanski was a serious contender, they would first have to spring him from Paris. Evans's own relationship with the LA law at the time was none too good, but contact was made and meantime, the bush telegraph was cranking up Polanski's image: Harrison Ford's very nice comments about him achieved wide coverage.

Nicholson was only one of a small group of Polanski's old friends in Hollywood who were secretly attempting to get him back. Polanski's agent since 1986, Jeff Berg, chairman of ICM, began overtures to the Los Angeles District Attorney, Ira Reiner, to discover if there was a possibility that the Polanski case might be reviewed.

Berg was told that any approach must be made through legal channels and so on Polanski's behalf, he hired the Californian lawyer Arthur Groman, a partner in a prestigious and influential law firm, to make contact. The idea was being floated that Polanski might return to Los Angeles, apologize to the court and perhaps undertake some community work.

261

In reality, the formalities involved in this procedure were far less promising. The only person who could revoke Polanski's prison sentence was a judge of the Superior Court of Los Angeles, and that could only be achieved if Polanski returned and placed himself in a position where probation reports could be obtained. Since he had no visa, there would be immediate problems with the US Immigration Department which had tightened its policy in regard to bail-jumping felons in recent years. The only route for his return would be to surrender himself to the American embassy and arrange to fly back under warrant. A resolution to these possibilities rested largely with the attitude of the District Attorney's office in Los Angeles.

At the beginning of May 1988, Groman heard back from Ira Reiner, who rejected any deal. Groman said, 'The DA gave me a fair hearing, but at the time, he believed that public opinion militated against Mr Polanski.'

So the risk remained. If Polanski returned, there was no guarantee that he would not be taken back to prison, and he would have been immersed in another year of sensational headlines just at the time when things were going his way in Paris. There was no guarantee that he would be allowed to work in the United States after he had completed whatever sentence, if any, was given to him. The move to get him back went no further. 'It became too intense,' admitted Robert Evans. 'It becomes not just a justice factor, but a media one. It doesn't take much to imagine the outcry that would be drummed up against him. The pressure would be too great; he wouldn't last five days in jail and no one's going to give him an airtight agreement that he wouldn't have to go back and do time.'

So Polanski was not going back.

Nicholson ended up directing *The Two Jakes* himself, as well as returning in the star role as Jake Gittes, the private eye whose nose Polanski had slit with a knife in *Chinatown*. Nicholson regretted his dual role afterwards and was honest enough to admit that it could have been a better film with a director who was not also the star.

And Polanski, who gave vague hints in interviews that he would like to return to America and Britain 'some day', got on with his life in exile.

Chapter Twenty-Five

*A*fter working with Polanski on *Frantic*, Witold Sobocinski observed that his life-style was still hectic, and he continued to immerse himself in an 'intensive social life' between films. His apartment in Paris was like a huge office, and he was constantly on the move, contacting people and talking about projects. 'I do not believe he makes big money out of it,' said Sobocinski, 'but he cannot live any other way. He started this way, and does not know how to do it differently.'

Sobocinski was also intrigued by Polanski's new girlfriend and made a point that others seemed to have missed. Emmanuelle Seigner bore physical similarities to Basia Kwiatkowska in her youth. Sobocinski found it striking that Polanski had been attracted by a girl of Slavonic looks, which had characterized most of the more permanent women in his life. 'Sharon Tate, Nastassia Kinski, and now Seigner,' said Sobocinski, 'they were all Slavonic types, slim, pretty blondes. Even Emmanuelle looks like a typical Polish woman – it was strange; after all, he could have found quite different types in the West but seemed drawn to those characteristics.'

Sobocinski also gave Roman some advice – to settle down, get married and have kids before it was too late. Polanski was ready. In the wake of the release of *Frantic*, and the publicity drummed up to promote the movie, Emmanuelle was already being dubbed the girl who finally tamed Polanski; by then she had been in his life for more than three years.

They would be married soon afterwards, and they kept it quiet until Polanski began to talk about his next project, the film *Bitter Moon*, in which the star was his new wife. In between times, they escaped the Parisian glare to his new retreat, a secluded house he had built on several levels overlooking the sea on the island of Ibiza. It was there that he began working on his screenplay which would take almost two and a half years to get to the cinema, going through the now obligatory routine of putting together the package, finding producers and money-men which, at the beginning of the nineties, seemed to take longer and longer for a director like Polanski whose American connections remained distant and apprehensive. In this he was assisted by Timothy Burrill, the old Etonian Britisher who had been working intermittently with Polanski since he was assistant producer on *Macbeth*, and who this time came in as producer. Polanski's new offering seemed to represent a return to basics, back into the realms of sexual voyeurism and black comedy where he had performed best, and in fact it was the graphics on a book cover conveying exactly those traits which had attracted him to the story.

The book was a best-selling French novel, Pascal Bruckner's *Lunes de Fiel*, and the cover showed a man and a woman viewed through the port-hole of a ship. He began reading and discovered a steamy tale of a tortured relationship between an ageing writer and a Parisian nymphet, of sado-masochism and rampant sex, which might become not so much a black comedy as a blue movie. There was naturally an immediate risk that some unkind press people might take this film to be the ultimate in autobiographical exposure. However, he pressed on, interrupting his film work for an acting stint on the movie *Back in the USSR*, and preparing to direct a production for the Bastille Opera. Then in May 1991 another kind of landmark was reached.

He was invited to be president of the jury at the 44th Cannes International Film Festival, which represented a certain achievement in view of his turbulent association with Cannes in the past, and what was at best an arm's-length relationship with French film-makers and the cinema-going public of France as a whole.

He was, after all, the man who had branded the French as pretentious in their films, and whose record at Cannes was controversial to the point of being farcical: the screening of *Repulsion* at which half the audience got up and walked out in 1965; the row with Godard and the rest after Polanski wanted to carry on with the Festival in the face of the riots in 1968; the hostility with which the French viewed *The Tenant* when he screened it at the 1976 Festival. And so on. Given that background, a certain aura of new respectability prevailed, though Cannes itself had changed by then too. Originality no longer commands the same kind of attention in a film world dominated by conveyor-belt production lines and run more ruthlessly than ever towards the mega-buck syndrome, regardless of quality or content. But, it might be countered, Polanski himself has suffered attacks of that very same syndrome in his endless battle with permutations of art, life and money.

264

As *Bitter Moon* began to take shape, those familiar with Polanski's earlier work might well have concluded that through it, he was seeking a return to acclaim, and perhaps fortune, by means of shock tactics expressed in terms of sexual psychosis worked out through a woman's body. And in this case, as in the deep past, that woman was his own wife in reality.

After the undeniable change of emphasis in which the complexes and anxieties which populated his more famous works gave way to the comparative mildness of his last three movies, *Tess*, *Pirates* and *Frantic*, *Bitter Moon* could be viewed as a veritable harvest of those more common Polanski traits and, in a way, it would be a test: to discover whether he still possessed that flair upon which he made his name, and whether he could reclaim the slot long ago taken over in Hollywood by modern directors like Brian De Palma, David Lynch and Jonathan Demme whose work was not interrupted by the physical restraints imposed upon him by the flight from American justice.

With Polanski stuck in Europe, the commercial aspects of his films were also governed by a limited choice. As always, the big studios had first grab at the big topics and the best-selling books, like *Silence of the Lambs* which Demme directed. If his ideas did not come from his own mind, he had to scour the lesser regions of the literary market. And once a story had been found, he then had to inject the elements that would make it a potential success in international cinema, and particularly in America. So the whole routine was becoming more difficult to establish.

As in *Frantic*, Polanski would have an eye on the American market with his central character for *Bitter Moon*, the ageing writer named Oscar who, while living in Paris, becomes infatuated with a young Frenchwoman named Mimi, to be played by Emmanuelle Seigner.

Their story is told in flashbacks. The technique is reminiscent of Polanski's Lodz graduation film, *When Angels Fall*, starring Basia Kwiatkowska – a story, it will be recalled, told through the recollections of a wrinkled old woman who is a lavatory attendant and whose day-dreams, while she remains oblivious to the splashing of the urinals around her, take her back through her life. Then, as now, Polanski's wife was the star of the flashbacks in a film noted for its crudity and cruelness.

In *Bitter Moon*, Polanski follows a similar pattern. Oscar, the ageing writer, by then in a wheelchair, is on a cruise, and daily recounts his experiences to a fellow passenger, a stiff-upper-lip Englishman who is on a marriage-mending trip. The mix of nationalities – French, English and American – is another favourite device which Polanski has introduced in the past to solve language problems for himself and his stars and to make the film internationally appealing. He used it in *Repulsion*, *Cul-de-Sac*, *Fearless Vampire Killers*, *Pirates* and *Frantic*.

The Englishman and his wife are the audience to Oscar's recollections, to the point that they also provide the humour through their reactions. Polanski had been hoping to get Jack Nicholson for the role of Oscar, but he was already committed well into the future. But the performance of Peter Coyote could not have been bettered. He reviles the full sordid detail of a disparate relationship between himself and Mimi which begins with grand passion and descends slowly into mutual hatred. The scenes move steadily and lustfully through the stages of Oscar's kinkiness, in which he is seen naked but for an animal mask crawling around the floor, while Mimi, pantie-less and in rubber gear, administers the leather-thonged correction. There is much sexual experiment and perversion and a good deal of nasty power-play. The twist in the tail of the story is the way in which the English couple find their own relationship torn further apart by the confessions of a sadist. The whole tale ends destructively, embracing weird behavioural explorations and death.

By the time the film was ready for the previews, sufficient detail had leaked out to get the newspapers into a state of anticipation that Polanski had directed another powerful cocktail of bondage and perverted sex. Naturally, Polanski did not try to dispel the rumour, and gave a flurry of interviews in which he talked at length about the fantasy and the reality of the subject matter, but prefixing every conversation with the assurance that he did not personally go in for sado-masochism, being well aware that writers tend to confuse art and life when discussing his films, just as they had when he was accused of dabbling in black magic to ensure ritual correctness in *Rosemary's Baby*.

Reviews were, to use that well-worn euphemism, mixed. In Britain, for example, Tom Hutchinson believed that Polanski had recovered some of the talent he showed in *Knife in the Water*. But *Variety* panned *Bitter Moon* as 'Polanski at rock bottom . . . while Seigner is eye-popping in the sex scenes, she sounds as if she is reading her dialogue off cue cards'. The reaction of women reviewers was also interesting. Zoe Heller, in the London *Independent on Sunday*, watched it 'in an agony of embarrassment, my views of the screen largely obscured by the hand which kept creeping up involuntarily to cover my eyes'.

Bitter Moon was a moderate commercial success and Seigner did not become an international star. But Polanski was back as a subject for discussion, to be taken seriously and to be placed on the couch for analysis. *Bitter Moon* provided cause for the motives and sources of his seemingly natural ability to tap into the subconscious to be re-examined after more than a decade in which Polanski's penchant for blood, gore and sex had been noticeably absent. To those who asked questions concerning his psychology and probed for clues to his mentality, he continued to insist that he was not interested in psychoanalysis.

The question had been asked of him many times in the past, and even the two psychiatrists who tried to delve into his subconscious at the time of the court case involving the thirteen-year-old girl were largely rebuffed and bemused. What intrigued them most was Polanski's own rejection of any kind of professional therapy. His answer then was the same as it is today, that he did not believe a shrink would enhance his intellectual capacity to explain or improve his emotional state, or even inspire him to make better films.

Henryk Kluba, as we have seen, has already provided a partial answer in that Poles have never been much interested in Freudian theories or self-discovery. Americans, on the other hand, are a nation obsessed with finding the hidden answers locked away somewhere in the mind. The most recent example is the craze for memory-recovery therapy which has led to all kinds of people accusing their parents of sexual abuse. The examining psychiatrists in the Polanski sex case were amazed that after all he had been through, he had not sought to take a guided tour of himself in the company of a qualified psychiatrist, that he had not sought counselling of any kind after Sharon's murder or that he showed no interest whatsoever in receiving psychiatric help after being arrested over the thirteen-year-old. They were more or less invited by Judge Rittenband, it will be recalled, to conclude that Polanski was a raving nut-case who urgently required treatment at a mental institution. They did not agree.

Even so, one of the reasons why Polanski could not begin to come to an arrangement with the Americans in later years was that he would have to show remorse. Harrison Ford, among others, had noted that if there was one thing that Polanski lacked when they were floating the idea of his return to the USA, it was remorse – he possessed none. 'He was not defiant,' said Ford. 'He was also not remorseful, and somehow you liked him better for it.' Polanski seems to believe that he is totally straight, mentally unaffected by what has happened in the past and only conscious that his life might have gone a different way if Sharon had not been murdered.

All these incidents were forced back to the surface with the coverage for *Bitter Moon*. What he had done in the movie, according to him, was touch strings that people would prefer to be left silent, because they recognized themselves in certain actions and attitudes. His stance remained as vigorous as ever: that while not going to the extremes he might express in his films, everyone had done things that they preferred not to talk about, which was a worrying generalization on his part – to assume that everyone was like himself.

As far as he was concerned, his movies were born out of reality – and not out of his own complexes or fantasies resulting from the Holocaust, lack of a mother's influence, the horror of the murders, guilt or anything else. He conceded, as he always has done, that the line between reality and fiction had been blurred for years past. But no, no, no – *Bitter Moon* was not about his own hang-ups.

Whether he liked it or not, they were there and visible and available for scrutiny. He does have hang-ups, and they appear when he is roused. Through three decades, it is possible to track him repeating various stories, such as the time he was beaten half to death when trying to buy a cycle and he remembers the blood running like water, or the time his father told him that his mother had been taken, or the way he was forced into Catholic worship in Wysoka. Basia Kwiatkowska's point about the way he portrays women in his movies, always in a down-trodden, sexually abused way, remains valid.

The purity of a woman's love, Basia observed, had not been evident since before she left him, and her reasoning that he was subconsciously taking revenge on her resounds down the years. He would doubtless dismiss that too, but Basia remains steadfast. 'This sexual exhibitionism, as in the perversity of *Bitter Moon*, is something that has always bothered me,' she said. 'And that he should expose his own wife in this way makes me feel that I escaped some danger.'

Of other events, such as the Sharon Tate murders, Polanski seldom attempts an explanation, never talks of reasons. At best he will speak in general terms, unconsciously quoting a line for which Charles Manson became famous – that no sense makes sense; that there was no sense in the way a gang of mad people killed his wife and unborn child.

Throughout these episodes and to the present day, he has maintained an extraordinary devotion to the unexplained life, and in many ways his autobiography, *Roman by Polanski*, provided a clinical record of his steadfastness in that respect. He told us everything, but nothing. His recollections were chillingly dispassionate, lacking in emotion, compassion or even confession. There was never time for tears. He held back on his revelations about his own sexual attitudes and gave away only enough in the field of sexual endeavour to help sell the book. When he wrote about sex, it all sounded very much like the conceit of a typical sixties' macho male – that the women were there, and he took them at will and whim, describing these encounters in a way that was as cynical as his views on religion and politics. And that is the way he continued through his life, until recently. Love? It was a word that seldom entered his vocabulary except when selected from that list of well-known macho lies: 'Of course I love you, darling . . .'

Emotion is a difficult area for Polanski. His love for Sharon Tate was marred by his promiscuity, and his fondness for his father was not, in the end, marked by any show of demonstrativeness. 'Ryszard died while visiting Romek in 1988,' said Zofia Komeda. 'He accompanied the coffin back to Krakow and at the airport he had a pick-up truck waiting to take the coffin to the cemetery. There was no big funeral – they just buried him in the tomb Ryszard had built for himself.'

Compassion was never part of the sixties' scene either, and Polanski is unperturbably, unapologetically a sixties' man. The liberation that characterized the sixties means so much to him to this day because he was the product of an oppressed society, hammered down by one of the most hard-line post-war Communist regimes outside the Soviet Union, from which he escaped at the very moment the Western world was embarking on an era of unimagined personal freedom. Like everyone else around him in the world of film, art and style, he also found freedom of expression and he used it without ever looking back. For reasons of his past, he more than most in his crowd could appreciate that freedom.

That he arrived in London when he did, just as the capital was swinging out, and went on to Hollywood just as the west coast was coming alive to the sound of screaming acidheads, was fortunate in one respect. In another age, when permissiveness had run out of steam – as he did when it did – he might have found difficulty in getting out of the starting gate.

He now talks with blithe fondness of the era that allowed him to prosper and, in spite of everything, he regrets little. Perhaps because of all that has happened, he refuses to consider the past as a reflection upon his present. The reason, notwithstanding his 'traumatic' childhood that we discussed in the early chapters of this book, or his anger that anyone should be capable of imagining what he went through by dismissing it with such an adjective, may well be the spectre of Charles Manson which clings to him and haunts him still.

No man, surely, is capable of ridding his imagination of visions of what went on in Cielo Drive that night, and especially a man who, as Basia confirmed, drew his inspiration from his mind's eye, his vision. More particularly significant for Polanski is the knowledge that the events of that night ended the era itself and brought the Age of Aquarius to a bloody close. As the American writer Joan Didion said in her essay 'The White Album', published in 1979, 'The tension broke that day, the paranoia was fulfilled.'

Just as the counter-culture group, the Weathermen, listed Sharon Tate along with Mayor Daley, Nixon, Johnson and Reagan as their enemies at that National War Council at Christmas 1969, so in another way Hollywood blamed the Cielo Drive victims by turning the murders into a terrible vicarious sideshow in which Polanski allowed himself to participate that day when he revisited the scene with a *Life* magazine reporter. He would never live down the mass of rumours about their life-style and their habits, however grotesque and exaggerated they may have been.

Manson must remain a spectre, and if Polanski has to deal with any guilt feelings in private, he may sometimes find himself wrestling with the thought that there was some underlying connection between the deaths and his film *Rosemary's Baby*, and that the murders were not just some accident of location, as he continues to maintain, of their living in Rudi Altobelli's house, in which Terry Melcher had also resided, when Manson's gang came to kill.

It is almost unimportant now, but the possibility continues to re-emerge from time to time in various ways. The hysterical publicity given to the upsurge of satanic practices and so-called satanic ritual abuse which occurred in the eighties, saw the image of Manson hoisted again by his supporters, along with those of various other murderers and serial killers. Remnants of The Process, the British-born movement to which Manson was affiliated, still bemoan the fact that he was 'a scapegoat' and worship his beliefs. To large sections of the satanic crowd, Manson remains a hero, and to them, the swastika emblem carved on his forehead is his badge of honour, while to his enemies it is the identification mark of absolute evil and madness. 'I am what you have made me,' said Manson when he last appeared on American television during Geraldo Rivera's special show, *Live From Death Row*. 'The mad dog devil killer fiend leper is a reflection of your society.'

From Manson's madness a peculiar truth emerged. Society, the movies, the media, writers, artists and social reformers were all wrapped up in something that got out of control. It is long past, now, and a sterner mood prevails, though Hollywood never learned any lessons. The legacy of the sixties was very visible in its output of the eighties and beyond – still more violence, more overt sex and an endless flow of blood that puts Polanski's most horrific scenes into a minor perspective. The two cannot be compared, however, either in intent or reason. Today's output is devoid of art, except the art of the spectacular; it has no sub-text, which is where Polanski at his best was outstanding. He did not regain his impact with *Bitter Moon*, either, and perhaps – like the sixties – his talent in that direction has run its course; only time will tell.

The list of Polanski's films, regarded by some as a remarkably slender record of accomplishment, belies a patchwork of tensions that were running through his own life and through society at large and cannot be discounted. Every one of his films has merit in that direction. *Knife in the Water, Repulsion, Chinatown* and, to a lesser degree, *Rosemary's Baby*, were in the present author's view masterpieces of modern cinema which cannot be repeated – as Nicholson found when he came to make *The Two Jakes*.

That is why it is too simplistic to say, as some do, that overall his list of credits is so lacking in quantity and so inconsistent in quality as to make him barely comparable with some of the great directors of his age. Perhaps there is no point in trying, anyway, because his contribution to the cinema is unique. As a director, Polanski has brought a style, an edge and influence to film, internationally, which was studied and analysed, dissected and copied, and which spawned a new 'new wave' of film people who liked to shock and scare. He is one of a dozen directors of the last fifty years whose work is interesting even in failure, and certainly few can match him in public awareness. His name carries instant recognition – but often for the wrong reasons.

It is this last aspect that makes him stand out in a crowd of often faceless practitioners of his craft. Apart from their variable artistic merit, his films consistently allude to his own personal mythology, reflecting his private dramas set against the backdrop of society at large.

Herein lies the irony of his situation.

Throughout his career as a film-maker, Polanski has stuck to the notion that the cinema is a form of entertainment for the voyeur. On film, he largely succeeded in that aim, and running parallel to his achievements on celluloid were the accidental, unplanned and media-hyped events that occurred in his own life. Here was reality: the 'traumatic'

271

life of Roman Polanski, played out in the most vivid, shocking and extraordinary episodes which made voyeurs of us all. Polanski himself became the natural and living companion to his films, part of the entertainment even in his most tragic and darkest hours.

There is a small coincidence in the fact that the date on the calendar as these words appear upon the author's PC screen is 9 August. It is twenty-four years to the day since Sharon Tate died and Polanski is just nine days away from his sixtieth birthday. A check with the American authorities reveals that as far as they are concerned Polanski's position is unchanged, and he cannot return to the USA without surrendering himself to the American embassy in Paris for onward transmission to Los Angeles where he would be arraigned before a judge. The District Attorney's office is still looking for an expression of remorse, but none is forthcoming. Polanski remains in Europe, attempting every now and again to find a backer for one of his films, which becomes increasingly difficult in the current economic climate of the film industry in general.

Otherwise, his life remains outwardly unaffected. The tabloids have long ago deserted his front door, and his media coverage now more usually takes the form of reviews and retrospectives of his work in the quality newspapers. At the beginning of 1993, Emmanuelle Seigner, Mrs Roman Polanski as is, presented him with a bonny baby girl named Morgan. As Polanski reaches sixty, she is twenty-six. The arrival of his first child followed a pattern among the old swingers. As the pressures upon the promiscuous became life-threatening in the eighties, Nicholson and Beatty, both five years younger than Polanski, also decided to settle down. The three boulevardies, as they were once known, simply could not keep on running.

Polanski set the style when his relationship with Seigner began to take on its air of permanence. Nicholson began a new family in 1989 with Rebecca Broussard, who appeared with him in *The Two Jakes* and the following year Beatty married his co-star in *Bugsy*, Annette Bening, in time to give their daughter his name. In that respect, Polanski had kept up with the fashion in Hollywood, where new fiftysomething dads were sprouting on every block.

A certain circle had been turned, albeit perhaps with a bumpy contour. It began to be drawn back in Poland when Basia declared that she was leaving Roman, and it ended up in Paris thirty-odd years later when he became a father, mellowing and contemplative and mixing in society. Ghosts occasionally walk across his grave, old friends from Hollywood drop by when they are in France, and he occasionally goes back to Poland, whose film industry, once so vibrant, ironically went into decline with the fading of the Communist system.

Sometimes there are brief encounters with women of his past, as when he and Emmanuelle went to a Vangelis concert in Paris in July 1993, and sat next to Nastassia Kinski, carrying her six-month-old baby from her relationship with producer Quincy Jones. The paparazzi snapped their pictures, but the best market they could find was the social pages of *Hello* magazine, reproduced small. In its way this summed up the new but old Polanski: married man, father, president of the jury at Cannes and all that . . . and one is drawn to a line spoken by John Huston in *Chinatown*: 'Politicians, ugly buildings and whores all get respectable if they last long enough . . .'

Filmography

Roman Polanski's career and reputation as a director began at Poland's National Film School at Lodz, where he made several short films which displayed early evidence of his talent for sophisticated characterization, his skill in kinetic arts and his voyeuristic predilection for psychological explorations, with ample sex and violence.

Shorts produced at Lodz were:

The Bicycle (1955; incomplete); *The Crime* (1957); *Toothy Smile* (1957); *Break Up the Ball* (1958); *Two Men and a Wardrobe* (1958), which gave him the breakthrough, achieving awards in European film festivals; *The Lamp* (1959); and his fifteen-minute graduation film which starred his future wife Basia Kwiatkowska, *When Angels Fall* (1959).

In Paris he directed and starred in *The Fat and the Lean* in 1961, and in 1962, temporarily back in Lodz, he made the award-winning *Mammals* which was financed by the father of his ill-fated friend Wojtek Frykowski.

Feature Films

KNIFE IN THE WATER (*1962, America*)

A psychological drama co-written with film school colleagues Jerzy Skolimowski and Jakub Goldberg, which tells the tale of a couple who take a young hitch-hiker aboard their yacht. The film won an American Academy nomination for best foreign film, was displayed at the New York Film Festival and gave Polanski his breakthrough. Remains one of his best, for which he was virtually outlawed in his home country. Starring Leon Niemczyk, Jolanta Umecka and Zygmunt Malanowicz.

THE MOST BEAUTIFUL SWINDLES IN THE WORLD
(1963, France)

Unsuccessful French-language compilation of crime stories. Polanski, out of work and struggling, wrote and directed a segment entitled *The Diamond Necklace*.

REPULSION *(1965, Britain)*

A young woman whose sexual repression leads to murder marks a return to the psychological theme with shocking undercurrents. Co-written with Polanski's creative partner Gerard Brach. His first English-language film, it won the Silver Bear award at the Berlin Film Festival. Starring Catherine Deneuve, Ian Hendry, John Fraser, Patrick Wymark and Yvonne Furneaux.

CUL-DE-SAC *(1966, Britain)*

A macabre black comedy, again from the Polanski–Brach partnership; the story of a nymphomaniac wife and a transvestite husband whose relationship becomes even more perplexing with the entry into their lives of a gangster on the run. Won the Golden Bear at Berlin. Starring Françoise Dorléac, Donald Pleasence, Lionel Stander, Jack MacGowran, William Franklyn.

THE FEARLESS VAMPIRE KILLERS, *or,* PARDON ME, YOUR TEETH ARE IN MY NECK *(American title), also known as* DANCE OF THE VAMPIRES *(1967, American production made in Britain)*

Spoof horror film written and originated by Polanski and Gerard Brach. Noted for the introduction in a major role of his lover and future wife, Sharon Tate. Two versions: the American print, heavily cut by the producers, which Polanski disowned and which flopped; and the European print, which was Polanski's own, and better, edited version. Starring Sharon Tate, Roman Polanski, Jack MacGowran, Alfie Bass, Terry Downes.

ROSEMARY'S BABY *(1968, America)*

Polanski's screen adaptation of Ira Levin's bestselling occult thriller concerning a young wife impregnated by the devil. The film was his first in Hollywood, and is among his career-best, a classic of its kind and his first major commercial and critical hit. His screenplay won an American Academy nomination and Ruth Gordon won an Oscar for best supporting actress. Starring Mia Farrow, John Cassavetes, Ruth Gordon and Ralph Bellamy.

MACBETH (*1972, Britain*)

Financed by *Playboy* (which caused much derision), co-written with Kenneth Tynan and dogged by rows over cost and delays, the film was panned in America for its excess of blood and violence (in the wake of the Sharon Tate murders) but fared far better with more objective British audiences. Starring Jon Finch, Francesca Annis, Martin Shaw and John Stride.

WHAT? *also known as* CHE? (*1973, Italy*)

A Polanski–Gerard Brach creation, backed personally by Carlo Ponti, *What?* was an unsuccessful and plotless semi-pornographic tale of a girl who proceeds through various sexual scenarios. Did nothing for his reputation except damage it. Starring Sydne Rome, Marcello Mastroianni.

CHINATOWN (*1974, America*)

The second and last of Polanski's Hollywood assignments before he fled the country; the quintessential seventies movie, and his personal best. Received six American Academy nominations, and Robert Towne won the Oscar for best screenplay. Starring Jack Nicholson, Faye Dunaway, John Huston, John Hillerman, Diane Ladd and Polanski himself in cameo.

THE TENANT *also known as* LE LOCATAIRE (*1976, France with American backing*)

Another Polanski–Brach original screenplay, Polanski also stars as the paranoid tenant of a Paris apartment building who finally dresses in women's clothes and commits suicide. Panned as a tediously morbid film and seen by some to be a self-parody, it still contained some first-rate subterranean movements and fine acting. Starring Polanski, Isabelle Adjani, Melvyn Douglas and Shelley Winters.

TESS (*1979, France*)

First film after his exile from America in the wake of the sex scandal, Polanski gives Thomas Hardy's novel, *Tess of the D'Urbervilles*, meticulously accurate, if occasionally tortuous, treatment; noted for the introduction of his young lover Nastassia Kinski. The film won three French Césars and three American Oscars (for cinematography, art direction and costume design), and an Academy nomination for best film. Starring Nastassia Kinski, Peter Firth, Leigh Lawson, David Markham and Richard Pearson.

PIRATES (*1985, France*)

This hollow tale of treachery on the Spanish main written years earlier with Brach finally came to the screen a decade out of date and was destined to become his biggest failure. It is the most expensive film he ever made and $33 million was lost at sea. Starring Walter Matthau, Damien Thomas, Richard Pearson, Roy Kinnear, Ferdy Mayne, Charlotte Lewis.

FRANTIC (*1988, France with American backing*)

Semi-return to Hollywood favour but still barred from US entry; a good thriller, written by Polanski and Brach, but lacks the twist in the tail. Notable for the introduction of Polanski's young lover and future wife Emmanuelle Seigner. Starring Seigner, Harrison Ford, Betty Buckley.

BITTER MOON (*1992, France*)

Unashamed Polanski voyeurism, and unashamed exploitation of the body of the actress who was now his wife and expecting his first child. The movie centres on one man's sexual obsession for a much younger girl. With obvious self-parodying connotations, it is both black comedy and blue movie, with kinky sex and distasteful S and M; but it also indicates that Polanski has not entirely lost his originality. Sterling performance by Peter Coyote. Starring Peter Coyote, Emmanuelle Seigner, Kirstin Scott Thomas, Hugh Grant.

Index

279